THE FOUNDATIONS
OF JEWISH ETHICS

THE FOUNDATIONS OF JEWISH ETHICS

Being Volume One of

THE TEACHINGS OF JUDAISM

From the Sources

COMPILED BY

DR. SIMON BERNFELD

For the Union of German Jews (Germany)

Authorized Translation
from the Second, Revised and Enlarged German Edition

BY

ARMIN HAJMAN KOLLER, Ph.D.

Assistant Professor of German in the
University of Illinois

INTRODUCTION BY
SAMUEL E. KARFF

KTAV PUBLISHING HOUSE, INC.
NEW YORK

LIBRARY OF CONGRESS CATALOG CARD NUMBER: 67-30441
MANUFACTURED IN THE UNITED STATES OF AMERICA

CONTENTS

INTRODUCTION VII

TRANSLATOR'S FOREWORD XXVII

PREFACE XXIX

CHAPTER

I. MORALITY AS A BASIC REQUIREMENT OF
JUDAISM 17
Introduction by Dr. Leo Baeck

II. FUNDAMENTAL VIEWS OF MORALITY 51
1. Doing and Believing 51
Introduction by Prof. Dr. I. Elbogen
2. Moral-mindedness 69
Introduction by Prof. Dr. I. Elbogen

III. PURITY OF SOUL 92
Introduction by Dr. A. Loewenthal

IV. FREEDOM OF WILL 102
Introduction by Dr. S. Bernfeld

V. REWARD AND PUNISHMENT 125
Introduction by Dr. S. Bernfeld

VI. EQUALITY OF ALL HUMAN BEINGS 150
Introduction by Dr. S. Hochfeld

VII. THE WILL TO LIVE 187
Introduction by Dr. Leo Baeck
1. Morality and Joy of Life 189
2. Temperance 217

VIII. KNOWLEDGE AND MORALITY 225
Introduction by Dr. S. Hochfeld

SOURCES 236

GENERAL INDEX 247

INDEX OF PASSAGES CITED 257

V

INTRODUCTION

When this volume first appeared its compiler promised the reader an objective source book on the foundations of Jewish ethics. Unlike those studies which reflected the prejudgments of the author, this work was to permit Judaism to speak "in its own words." The perspective of our time has not tarnished the considerable value of this compendium. It will repay the careful scrutiny of a contemporary reader, offering him a rich sample of Jewish ethical thought from the biblical to the early 20th century.

Ironically, one value of this book lay in its failure to fulfill the major claim of the compiler. Inescapably, a compendium is an interpretation reflecting the author's ideological perch. This should neither surprise nor disenchant us. Jewish tradition itself bears witness to many universes of discourse. Philo's midrash on Abraham extracts different truths from the biblical text than those extracted by the talmudic rabbis. Maimonides' understanding of divine retribution is not simply deducible from that of the deuteronomists. Not surprisingly, therefore, this work reveals as much about the spirit of 19th century German Jewish scholarship as about the foundations of Jewish ethics.

I

Simon Bernfeld, the principal editor, was born in Stanislawow, Galicia, in 1860. He died in Berlin in 1940. His productive and eventful career encompassed years of study at the University of Berlin and the Hochshule (later the Lehrenstaat) für die Wissenschaft des Judentums. Before settling in Berlin permanently to engage in extensive study and publication, Bernfeld spent seven years as Chief Rabbi of the Sephardic community in

Belgrade, then the capital of Serbia. A gifted popularizer, he wrote extensively in Hebrew and German, focusing in particular on the earlier decades of Jewish emancipation. These monographs include *Dor Hacham* (Warsaw, 1896), biographical sketches of Jewish scholars of the 19th century; *Toledoth Hareformatzion Hadathith* (Cracow 1900), a history of the Reform movement in the 19th century; and *Dor Tahpuchoth* (Warsaw 1897), a study of the age of Moses Mendelsohn.

The present work appeared originally as a series on "The Teachings of Judaism," *Die Lehren des Judentums*. In form and content it remains a classic model of 19th and early 20th century German Jewish apologetics. The selection of sources, the introductory paragraphs, the Christian affidavits, the major categories themselves, reflect a congeries of illuminating if not always incontestable assumptions.

These include, in part, the following:

(1) An educated Jewish and Christian layman needs to be disabused of the false notion that Judaism is primarily a regimen of ritual acts. On the contrary "to seek God means to strive after the good." (p. 33)

(2) German idealism's understanding of history as the progressive unfolding of the Divine Spirit is consistent with, perhaps even borrowed from Jewish messianism: "The interpretation of history is that the existence of good shall continually increase." (p. 80)

(3) The Jewish view of man is far closer to that of enlightened German philosophy than the Christian concept of human depravity:

> While it [Judaism] also takes cognizance of the inclination to sin present in sensuous man, nevertheless it asserts that he can conquer it in himself, requires this of him and also credits him with the strength required to efface the sinful disposition himself and to make amends for the sin committed through his own repentance. (p. 93)

(4) The concept of Israel's election attributes to this people no special virtue nor any exclusive privilege. Israel's birth and rationale for continued existence are linked to its role as the vanguard of enlightened men. Israel has "a mission to influence the rest of mankind by leading the way in morals." (p. 151)

Dr. Bernfeld, aided by his worthy collaborators, assembled this work for publication in Berlin in 1922. It was his avowed purpose to improve the level of Jewish self-knowledge and the Jew's measure of acceptance by German citizenry. Professor Armin Koller's translation, published in the United States in 1929, was similarly conceived. The underlying humanistic goals of Bernfeld and Koller were dealt a cataclysmic blow by the Age of Hitler. It is difficult to conceive that this compendium with its prevailing tone of urbane rationalism and gentle meliorism appeared originally only a decade before *der Führer's* rise to power.

To pretend that *The Foundations of Jewish Ethics* has not been shaken by the intervening apocalypse is to insult the integrity of its authors and to mock the martyrs of our people. Chastened veterans of 20th century madness, Jews will now read this volume with different eyes. We must presume also that, were its authors to assemble their sources and write their introductory paragraphs this day, these would poignantly reflect the events of recent decades.

II

One of the central foundations of Jewish covenant ethics is the faith that He who holds man accountable for the moral demand is active in history to fulfill His purposes. He who commands Israel to refrain from oppressing the stranger is the God who acted in Israel's history to liberate oppressed slaves. Pharaoh learned that the moral imperative may not be ignored with impunity. There were times in Israel's history when the affirmation

of divine justice and power required an accentuation of
the covenant people's culpability: "Because of our sins
we were exiled from our land." And there were times
when Israel's vulnerability to disaster was deemed an
inescapable risk of responding to the divine commandment in a world not yet "perfected under the kingdom
of the Almighty." Repeatedly the believing Jew encountered this major stumbling block to faith: good men do
suffer—history is not always a reliable witness to a transcendent moral order.

Jewish eschatology, through its projection of history's
redemption to the end of days and its vision of a personal postmortal reward for faithful men, helped sustain
Israel's confidence in the spiritual order of the universe,
despite the perplexing testimony of "current events."

Nineteenth century German Idealism, influenced by
Hegel, conceived of the historic process itself as a progressive unfolding of the Divine Spirit. Not surprisingly,
history's newest offspring, the nation-state, and particularly the German State was heralded as a triumph of
Divine Reason.

Many Jewish thinkers on the European continent, and
particularly in Germany, avidly embraced these assumptions. On the very threshold of American entry into
World War I, Hermann Cohen (1842-1918), founder
of the Neo-Kantian School of Philosophy, and one of the
most respected thinkers of his time, reminded his
American coreligionists of their debt to Germany in
these words:

> Dear Brethren in America: You will understand me now if
> I say to you every Jew of the Occident must, in addition to
> his political fatherland, recognize also the motherland of
> his religiosity as the basic esthetic force and center of his
> cultural sentiments—that it is Germany which he must
> honor and love. . . . Germany, the homeland of humani-
> tarianism, of the freedom of conscience and of social wel-
> fare policies, has been called to battle by its enemies all
> around who, though they are civilized nations have made
> a compact with Russia . . . every Jew who is convinced of

the cultural power of Israel's religion and therefore of its right to life must deem himself happy if his patriotism accords to him at least neutrality in this war, but he must envy us German Jews who can battle for our fatherland borne at the same time by the pious conviction that we will obtain human rights for the greater part of our coreligionists. Germany, the motherland of occidental Jewry, the land of intellectual freedom and ethics, Germany will, by its victory found justice and peace amongst the peoples of the world. We trust in the logic of our fate and of our history. (Cited in W. G. Plaut *The Growth of Reform Judaism*, UAHC, N. Y., 1965, p. 78)

No generation is more keenly aware than ours of history's ambiguous testimony to the power and goodness of God. None is more sensitive to the danger of identifying any ideology, social system or historic event with the footsteps of the Messiah. Understandably, we bridle at the assumption that "the interpretation of history is that the existence of good shall continually increase." We are forced to take more seriously, if not literally, the temper of some talmudic statements which are conspicuously absent from this compendium. Forsaking the notion of a progressive ascent toward the millennium, our generation finds more meaning in the notion that history may hurtle man to the depths of despair before the Messiah will appear.

> In the footsteps of the Messiah insolence will increase and honor dwindle . . . the meeting place (of scholars) will be used for immorality . . . the wisdom of the learned will degenerate, fearers of sin will be despised, and the truth will be lacking. Children shall shame the elders and the elders shall rise up before the children. . . .
>
> (*Mishneh Sotah* 9:15)

III

Through a generous array of sources, the first section of the volume contends that ethical conduct is the touchstone of covenant fidelity. Prophetic literature veritably pulsates with this teaching. Animal sacrifices are not an acceptable substitute for elemental decency; fasting is no proxy for righteousness. These assertions, hardly de-

batable, are amply and eloquently corroborated by the
sources. (pp. 20–38)

It may be argued further that many "cultic" acts were
a way of refining the Jew's moral sensitivity. The Seder
ritual commands him to imagine that he is reliving the
Exodus from slavery to freedom in order that he may
celebrate God's redemptive power and confirm his own
obligation to "know the heart of the stranger." Even the
ritual slaughtering of an animal was merely to refine the
character of its observer. Rav said:

> The Mitzvot were not given save to purify God's creatures.
> For what difference does it make to God whether one
> slaughters [an animal] from the back of the neck or the
> front of the neck; hence the commandments were not given
> save to purify God's creatures. (*Genesis Rabbah* 44:1;
> *Leviticus Rabbah* 13:3)

Having conceded this, we must add that the very attempt to treat *The Foundations of Jewish Ethics* apart
from a more comprehensive view of the Jewish "idea of
the holy" is replete with difficulties and dangers. It may
lead one to suggest, however erroneously, that the holy
and the ethical are synonymous, and the terms "good
Jew" and "good man," virtually interchangeable. Nineteenth century German liberalism was vulnerable on
this score, as is the present compendium.

In his introductory paragraphs Leo Baeck writes
"Only by loyalty to God's commandment, to the moral
law that He has given to humanity, can man approach
the one God in order to serve Him." This statement is
subsequently supported by such citations from the tradition as: "And now Israel what doth the Lord thy God
require of thee? To fear the Lord thy God, to walk in
all His ways and to love Him and to serve the Lord thy
God with all thy heart and with all thy soul." (Deut.
10:12)

In its original context this biblical commandment can
hardly be reduced to an observance of "the moral law."
Such Service of God included animal sacrifices offered

at the central sanctuary in Jerusalem. The attempt to impose the distinctions of 19th century apologetics upon biblical or rabbinic texts is at the very least misleading. In truth covenant faithfulness embodied an integrated system of "ethical" and "ritual" acts.

It may be more helpful to speak of Torah as an all-encompassing way of life through which the man born Jew nurtures his humanity and fulfills his particular divine vocation in the world. Thus a Jew who fails to identify with his people's redemption from Egyptian bondage (who says "What mean ye by this service?") and who denies the claim of mitzvot relating to Passover, is surely rejecting the covenant of his fathers. Shall we describe this rejection in ritual or ethical terms? While his neglect of a Seder observance may be characterized as a failure to perform certain ritual acts, it may also betoken a lack of self-respect, of reverence for the sources of his being, and therefore be deemed an offense against his humanity, his people and the God of the covenant. Significantly, the Haggadah designates such a Jew as *rasha*, an evil man. A Christian who fails to observe the Passover is not similarly culpable. Morality as "a basic requirement of the religious life" has distinctly Jewish as well as universal overtones. This is not made clear in the volume.

The equation of holiness and morality neglects another foundation of Jewish ethics—the Jew's acknowledgment of his reliance on divine love and forgiveness. "In a moral action," we are told, "man becomes conscious of the power latent within him" (p. 19); but man may also become aware of his moral inadequacies. This awareness entails more than acknowledgment that when man fails "he can accomplish his own atonement and his own purification by his deeds, his own moral choice." It calls for the affirmation that our worth is not totally contingent upon our performance, and that despite our acts of penitence we neither fully redress our sins nor measure up to the fullness of divine expectation. He who regards fasting or prayers as atonement for sin against his neighbor has failed to grasp the Torah. Neither has he who believes that by his initiative, cultic or "moral," the slate is made fully clean. The affirmation of man's inescapable reliance on a divine margin of unmerited forgiveness is a foundation of the covenant.

Jewish ethics is rooted in a twofold relation between God and man. The conditional aspect of the covenant highlights Israel's (man's) spiritual potential: "Let a man ever regard himself as if he were half guilty and half innocent; if he then performs a mitzvah how fortunate is he, for he has thus determined the balance in favor of his innocence. . . ." (*Kiddushin* 40b)

The unconditional dimension of the covenant acknowledges Israel's (man's) spiritual finitude. The *Ashamnu* prayer of the High Holyday liturgy illustrates this well:

> Endless would be the sacrifices due unto Thee according to ancient rite, and numberless would be the guilt-offerings required because of our sins. But Thou knowest that our end is but dust and ashes and therefore Thou hast multiplied the means by which we may seek Thy forgiveness. What are we? What is our life? What our piety? What our righteousness? What our help? What our strength? What our might? What shall we say before Thee, O Lord our God and God of our fathers? Are not all the mighty ones as naught before Thee? Are not wise men as though without knowledge and men of understanding as though without discernment? For the multitude of their works is emptiness, and the days of their lives are vanity before Thee; and the days of their lives are vanity before Thee; and the pre-eminence of man over beast is naught; for all is vanity, except the pure soul which must hereafter give accounting before the throne of Thy glory.
> From the beginning, Thou hast distinguished man by endowing him with reason and filled him with the desire to seek Thy presence. (High Holiday Prayer Book, Publ. by Prayer Book Press, compiled and arranged by Rabbi Morris Silverman)

Although 19th century apologetics accentuated the former dimension, the tradition itself conveys more of an enduring and creative tension between accountability and forgiveness, justice and unconditional love. One of the foundations of Jewish ethics is an affirmation of one's dependence on divine gifts, including the grace of forgiveness. Without compromising the necessity of human initiative, it requires a profound awareness of the immense gap between what we are and what we have been called to become. To profess the need for divine grace transports us across the boundary from humanism to *kedusha*, holiness.

A compendium of Jewish ethics composed "after Auschwitz" would doubtless also linger more appreciatively on those traditional sources which, without denying man's embryonic "purity of soul," soberly rehearse his demonic potential and his ever tenuous claim to *menshlichkeit*. In addition to those sources cited on pages 95 and 96 one might suggest the following samples:

> Rabbi Simeon ben Levi said "The evil *yetzer* of man waxes strong against him day by day and seeks to kill him, and if God did not help him, man could not prevail against it." (*Kiddushin* 30b)
> The Israelites say to God: "Lord of the World, Thou knowest how hard is the strength of the evil inclination." God said "Remove it a little in this world, and I will rid you of it altogether in the world to come." (*Numbers Rabbah* 15:12)
> Rabbi Simai said "The Evil *yetzer* is like a great rock which stands at the crossroads and people stumble against it." The King said "Crush it little by little till I come and remove it altogether." So God says "The evil inclination is a great stumbling block, crush it little by little, till at the last I remove it from the world." (*Pesikta De Rav Kahana* 165a)

The absence of such sources which attest the difficulty of molding men into faithful covenant partners is more a reflection of nineteenth century optimism than an objective mirror of the Jewish tradition.

IV

No discussion of *The Foundation of Jewish Ethics* may ignore the issue of freedom and determinism. To deny the reality of human freedom is to forfeit the ground of accountability. To deny that external and internal forces impinge on that freedom is to flout the canons of common sense. Covenant ethics is rooted in man's power to obey and betray the will of God. The traditional celebration of this power is aptly sampled in this work. Once acknowledging the reality of freedom, a meaningful discussion may focus on the factors which enhance or diminish it.

Modern jurisprudence grapples with the categories of sanity and insanity. The "McNaughton Rule" grants immunity to a man who at the time he committed a crime did not "know" that his act was legally wrong. Psychiatry reveals the woeful inadequacy of this rule. A man may know that an act is legally and morally wrong, and yet, at the fateful moment, possess little if any power to control it. On the other hand, the danger of simply reducing crime to sickness is that morality then becomes a function of mental health and all ground for moral judgment disintegrates. A psychiatric perspective on crime must therefore acknowledge both the limits and reality of freedom. No simple formula has yet been devised to establish or define a neat line of demarcation.

Nor does psychoanalysis provide warrant for denying the reality of human freedom. The success of treatment depends in part on the patient's willingness to overcome a "resistance" to self-understanding, and psychoanalytic theory posits a correlation between consciousness and ego control: Man's self-understanding increases his power to mediate rationally—freely—among the competing and conflicting claims of his life.

The Jewish tradition is also mindful of the variability of human freedom and considers the factors which increase or diminish it. Thus, the more wrong decisions one makes in freedom, the less free we become to choose the good. "At first the evil inclination in man is like a cobweb but afterwards like strong thick ropes." (*Sukkah* 52b)

When Pharaoh is commanded to free the Israelites he alternates between consent and refusal. Bowing to the threat of divine sanction he acquiesces. Once the threat is removed, he reneges on his pledge. Pharaoh's "hardening of the heart" is subsequently imputed to divine intervention: "And the Lord said unto Moses 'Go in unto Pharaoh for I have hardened his heart and the heart of his servants that I might show these my signs in the midst of them.'" (Exodus 10:1) The rabbis ask: If man is free to choose between good and evil, why was Pharaoh denied the freedom to make the right choice? Rabbi Simeon ben Lakish answered: "When God warns a man once, twice, or even three times and still he does not repent, then God closes His heart. . . ." (*Exodus Rabbah* 13:3).

Man's freedom, itself a God-given gift, expands or contracts with his exercise thereof. The more consistently one embraces a pattern of conduct, good or evil, the more difficult it becomes to alter the pattern. Here in part is the significance of the rabbinic dictum: "If God created the evil inclination, He also created the Torah with which to temper it." If Torah functions in a man's life as a structured system of acts and restraints, his power to pursue the good has found sturdy anchorage.

In the rabbinic play on the words *chārut* and *chärut* one may find another enduring insight which the tradition contributes to a discussion of human freedom. The Hebrew slaves experienced their greatest birth of freedom not at the Red Sea, but at Sinai. Their freedom *chārut* was bound up with their acceptance of the covenant and the engraved (*chärut*) tablets of law. At that hour, they ceased being servants of men and became servants of God (See *Avot* 6:2). Freedom may not be simply defined as a rejection of authority. It is the exchange of one kind of loyalty for another; in religious terms, a rejection of idolatry for commitment to God.

The man who exercises freedom must choose between conflicting claims. His freedom to choose one or the other depends on his assessment of their relative value. How free is a man to stand out in a torrential downpour to purchase an advance ticket for a theatrical performance? The answer depends measurably on how high "love for the theatre" ranks in his order of passionate loyalties or values. An infant's freedom to restrain his aggression is linked to the value he attaches to maternal love. The traditional Jew's freedom (his power) to observe the demands of the covenant—even under duress—is related to the value he places upon doing the will of God. " 'Of them that love me and keep my commandments' [Exodus 20:6] refers to those who dwell in the land of Israel and risk their lives for the sake of the commandments." (*Mekilta Bahodesh,* Vol. II, Lauterbach edition p. 237)

Rabbi Eliezer ben Azariah envisages Jews who are tempted to eat pork or who will wish to violate the laws of sexual purity, but who conclude: "What can I do in as much as my Father in heaven has decreed that I do otherwise" (*Sifra* 93b). Man's freedom (power) to serve God is contingent upon the place such divine service occupies in his hierarchy of concerns. We are partly free to choose our values and those values in turn help define the perimeters and substance of our freedom.

V

In this compendium as in any discussion of the foundation of ethics, freedom is closely linked to punishment and reward. If the correlation between service of God and the receipt of earthly rewards seems too rigorous, such divine service can be reduced to a simple act of prudence, very much as when a child learns not to place his finger on a hot stove. We are not prone to characterize such learning on a child's part as a great triumph for freedom or virtue. Conversely, if the service of God receives no positive reinforcement, man's freedom (power) to be a faithful servant will be seriously attenuated.

An animal's capacity to choose the right course is nurtured by a system of reward and punishment. At its moral peak it will perform sacrificial acts of self-denial to please its master and preserve his love. An infant's responsiveness to parental authority is quite analogous. But the moral adult is presumed capable of committing himself to a far broader range of spiritual goals. He can articulate, empathize with and expend energy in behalf of moral ends which do not directly relate to the satisfaction of his basic drives. An adult may fast, for example, in order to share or dramatize the anguish of "oppressed people" whom he has never met, who may even reside in another corner of the globe. He may choose to devote his entire life to their welfare.

The hallmark of a morally sensitive adult is purportedly his capacity to pursue the right "for its own sake." But has such a person totally emancipated himself from a system of reward and punishment, or is he distinguishable by the kind of reinforcement to which he responds? A child's moral sustenance may require the physical presence of a parent who periodically imparts or withholds approval and more concrete benefits. An adult may find adequate reinforcement by believing "If he were alive he would be proud of me today." In either case, *fidelity to a bond of love or fear of its betrayal undergirds a man's moral resolve.*

Careful scrutiny reveals that concern for the integrity of a precious human relationship inspires the man who does the right "for its own sake." At this point, fear and love converge. He who controls his aggression may be impelled by (1) love for a person or (2) by fear of losing a person's love. Theoretically, the former motive has prevailed if the actor seems more concerned about giving love than receiving it. In reality, the distinction is shadowy, and no society has relied entirely on either to secure adherence to its norms. More mundane reinforcements (public ridicule, fines, incarceration, death penalties) remain man's durable instruments of social control.

Let us now consider the role of reward and punishment in a theistic ethical system. What distinguishes man from animals is his need for, or at least his capacity to respond to, the Ultimate Power of the universe, an unseen reality whom he may inadequately but inevitably conceptualize as universal "Father" or "King." Man alone experiences the presence of God and stands accountable to Him. If, as in a covenant ethic, God is Supreme Lawgiver, then good and evil become *chesed*, faithfulness to and *Chat,* betrayal of divine expectations.

Reward and punishment remain a constant foundation of covenant ethics. At the "lowest" level man conceives of obedience and disobedience as a choice between plenty and drought, health and pestilence. "I have set before thee this day life and prosperity, death and adversity . . ." (Deut. 30:15) When in his personal life there seems to be no direct correlation between piety and reward, the religious man may conclude that he is less deserving than he imagines, or that reward is being deferred to some postmortal realm, or that God is testing him.

It is often presumed that the truly pious man has emancipated himself from a concern for reward and punishment . . . "If man," says Maimonides, "loves God with true love, he will, out of love for Him, soon be doing everything that is commanded of him. . . ." (*Mishneh Torah, Hilchot Teshuvah*, X,2) A man overcome by divine love will say: "The recompense of a mitzvah is the awareness of having performed a mitzvah and the punishment for a sin is the knowledge that one has committed a sin." (*Avot* 4:2) Maimonides supports his definition of true piety by quoting Antigonus' dictum: "Be not like servants who minister to their master upon the condition of receiving a reward. . . ." (*Avot* 1:3)

In truth such a man may be quite responsive to reward; only the nature of his cherished reward distinguishes him from less morally mature men. His recompense is the awareness that he is living in accord with the will of the Master of the Universe before Whom he stands in awe, Whose approval and love he cherishes and from Whom he cannot bear to be estranged. To foster this relation by his conduct is ample reward. To threaten its rupture by default is an ominous prospect scrupulously to be avoided. In this context the sequel to Antigonus' admonition, "And let the fear of heaven be upon you," may be rendered as follows: The faithful covenant man is motivated not primarily by the fear of pestilence, premature death, etc., but by fear of alienating himself from God.

Again, it is evident that *Yirat Shamayim,* "fear of heaven," and love of God are interrelated. When apprehension about the integrity of the relationship is overshadowed by a compelling desire to do something for God, we may speak of an act as prompted by the "love of God." The actual life situation makes such neat distinctions difficult, at best. Moreover, even in the premodern era both reverence and love were deemed transitory peaks rather than sustained achievements. Covenant ethics never dispensed with the promise of more mundane reward and punishment in this world or the world to come, and in some measure their distribution was not confined to the vagaries of divine action. In God's name "religious leaders" have always imposed sanctions which, if they did not enhance the love or fear of God, reinforced man's fear of man.

VI

Since the emancipation, a theistic ethic has been less able to employ political sanctions in its behalf. A rabbi

may counsel Jews to observe the Sabbath or be scrupulous in the marketplace, but whether he appeals to their
quest for prosperity, immortality, or their love of God
he knows that the sanctions to which most men respond
most readily are not in his power to dispense or with-
hold.

With the dawn of secularity men have also taken traditional religion's promise of divine punishment and
reward far less seriously. The concern with man's postmortal destiny has waned decisively and the validity of
the deuteronomic admonitions has been profoundly
questioned. Yet even the secularist must at times grapple
with the possibility that there is an order of life which
men may not violate with impunity. Two of the most
pressing challenges confronting our society provide lurid
illustrations:

Man's technology has unleased the power of the atom.
Whatever restraint the nuclear nations presently exercise towards each other derives principally from the fear
of a retaliatory potential. The future security of all nations, the very endurance of civilization, depends on
man's capacity to regulate the use of atomic energy. The
believing Jew will discover in this situation a divine
address: "I have set before thee life and death . . ."

We live at a time of "rising expectations." The American Negro is determined to share the affluence of our
society. As his disaffection imperils "domestic tranquil-
ity" it is becoming increasingly obvious that our cities
cannot endure half slum and half suburb. Even the
secularist may appreciate Isaiah's formula for domestic
peace: "Give rest to the weary" (Isaiah 28:12). The believing Jew will find therein God's condition for human
fulfillment.

With the rapid advance of secularity men are also far
more likely to define the loftiest foundations of ethics
in non-theistic terms. God's role as source of value is
itself challenged. The concept of *mitzvah,* of divine commandment, or of God as the source of the moral law has

been commonly dismissed as a sociologicàl stratagem. Man, it is claimed, gives himself Torah in order to establish a viable social order. Pragmatism and ethical subjectivism have eclipsed the concept of accountability to God.

Martin Buber (1878–1965) whose earliest writings are referred to in the bibliography of the compendium, but whose most significant work appeared after its publication, took seriously the "eclipse of God" but refused to surrender the ultimate ground of covenant ethics. For Buber, God remains a source of value, and love between persons is its classic paradigm. In *I and Thou*, Buber distinguished two postures which characterize man's relation to the world. *I-it* is a symbol of man's power to treat things or persons as objects for study, analysis and use. The physical and social sciences are the fruits of man's detached analytical prowess. *I-Thou* is a symbol of man's capacity to enter into a relation with the world characterized by full involvement, mutual confirmation of being, and unconditional love. The love between persons is its supreme visible model. Love, claims Buber, is not a feeling within but a relation between persons: "Feelings dwell in man but man dwells in his love . . . love does not cling to the I in such a way as to have the Thou only for its object; but love is between I and Thou. The man who does not know this . . . does not know love; even though he ascribes to it the feelings he lives through, experiences, enjoys and expresses. (*I and Thou*, translated by R. G. Smith, Charles Scribners Sons, N.Y., 1937, p. 14f)

"Love," writes Buber, "is the responsibility of an I for a Thou." In moments when man's human relationships bear witness to this responsibility, he is expressing love of God, the Eternal Thou and fulfilling the meaning of his life. Love, as Buber defines it, is the supreme norm of human existence. This norm is man's discovery, not his creation.

One can believe in and accept a meaning or value, one can set it as a guiding light over one's life, if one has discovered it, not if one has invented it. It can be for me an illuminating meaning, a direction giving value only if it has been revealed to me in my meeting with Being, not if I have freely chosen it for myself from among the existing possibilities and perhaps have in addition decided with some fellow creatures: This shall be valid from now on. (*Eclipse of God*, Harper Torch Book Edition, N. Y., 1957, p. 70)

The foundation of covenant ethics remains, for Buber, as for Jewish tradition, man's responsibility towards and his love for God, Who called him into being and reveals to him the goal of his life.

But Buber the "Jewish existentialist" departs from the tradition in his denial that such a norm may be ultimately validated or reduced to specific obligations by appeal to the written and oral law as interpreted by the authoritative teachers of a particular generation. Instead he avers: "Only out of a personal relationship with the absolute can the absoluteness of the ethical coordinates arise. . . . Even when the individual calls an absolute criterion, handed down by religious tradition, his own, it must be forged in the fire of the truth of his personal essential relation to the absolute if it is to win true validity. But always it is the religious who bestows, the ethical who receives." (*Eclipse of God*, p. 98)

Those moderns who deny Buber's "accountability to the Eternal Thou" or who refuse to acknowledge a transcendent source of "the good" must still grope for the ultimate foundation of their value system. Why, for example, is it wrong to demean, degrade, or exploit another person? Should man's increasing dominion over the earth make it technically possible to breed a race of docile imbeciles—why would it be wrong to do so? To answer this question in its ontological depth, is to imply that there is an order of creation which man should not violate. At the heart of this order is "the sacredness of the human personality" or what ben Azzai called the most important sentence in the Torah: "This is the

Book of the generations of man. In the image of God created He him." (*Genesis* 5:1). To explore the foundation of ethics is to point toward if not explicitly to affirm the God who is the "Giver of Torah."

VII

At the very outset we noted that among the primary pillars of a theistic ethic is a faith that the God who gives the command is also active to fulfill it, that man is not alone in his struggle to attain the promise of creation. The Holocaust has irrevocably shattered the urbane optimism of 19th century German Jewish liberalism. History provides, at best, an ambiguous testimony of God's unfolding purpose. Nevertheless, covenant man does not surrender the hope that "the mountains may depart and the hills be removed but My kindness shall not depart from thee, neither shall My covenant of peace be removed, saith He-Who-Is, that has compassion on thee." (Isaiah 54:10)

These words were cited by a contributor to this compendium after he had endured and survived the Nazi era. Rabbi Leo Baeck (1873–1956) who savored man's demonic potential and history's apparent madness at Theresienstadt, emerged to declare:

> "As true as My Covenant is"—this was the word of the Eternal One heard by the prophet when he thought about his people in a time of oppression and dark destiny, and certainty entered him. The question of all questions, that of the entrance of the Eternal, the unending, the One into the domain of the many, the terrestrial, the passing, this question in which the searching, the thinking, the hope of this people has always lived, in which it once grew and in which it was ever reborn—this question itself possessed the answer: "as true as My Covenant is." (*This People Israel* translated by Albert Friedlander, Holt Rinehart Winston, N.Y., 1964, p. 403)

Despite the anguish of the Nazi inferno, Leo Baeck refused to trade the faith of Israel for the myth of Sisyphus. If history is not a simple progressive unfolding of

God's design, neither is the pursuit of justice an exercise in futility. Covenant man denies that the world is absurd. Chastened but unbowed, he struggles for the assurance that, as Baeck phrased it, "acting in God's ways . . . is not only morality but also the beginning of wisdom."

SAMUEL E. KARFF

FOREWORD

Ever since the appearance in Germany of the first volume of *Die Lehren des Judentums,* the translator has felt the need of rendering that work into English in order to give American and English readers the opportunity not only of deriving due benefit from the sublime ideals of conduct and ethical treasure garnered in the book, but also of availing themselves, particularly the scholarly-minded, of the sources quoted therein. He therefore welcomed the authorization to translate it.

The reader is not interested in any recital of the difficulties encountered in the translation of a work of this type. Suffice it to say that the translator has scrupulously avoided taking any liberties with the text, and has tried at all times to give a faithful rendering both of the letter and the spirit of the German original. If an acceptable English translation of a given passage were already available, use was made of it. In all such instances, except where the citations were from the Bible, the source is fully acknowledged. For the Biblical passages, the New Translation of the Holy Scriptures, published by the Jewish Publication Society of America, was consulted—and nearly always followed; sometimes also Isaac Leeser's The Holy Scriptures (New York, Bloch), as well as the translation of the Holy Bible published at Oxford;

and occasionally, particularly in cases of divergence between the German and the English rendering of a Scriptural passage, recourse was had to the original Hebrew text. Attention is called to divergences of this kind in brief translator's notes. The translator endeavored to mark any addition or change made by himself.

In the present state of the world, both among adolescents and adults, good should come in the Christian, as also in the Jewish camps, of reaffirming the eternal verities of Judaism, the rejuvenating fountainhead of the ideals of human conduct, and from direct contact with the standard and ideal pattern of moral behavior. It is not too much to hope that such contact may result in a moral betterment of mankind.

Before going to press, the manuscript was read by Professor E. C. Baldwin and Dr. M. Jung. I wish to thank them both for a number of suggestions pertaining to English diction, and Dr. Jung especially for references to the passages from Bailey and Kent, from Isaacs, and from Alexander.

My principal obligation, which I here gratefully acknowledge, is to Rabbi Joseph L. Fink, spiritual leader of Temple Beth Zion, Buffalo, New York, whose sympathetic encouragement and suggestions helped me most in seeing the manuscript through the press.

ARMIN H. KOLLER.

Urbana, Illinois
March 22, 1929

PREFACE

From its earliest periods to the present day, the content of Judaism has been made the subject of research by many minds. It has been portrayed, either as a whole or in single phases, in an uncommonly large number of treatises and essays.

Until now, the reporting method has been the treatment employed throughout this immense literature. In it the results of research are drawn up in summaries and documented with mere references to the sources. Although the reader is thus supplied with the means of testing their correctness for himself, still such expositions consist by their very nature of reports *about* Judaism and do not let its teachings speak in their own language. With all the objectivity for which the investigators may have been sedulously striving, they inevitably look at and value things from their own viewpoint. Often a judgment of their own lies implicit in the very manner of reproducing the passages quoted from Jewish literature, and the subject under discussion thereby receives a coloring that biases the judgment of the reader in one direction or another.

In this work, the first volume of which is here made public, a different method is employed. The teaching of Judaism in respect to its principles and its manifold application to life speaks here in its own words. *What* Judaism teaches and *how* it teaches will be made manifest in this account of it. The brief introductions that precede each chapter are either simple recapitulations of the leading ideas of the passages cited in the text, or they are inserted to throw light on the historical development undergone by certain religious conceptions in Judaism, and on whatever differences of opinion have existed.

The first volume of the work contains "The Foundations of Jewish Ethics."

The second volume, "The Ethics of the Individual," and the third volume, "Social Ethics in Judaism," will deal with the duties which Jewish ethics enjoin upon the individual and upon communities.

The fourth volume will be entitled "God." It will contain the teachings of Judaism concerning the One and Only, the God who is Spirit, the God of all mankind, who is the sum total and the essence of holiness, righteousness, and love.

The fifth volume will throw light upon "Judaism among the Religions," having to do with its position in comparison with the religions of antiquity, and also in comparison with the Christian religion, which sprang from it. It will describe what Christianity has taken from Judaism and wherein it differs from it in principle.

Judaism will be treated in this work only in its doctrinal and ethical content. The ceremonial law with its exhaustive detail has already been handled in a number of compendiums and is outside the scope of the present undertaking.

In pursuance of the method employed, the teachings of Judaism are assembled in each chapter in quotations and passages given in historical sequence from the whole range of its entire literature. Those from the Bible are followed by others from the Palestinian Apocrypha and Pseudepigrapha—that is, those originally written in Hebrew or Aramaic. These, in turn, are followed by the Greek Apocrypha and the Jewish-Hellenistic literature. To these are added passages from the prayers and poetry of the synagogue, from the Talmud and the literature related to it, from the Jewish philosophy of religion of the middle ages, from the popular ethical literature and from other Jewish writings. Quotations are then given from Jewish scholars, of modern times, who derive their teaching of the principles of Judaism from the old Jewish literature. The concluding part is formed by extracts from works of Christian authors who have made a scientific study of Judaism.

The passages from the older religious works in the Hebrew, Aramaic, or Greek language have been rendered in a translation that is true to the letter and to the spirit of the original, faithfulness to the original text having been the translator's aim. Occasionally an elucidating word—in square brackets—has had to be inserted in the text.

Wherever Hebrew or Aramaic words have had to be used in the text, they have been reproduced in Latin script with phonetic spelling corresponding with the so-called Portuguese pronunciation.

In all quotations from the apocryphal and pseudepigraphic literature, the verse numbers in Kautzsch's edition of *Die Apokryphen und Pseudepigraphen des Alten Testaments* have been used, although they do not always agree with the numbering in the Greek editions. In passages from the Proverbs of Ben-Sira, where the Hebrew original has recently been rediscovered and published, this original has been used, otherwise the old Greek translation has been followed.

Passages from Philo's works have been cited in part as found in the old edition by Mangey (London, 1742) =M., and in part from the more recent edition by Cohn-Wendland (Berlin, 1896ff.) =C.-W., while the German translation issued by Leopold Cohn (Breslau, 1909ff.) but not yet completed, has been made use of wherever possible.

The Talmudical works have been named by their Hebrew or Aramaic titles, which are well known in scientific literature. In the case of medieval writings with less familiar titles a German (in this case, an English) translation of the title has been added to the first excerpt in any chapter, and this translated title is then used thereafter.

This work aims at a presentation of the true ethical and religious content of Judaism as vouched for by its original documents. May it be instrumental in removing prejudices and in creating far more just appreciation of Judaism! May the teachings of Judaism, which were not proclaimed for Israel alone, be taken to heart by all mankind and be incorporated in its life to its lasting happiness and salvation!

The material for the work has been assembled largely from the archives established by the Union of German Jews (*Verband der Deutschen Juden*) at the instigation of Rabbi Dr. Benno Jacob of Dortmund and Rabbi Dr. Josef Eschelbacher (since deceased), following a proposal of Advocate Dr. Alfred Klee's. Since their establishment these archives have been built up by continuous diligence in collecting material from Jewish and non-Jewish literature.

Utilizing proposals of Rabbi Dr. Ziegler of Carlsbad, the classification of the archives was planned and worked out in detail by Counselor Felix Makower. The collecting and arranging of all this copious material was done by Dr. Simon Bernfeld, assisted by a staff of readers under his direction. In the editing of this work, the arrangement of which is based upon the classification used in the archives, Counselor Makower and Advocate Max J. Loewenthal have collaborated with Rabbi Dr. L. Baeck, Prof. Dr. I. Elbogen, Rabbi Dr. S. Hochfeld, Director Dr. M. Holzman, and Rabbi Dr. A. Loewenthal.

For the second edition of this work all the material has been again subjected to careful scrutiny and a number of passages from old Jewish literature has been added. A list of these additional passages will be found at the end of the book.[1]

SIMON BERNFELD

Berlin, July, 1922.

[1] Herein omitted as of no interest to the reader in this first English edition.—Tr.

I

MORALITY AS A BASIC REQUIREMENT OF JUDAISM

Introduction by Dr. Leo Baeck

The insistence upon morality, as a principle of religion, is the very core and backbone of Judaism. In it, ethics does not need to be added to religion because it is already an essential part of it; without ethics there can be no belief in its judgment, in the meaning of this life, nor in that which pertains to the life beyond. This definite ethical character, which is peculiar to it, is the root of the new thing that the faith of Israel has contributed to the world.

The monotheism of Israel is ethical monotheism. The Oneness of God was recognized because His divine holiness was recognized. The one God whom the prophets have proclaimed is One not because He is the summation of all the gods of the heathen, but He is One because He differs from them in that the reality and certainty of the one good finds its seat in Him. Besides the one flawlessly moral God there can be no other gods, because the one morality does not tolerate anything contrary to itself. The One and Only God, and the Holy God, signify here the same thing. The One God pro-

claims to human beings what the one good is—to
practice righteousness and love.   This is the essential difference between Him and the many gods.

The belief in the One God has thus grown out
of the indivisibility of the demand of conscience for
holiness.   The thesis "Hear, O Israel, the Eternal
is our God, the Eternal is One," and the other thesis,
"Thou shalt love the Eternal, thy God, with all thy
heart, with all thy soul, and with all thy might,"
belong indissolubly together.   With all that we in-
wardly are and all that is given us, we can serve
only the One God; only the One God can command
that with our whole heart, our whole soul, and our
whole strength we shall surrender ourselves to Him.
In the moral unity of his soul, the Israelite became
conscious of the unity of God.

In Judaism, to know God does not imply an understanding of the nature of His Being but a knowledge of His government, a perception of and an effort
to follow the right way, the way which God has revealed and which is the same for all types of human
beings.   It is incumbent upon every human being to
seek to know His ways.   By this means he can approach God and learn to cleave to Him.   Only by
loyalty to God's commandment, to the moral law
that He has given to humanity, can man approach the
one God in order to serve Him.   The stronger our desire to be true moral human beings, the nearer we are
to God and the more accessible is He to us.   We can
always find Him if with our whole heart we seek to
obey His commandments.

In this way human life acquires meaning.   Herein is reality, that is, the good. And this good, this moral force, man has it in his power to create and to realize in his life. Therein he has his real existence; he becomes a creator of the good, the image of the one God. The amount of good existing upon the earth is the amount that man himself calls into being. Life is given to man by God and man himself has the task of shaping and forming it. By doing what is right, man "chooses life," he becomes the creator of his existence.

In a moral action, man becomes conscious of the power latent within him. By a moral act he makes a decision and in so doing realizes his freedom. Good and evil are placed before him that he may choose between them. Freedom also is a moral obligation that God has laid on human life. The will to the good is the will to freedom and the will to life. To choose life and to shape it, that is the demand that Judaism makes of the human being.

The life of man does not lie under the decree of a fate ordained for him but is shaped by the decisions that he himself makes. His goal is set before him, he is free to attain to it. He has the capacity, if he has swerved from it, to turn back into the way which leads to God. He can accomplish his own atonement, his own purification, by his deeds, his moral choice. No miracle, no sacrament performs this for him, but the freedom that is within his own soul. In so atoning, man procures for himself new freedom and new responsibility. He is led ever to new tasks.

The same goal is set forth for the individual and for mankind. This goal is the fulfillment of the good upon earth, in the realization of which alone mankind finds its true purpose and chooses its true life.   Above mankind stands the infinite moral commandment ever admonishing and making its demands.   The future thus becomes a task to be worked out.   The interpretation of history is that the existence of good shall constantly increase.   History has continuity and permanent meaning only in the good; only that keeps on living that wills to live through moral action.   The belief of Judaism in the future is based on this certainty.

Within Judaism there have been divergent currents of thought, but on this one point there has always been agreement and an ever increasing insistence, namely, that piety and the fear of God are grounded in moral action and that man can only apprehend God as he realizes that in the fulfillment of the good lies the *raison d'être* of his existence.

BIBLE

I,   1: I have known him [Abraham], to the end that he may command his children and his household after him, that they may keep the way of the LORD, to do righteousness and justice.—Genesis xviii. 19.

2: Ye shall be holy; for I the LORD your God am holy.—Leviticus xix. 2.

3: And now, Israel, what doth the LORD thy God require of thee, but to fear the LORD thy God, to walk in all His ways, and to love Him, and to serve the LORD thy God with all thy heart and with all thy soul.—Deuteronomy x. 12.

4: For this commandment which I command thee this day, it is not too hard for thee, neither is it far off.   It is not in heaven, that thou shouldest say: 'Who shall go up for us to heaven, and bring it unto us, and make us to hear it, that we may do it?'   Neither is it beyond the sea, that thou shouldest say: 'Who shall go over the sea for us, and bring it unto us, and make us to hear it, that we may do it?'   But the word is very nigh unto thee, in thy mouth, and in thy heart, that thou mayest do it.—Deuteronomy xxx. 11-14.

5: Wash you, make you clean, put away the evil of your doings from before Mine eyes, cease to do evil; learn to do good; seek justice, relieve the oppressed, judge the fatherless, plead for the widow.—Isaiah i. 16-17.

6: He that walketh righteously, and speaketh uprightly; he that despiseth the gain of oppressions, that shaketh his hands from holding of bribes, that stoppeth his ears from hearing of blood, and shutteth his eyes from looking upon evil; he shall dwell on high; his place of defence shall be the munitions of rocks; his bread shall be given, his waters shall be sure.—Isaiah xxxiii. 15-16.

7: Thus saith the LORD: keep ye justice, and do righteousness; for My salvation is near to come, and My favor to be revealed.—Isaiah lvi. 1.

8: Behold, the days come, saith the LORD, that I will make a new covenant with the house of Israel, and with the house of Judah; not according to the covenant that I made with their fathers in the day that I took them by the hand to bring them out of the land of Egypt; forasmuch as they broke My covenant, although I was a lord over them, saith the LORD.   But this is the covenant that I will make with the house of Israel after those days, saith the LORD.   I will put My law in their inward parts, and in their hearts will I write it; and I will be their God, and they shall be My people.—Jeremiah xxxi. 31-33.

9: It hath been told thee, O man, what is good, and what the LORD doth require of thee: only to do justly, and to love mercy, and to walk humbly with thy God.—Micah vi. 8.

10: LORD, who shall sojourn in Thy tabernacle? who shall dwell upon Thy holy mountain? He that walketh uprightly, and worketh righteousness, and speaketh truth in his heart; that hath no slander upon his tongue, nor doeth evil to his fellow, nor taketh up a reproach against his neighbor; in whose eyes a vile person is despised, but he honoreth them that fear the LORD; he that sweareth to his own hurt, and changeth not; he that putteth not out his money on interest, nor taketh a bribe against the innocent.   He that doeth these things shall never be moved.—Psalms xv.

11: Who shall ascend into the mountain of the LORD? and who shall stand in His holy place? he that hath clean hands, and a pure heart; who hath not taken My name in vain, and hath not sworn deceitfully.   He shall receive a blessing from the LORD, and righteousness from the God of his salvation.—Psalms xxiv. 3-5.

12: The fear of the LORD is to hate evil.—Proverbs viii. 13.

13: And unto man he said: 'Behold, the fear of

the LORD, that is wisdom; and to depart from evil is understanding.'——Job xxviii. 28.

14: If I did despise the cause of my man-servant, or of my maid-servant, when they contended with me—what then shall I do when God riseth up? and when He remembereth, what shall I answer Him? did not He that made me in the womb make him? and did not One fashion us in the womb? If I have withheld aught that the poor desired, or have caused the eyes of the widow to fail; or have eaten my morsel myself alone, and the fatherless hath not eaten thereof—Nay, from my youth he grew up with me as with a father, and I have been her guide from my mother's womb. If I have seen any wanderer in want of clothing, or that the needy had no covering; if his loins have not blessed me, and if he were not warmed with the fleece of my sheep; if I have lifted up my hand against the fatherless, because I saw my help in the gate [at court]; then let my shoulder fall from the shoulder-blade, and mine arm be broken from the bone. For calamity from God was a terror to me, and by reason of His majesty I could do nothing. If I have made gold my hope, and have said to the fine gold: 'thou art my confidence'; if I rejoiced because my wealth was great, and because my hand had gotten much; if I rejoiced at the destruction of him that hated me, or exulted when evil found him—Yea, I suffered not my mouth to sin by asking his life with a curse. The stranger did not lodge in the street; my doors I opened to the roadside. If after the manner of men I covered my transgressions, by hiding mine iniquity in my bosom—If my land cry out against me, and the

furrows thereof weep together; if I have eaten the
fruits thereof without money, or have caused the til-
lers thereof to be disappointed—let thistles grow instead of wheat, and noisome weeds instead of barley.
—Job xxxi. 13-25, 29, 30, 32, 33, 38-40.

PALESTINIAN APOCRYPHA

IIa,   1: All wisdom is the fear of the Eternal; and
in all wisdom is the fulfilling of the Torah.—Ben-
Sira (variously cited as: Proverbs of Ben-Sira;
Sirach; Ecclesiasticus; Ben-Sira's Book of Wisdom—
Tr.) xix. 20-21.

2: To depart from wickedness is a thing well
pleasing to the LORD; and to forsake unrighteousness is a propitiation.—Ben-Sira xxxii. 5 (=xxxv. 3).

3: And now, my children,
    Make your hearts good before the Lord,
    And your ways straight before men,
    And ye shall find grace before the Lord and
men.—*The Testaments of the Twelve Patriarchs*, II.
5, 2 [Charles, in *The Apocrypha and Pseudepigrapha
of the Old Testament in English* (ed. by R. H.
Charles, Vol. I, *Apocrypha*, Vol. II, *Pseudepigrapha*,
Oxford, Clarendon Press, 1913), Vol. II].

4: Keep, my children, the law of God,
    And get singleness,
    And walk in guilelessness,
    Not playing the busybody with the business
        of your neighbor,
    But love the Lord and your neighbor,
    Have compassion on the poor and weak.—
Ibid., V. 5, 1-2 (Charles, *l. c.*).

5: Take heed to thyself, my child, in all thy works, be discreet in all thy behavior. And what thou thyself hatest, do to no man.—Tobit iv. 14-15 (Simpson, in Charles, *l. c.*, I).

JEWISH-HELLENISTIC LITERATURE

III,   1: The sacred commandments were given for the sake of righteousness, to arouse pious thoughts and to form character.—*The Letter of Aristeas*, 144; see also *ibid.*, 168. [To watch for men's destruction is an unholy thing. And our law forbids us to injure anyone either by word or deed . . . . all our regulations have been drawn up with a view to righteousness, and nothing has been enacted in the Scripture thoughtlessly or without due reason, but its purpose is to enable us throughout our whole life and in all our actions to practise righteousness before all men, being mindful of Almighty God (Andrews, in Charles, *l. c.*, II).—Tr.]

2: And there are, as we may say, two most especially important heads of all the innumerable particular lessons and doctrines: the regulating of one's conduct towards God by the rules of piety and holiness, and of one's conduct towards men by the rules of humanity and justice.—Philo: *On the Special Laws*, II; *On the Number Seven* (M. II, 282; C.-W. 63) (*The Works of Philo Judaeus, the Contemporary of Josephus*, tr. from the Greek by C. D. Yonge, London, 1855-99).

3: It is a felicitous and true saying of one of the wise men of old, that men never act in a manner more resembling God than when they are bestowing benefits; and what can be a greater good than for mortal men to imitate the everlasting God?—Philo: *On Special Laws*, IV; *On the Office and Character of a Judge* (M. II, 347; C.-W. 73).

4: And this [reconciliation] is an object which the most holy prophet [Moses] is endeavoring to bring to pass throughout the whole of his code of laws, studying to create unanimity, and fellowship, and agreement, and that due admixture of different dispositions by which houses, and cities, and altars, and nations, and countries, and the whole human race may be conducted to the very highest happiness.— Philo: *On Virtues, On Humanity* (M. II, 395; C.-W. 119).

5: All men ought to follow and worship God in the exercise of virtue; for this way of worship of God is the most holy.—Josephus, *Against Apion*, II, 23 (*The Works of Josephus Flavius*, Whiston's tr. revised by A. R. Shilleto, 5 vols., London, 1898-1903).

TALMUDICAL LITERATURE

V,   1: Simon the Just . . . used to say, 'On three things the world standeth: on the Torah,[1] and on the Service, and on the doing of kindnesses.'— *Ethics of the Fathers*, I, 2 (Herford, in Charles, *l. c.*, II).

---

[1] "The word Torah is left untranslated. It is variously used for the Pentateuch, the Scriptures, the Oral Law, as well as for the whole body of religious truth, study and practice" (Singer's *The Standard Prayer Book*, Bloch, 1924, p. 271, n.).
"Torah. A technical term not identical with 'Law.' *Torah*—teaching—denotes the revelation which God gave to Israel by Moses, supposed to be complete and final.

2: Another heathen came to Shammai saying: "Convert me to Judaism [*gajjereni*] [make me a proselyte] on the condition that thou teach me the whole Torah while I stand on one foot." Shammai pushed him away with the builders' measure he held in his hand. He thereupon came to Hillel, and the latter accepted him [*gijjero*] [made him a proselyte]. He told him: "What is hateful to thee, do not unto thy fellow: this is the whole Torah. All the rest is commentary; go and learn it."—*Shabbat* 31a. [See Abraham Geiger, *Judaism and Its History*, tr. by Newburgh, p. 116: "Hillel said to him: 'Whatever is displeasing unto thee, do not unto another; that is the foundation and root of Judaism; the rest is commentary which you may learn at your leisure'"; see also *The Testaments of the Twelve Patriarchs*, VIIIb, 1, 6 in Charles, *l. c.*: "But He hath not created the world for nought, but that His creatures should fear Him, and that none should do to his neighbor what he doth not like for himself"; see also *Tobit* IV. 15: "Do that to no man which thou hatest"; see also Philo, *Fragments* (M. II, 629), in Yonge: "Moreover, it is ordained in the laws themselves that no one

The Pentateuch is the written record of that teaching; hence the name Torah is often applied to the Pentateuch. But Torah included also the unwritten tradition whereby the implicit contents of the revelations were made explicit by successive interpretations. No English word is equivalent to Torah" (Herford).

"Torah (Heb. instruction). Used in a wide sense to denote the whole body of Jewish teaching as contained in the Scriptures and the traditions connected therewith. It is also employed to mean the Pentateuch, as distinct from the Prophetical books. On the Rabbinic conception of *Torah*, see W. O. E. Oesterley and G. H. Box, *The Religion and Worship, of the Synagogue*, 2d ed., 1911, Chap. VII; R. T. Herford, *Pharisaism*, [Chap. II]; and Schechter, *Aspects of Rabbinic Theology*, Chaps. VIII-XI."—(Rev. A. Cohen, *The Babylonian Talmud: Traktate Berakot*, tr. into English for the first time. Cambridge University Press, 1921, Glossary, p. 430).

See also Herford, *The Pharisees*, New York, Macmillan, 1924, Chap. III, "Torah and Tradition," pp. 53-87; Chap. V, D, "The Torah and the Moral Law," pp. 138-146—Tr.

shall do to his neighbor what he would be unwilling to have done to himself."]²

3: "Thou shalt love thy neighbor as thyself" Leviticus xix. 18. Rabbi Akiba taught: That is a chief principle [*kelal gadol*]³ of the Torah. Ben Azzai taught: There exists a still more important principle: This is the book of the generations of man [human being] . . . *in the likeness of God created He him* (Genesis v. 1).—*Siphra, ad loc.;* compare Albo, *Ikkarim* (Book of Principles), I, 24.

4: Rabbi Simlayi taught: The Torah contains six hundred and thirteen commandments; two hundred and forty-eight of them positive: "Thou shalt," corresponding to the two hundred and forty-eight members of a man's body; and three hundred and sixty-five negative; "Thou shalt not," corresponding to the three hundred and sixty-five days in the solar year. King David condensed all of them to eleven. For it is said, "Lord, who shall sojourn in Thy tabernacle? Who shall dwell upon Thy holy mountain? He that walketh uprightly, and worketh righteousness, and speaketh truth in his heart; that hath no slander upon his tongue, nor doeth evil to his fellows, nor taketh up a reproach against his neighbor; in whose eyes a vile person is despised, but he honoreth them that fear the LORD; he that sweareth to his own hurt, and changeth not; he that putteth not out his money on interest, nor taketh a bribe against the innocent. He that doeth these things shall never be moved" (Psalms xv).

---

² The last three passages are referred to, but not cited in the German text.—Tr.
³ "The all embracing principle of the divine law."—M. Mielziner, *Introduction to the Talmud* (2d. rev. ed., New York, Funk and Wagnalls, 1903), p. 279.—Tr.

The prophet Isaiah condensed them to six (xxxiii. 15-16): "He that walketh righteously, and speaketh uprightly; he that despiseth the gain of oppressions, that shaketh his hands from holding of bribes, that stoppeth his ears from hearing of blood, and shutteth his eyes from looking upon evil; he shall dwell on high; his place of defence shall be the munitions of rocks; his bread shall be given, his waters shall be sure."

The prophet Micah condensed them to three (vi. 8): "It hath been told thee, O man, what is good, and what the LORD doth require of thee: Only to do justly, and to love mercy, and to walk humbly with thy God."

Then Isaiah condensed them again to two (lvi. 1): "Keep ye justice, and do righteousness; for My salvation is near to come, and My favor to be revealed."

At last the prophet Habakkuk condensed them into one sentence (ii. 4): "The righteous shall live by his faith."—*Makkot* 23b-24a.

5: The Torah has been revealed only for the purpose of purifying human beings.—*Bereshit Rabbah,* c. 44.

6: "Every one of the divine works is pure" (Proverbs xxx. 5): this means that the laws have been given to Israel to purify it and to cleanse it from fleshly appetites.—*Vayyikra Rabbah,* c. 13.

7: The human being shall ever so conduct himself as if the Holy One dwelled in him.—*Taanit* 11a.

8: Keep thy mouth from all sin, and purify and sanctify thyself from all guilt and iniquity. Then shall I be with thee everywhere.—*Berachot* 17a (Rev. A. Cohen, *l. c., p.* 111).

MIDDLE AGES

VI, 1: The ray of divine holiness [*Shechinah*][4] rests upon everyone in Israel whose actions are clean, whose heart is pure, and whose soul is wholly with the God of Israel.—Yehudah ha-Levi, *Kuzari*, V, 23.

2: What the Torah commands Israel has the sole purpose of maintaining among human beings mutual love and peace.—*Book of the Pious*, §956 (567).

3: The commandment to walk in the ways of God has been explained by our sages thus: as God is love, so must thou also become loving; as God is merciful, so must thou also become merciful; as God is holy, so must thou also become holy. So the prophets have spoken of God as forbearing, gracious, and just: —in order to make it known that these are the good and straight ways upon which man shall walk so as to become like unto God, according to the measure of his capacity.—Maimonides, *Mishneh Torah Hilchot Deot* (Ethics), I, 6.

4: Do not let God be far from your thoughts; forget not what He has done for you; do not let that strange idol, your voluptuousness, rule over you. Act so that you do not have to blush before yourself; lend no ear to appetite; do not sin and say that afterward you would do penance; never let an oath pass your lips; never let arrogance rise in your mind; do not

---

[4] *Shekinah* (Heb. abiding). The Divine Presence as manifested on earth; the Spirit of God immanent in the world. See Oesterley and Box, pp. 217ff.; Abelson, *Immanence of God in Rabbinic Literature*. Chaps. IV-XII. (Rev. A. Cohen, l. c., Glossary, p. 430). For *Shechinah* see also Herford, *The Pharisees*, pp. 153f.—Tr.

follow the lust of the eyes. Banish guile from your heart, insolence from look and spirit. Never speak vain words, do not quarrel with anyone, do not attach yourself to scoffers, do not wrangle with the wicked. —R. Eleazar b. Yehudah, *Rokeach* (Zunz, *Gesch. u. Lit.*, p. 132).

5: Pure love of the Creator is the highest divine service.—R. Moses b. Jacob of Coucy: from the *Great Law Book, Prohibitions* 2, 64, 170; *Precepts* 3, 16, 74.

6: Furthermore, do not walk in the ways of thy heart, but in the fear of God and in conscientiousness toward His precepts: in chastity, modesty, purity, and holiness. Let pious thoughts always be in thee.— Moses Cohen b. Eleazar, the smaller *Book of the Pious*, p. 2.

7: We might assume that Maimonides did not wish to set up dogmas of faith by which Judaism stands and falls, but only important principles of Judaism. If that is the case, I propose to state this as an important principle of Judaism: that we Jews believe that there is communion between God and the human being, and that God's holiness is ever present among us.—Joseph Albo, *Ikkarim* (Book of Principles), I, 3.

8: The Torah admonishes to love of humanity: "Thou shalt love thy neighbor as thyself" (Leviticus xix. 18). The Torah removes hatred: "Thou shalt not hate thy brother in thy heart" (*ibid.*, 17). The Torah commends love for the stranger: "Love ye therefore the stranger" (Deuteronomy x. 19). The Torah forbids us to oppress and harass him: "He shall dwell with thee, in the midst of thee, in the place which he shall choose within one of thy gates, where it liketh him best; thou shalt not wrong him" (*ibid.*, xxiii. 17). And this does not refer only to the converted stranger but also to the mere "sojourner" if he does not worship idols.—Joseph Albo, *l. c.*, iii, 25.

Modern Jewish Literature

VII,   1: For the prophets to know the nature of God means to know that He is righteous and incorruptible, that He is merciful, gracious, and forbearing, that He tries the heart of man, that He has destined him for the good. The knowledge of God instructs us in what man shall be; the Divine tells us what is human. The ways of God are the ways in which men shall go—"they shall observe the way of the Eternal, to do righteousness and justice." To understand a human being means, therefore, to comprehend what God has given him and requires of him, to comprehend that he is created to be righteous and good, holy as the Eternal his God is holy. The revelation of God and the revelation of the moral element in humanity thus meet. Not a revelation concerning God's nature falls to the lot of the prophet and through him to us; but a revelation concerning God's will and commandment. In learning to know God, we learn to understand ourselves, we learn to be true human beings. "He hath told thee, O man, what is good." What God reveals to us is the good that He requires of us for the sake of our true life. Along the path of the right alone do we thus reach our

God.   The more we desire to be true human beings, the nearer we are to Him, the nearer is He to us.   To seek God means to strive after good; to find God means to do good.   Do what God commands you, then you will know who He is.   That is the apprehension of God as the prophets experience and teach it; the way that leads to God.   "Know Him upon all thy ways."   "Return to thy God, practice true love and justice and ever wait for thy God."   "Seek the *Eternal*, then ye shall live: .   .   . seek the *good* and not the evil, that ye may live; then the Eternal, the God of hosts, will be with you, as ye have said." —Leo Baeck, *Das Wesen des Judentums* (2d ed.), pp. 29-30.

2: Its ethical character, the basic significance which it sees in the moral action, is the primary thing in the religion of Israel.   No matter at what date one may fix its origin and no matter how one may view the question of its progress, one thing is certain, that since that Israelitish, prophetic religion began, which is the true religion of Israel, the moral law has formed its cardinal point.   Judaism is not only ethical, but *ethics constitute its principle, its essence and nature.* —Leo Baeck, *l. c.,* p. 54.

3:   To love God supremely, and one's fellow creature as oneself, this is what is required by the revealed teaching and the moral law.—M. Bloch, *Die Ethik in der Halacha,* p. 9.

4:   Ethics is the vital principle, the soul of Judaism.   Its religion wills to be moral teaching and is moral teaching.   The love of God is the knowledge of God.   And the knowledge of God is the knowledge of the ultimate moral purpose of the human race.— Hermann Cohen, *Innere Bezhg. d. Kant. Philos. z. Judentum,* pp. 59-60.

5: The Pharisaic view of religion never underestimated lightly the importance of moral works, of compassion and brotherly love; but in conformity with the prophets always represented them as the highest and final goal of religious life. "Righteousness and beneficence counterbalance all religious precepts." "To him who in his general conduct and contact with his fellows is guided by *honesty and loyalty,* it is accounted as if he had fulfilled the whole Torah."—J. Elbogen, *Die Religionsanschauungen der Pharisäer,* pp. 27-28.

6: Virtue and morality were esteemed as a phase of piety that was inalienable from the worship of God. The literature of Judaism is permeated by religious and ethical thoughts. These abound not merely in innumerable moral writings, books of exhortations, sermons of reproof, and penitential poems, with their severe moral demands and inexorable scourging of moral wrongs, but also in the legal opinions which often consist simply of a practical application of what is taught in those books on morals, and in sermons which give ethical expositions of the Holy Scriptures. The same moral content is seen in the actual life of the people—a people harshly persecuted and scornfully regarded, but none the less morally sound.—J. Freudenthal, *Spinoza,* I, pp. 29-30.

7: But Judaism was not simply to introduce a new conception of God into the world, but also to dignify and ennoble all human relations. The men who taught in ancient time, "The true foundation and the nerve of the Law is, whatever displeases thee, do not unto others; that is the essence and the root of the Law, all the rest is commentary which thou mayest learn at thy leisure"; or, "Thou shalt love thy neighbor as thyself, that is the great comprehensive principle of the law"; or, " 'This is the book of the generations of man'; here is still a greater principle: to be a man and to recognize all men under all conditions as equals and peers";—the men like Hillel, Akiba, and Ben Soma (Asai), who taught such lessons, are the very props and pillars of Judaism, and we must take their words seriously to heart.   Judaism, I repeat, did not come into this world simply to present a new conception of God, but to illumine and ennoble all human relations and to teach the proper recognition and estimate of man.—Abraham Geiger, *Das Judentum u. s. Geschichte*, I, p. 41 (*Judaism and Its History*, in two parts, tr. from the German by Charles Newburgh, New York, Bloch, 1911, Part One, pp. 53-54).   (Revised by Tr.).

8: This is the teaching of Hillel: "Whatever would be odious to thee, do not to thy fellow man," and he could, therefore, give this sentence as the fundamental principle of the whole law, for all laws are but to inculcate righteousness and love toward all beings—or an education toward that end.—S. R. Hirsch, *Choreb*, c. 91, p. 586.

9: First of all, we may establish the brief proposition: *Judaism has for the first time connected religion and morality together with a truly ideal con-*

sistency.—Max Joseph, *Zur Sittenlehre des Juden-*
tums, p. 4.

10: All of them [the prophets] say this clearly
and distinctly: Wilt thou truly worship God, practice first of all righteousness and love! wilt thou find
favor in the eyes of God, first of all lead a pure, morally consecrated life!—Max Joseph, *l. c.*, p. 9.

11: Judaism alone fully realized the moral nature
of the Deity. This was done by investing the term
"holiness" with the idea of moral perfection, so that
God became the ideal and pattern of the loftiest morality. "Be ye holy, for I the LORD your God am
holy" (Leviticus xix. 1). This is the central and cul-
minating thought embodied in the Jewish law. Holiness is the essence of all moral perfection; it is purity
unsullied by any breath of evil.—Kaufmann Kohler,
Theologie des Judentums, p. 76 (*Jewish Theology,*
Systematically and Historically Considered, New
York, Macmillan, 1918, p. 101). (Revised by Tr.)

12: The problem of human destiny is met by
Judaism with the idea that God is the ideal and pattern of all morality. The solution is "To walk in
the ways of God, to be righteous and just," as He is
(Genesis xviii. 19; Deuteronomy viii. 6; x. 12;
xxxii. 4).—Kaufmann Kohler, *l. c.*, p. 165 (*ibid.*, p.
218). (Revised by Tr.)

13: The same thought runs through the whole
of Rabbinic literature. Knowledge of the Divine Being and therefore the knowledge of His moral attributes, combined with the endeavor to emulate them
in man's finite way, constitute at once the rule and the
reason of morality.—M. Lazarus, *Die Ethik des Ju-*

dentums, I, p. 87   (*The Ethics of Judaism,* tr. from the German by Henrietta Szold, Philadelphia, The Jewish Publication Society of America, 1900, Part One, p. 113). (Revised by Tr.)

14: From all this we deduce the following as the essential doctrine of Judaism: Morality is its own reason and aim; it is man's vocation and the vocation of all spiritual beings. It may not serve any purpose outside of itself; it is its own purpose, and to all other purposes that man seeks to realize, it assigns their proper value and due proportion.—M. Lazarus, *l. c.,* p. 118 (Szold, ibid., p. 154). (Revised by Tr.)

15: It is characteristic of the fundamental doctrine of Judaism that morality is looked upon as absolute, as unconditioned. In this life, as in the world beyond, morality is the highest aim and its value as such is eternal. In our very conception of God ethical ideas are fundamental. Through them man is enabled to attain to a clearer understanding of the divine essence than through any others.—M. Lazarus, *ibid.,* p. 202 (Szold, *ibid.,* Part Two, p. 22). (Revised by Tr.)

16: The command to walk in the ways of God includes the whole formation of character. That is what our sages mean by the words: As He is merciful, be thou likewise merciful. The purport of it all is that a human being shall determine all the qualities of his character and all his actions in accordance with uprightness and morality.—Moses Chayim Luzzatto, *Mesillat Yesharim* (The Path of the Pious).

17: The nature of holiness consists in the fact of a human being adhering to his God so entirely that in no action that he performs does he dissociate himself from Him; so that he is not pulled down from the heights of communion with God by occupation with earthly things, but on the contrary, earthly things are exalted by his concerning himself with them—Moses Chayim Luzzatto, *l. c.,* c. 26.

18: The prophetic commands are centered around the teaching that all piety and devotion must begin with love of mankind and can be realized only within that love.   Religion and morality, the way to God and the way to man coincide, are to be reckoned as one.—Max Wiener, *Die Religion d. Propheten,* pp. 11-12.

19: There is no period in the development of the Israelitish religion in which the relation of *YHVH* to his people was not radiantly evident as a rigorously moral one.—Max Wiener, *Die Anschauungen d. Propheten v. d. Sittlichkeit,* p. 35.

20: The holy God desires a holy, pure life . . . It is scarcely possible to coin a clearer expression for the indissolubility of true religion and true morality. —Max Wiener, *ibid.,* pp. 47-48.

See also:

ALBERT BACH, *Erlösung,* 1917, p. 19.

M. BLOCH, *Die Ethik in der Halacha,* 1886, p. 4.

H. COHEN, *Religion u. Sittlichkeit,* 1907, pp. 124f.

MAX ELLGUTHER, *Die soz.   Gesetzgebung d. Bibel,* 1902, pp. 21f.

J. FREUDENTHAL, *Spinoza,* I, 1904, pp. 21f.

ABRAHAM GEIGER, *Das Judentum u. s. Geschichte,* I, 1865, p. 36.

M. GÜDEMANN, *Das Judentum i. s. Grundzügen,* 1902, p. 104.

LEVI HERZFELD, *Geschichte d. Volkes Jisrael,* 1847, p. 61.

EMIL G. HIRSCH, *Die Beitr. d. Judentums z. lib. Rel.*, 1911, p. 466.

S. R. HIRSCH, *Choreb*, 1837, c. 72 §481; c. 75 §491; c. 95 §597; c. 98 §616.

———— *19 Briefe*, 1836, pp. 17f., 20f., 52ff., 57ff.

———— *Ges. Schr.* I, 1902, pp. 50, 394; II, 1904, p. 164; III, 1906, pp. 111, 456.

WILHELM JERUSALEM, *Der Kulturwert des Judentums* (in *"Der Jude,"* Nr. 7, 1917), p. 479.

M. JOEL, *Religionsphilosophische Zeitfragen*, 1876, p. 82.

MAX JOSEPH, *Zur Sittenlehre d. Judentums*, 1902, pp. 7f., 24.

BENZION KELLERMANN, *Der ethische Monotheismus d. Propheten*, 1917, p. 27.

KAUFMANN KOHLER, *Grundr. e. syst. Theol. d. Judentums*, 1910, pp. 5, 11, 16, 18f., 26, 180, 182f., 268.

L. LAZARUS, *Zur Charakteristik d. talmud. Ethik*, 1877, p. 16, note 9.

M. LAZARUS, *Die Ethik d. Judentums*, I, 1899, pp. 33, 74, 84ff., 89, 91f., 99, 101f., 105ff., 118, 123, 193, 198f., 310, 248.

RUDOLF LESZYNSKY, *Pharisäer u. Sadduzäer*, 1912, pp. 59f.

SALOMON MAIMON, *Lebensgeschichte*, 1792, pp. 76ff.

MOSES MENDELSSOHN, *Jerusalem*, 1783, pp. 142, 197.

FELIX PERLES, *Bousset's Religion d. Judentums*, 1903, p. 114.

H. STEINTHAL, *Über Juden u. Judentum*, 1906, pp. 16f., 122f.

———— *Zu Bibel u. Religionsphilosophie*, 1895, II, p. 9.

LUDWIG VENETIANER, *Jüdisches im Christentum*, 1913, p. 30.

MAX WIENER, *Die Anschauungen d. Propheten v. d. Sittlichkeit*, 1909, pp. 35, 47f.

———— *Die Religion d. Propheten*, 1912, pp. 41, 75.

NOTE—For a bibliography of "The Hundred Best Available Books in English on Jewish Subjects," see *The American Jewish Year Book*, Vol. 6, pp. 309-317; Vol. 27, pp. 260-273.

For "A Classified List of Standard Books on Jewish Subjects," see *ibid.*, Vol. 25, pp. 204-255.—Tr.

CHRISTIAN AUTHORS

VIII, 1: The basic character, then, of Jewish ethics is *thoughtful prudence* in the good sense of the word, *serene moderation, tranquil kindness and friendliness that are not carried to excess.* Its supreme ideal is righteousness (*Tzedakah*) (δικαιοσύνη) which is at the same time goodness (mercy) (ἐλεημοσύνη) and justice which gives everyone his due; friendliness, humaneness, meekness, and avoidance of haughtiness; civility and complaisance, willing readiness to help others in the difficulties and troubles of everyday life; peaceableness, forbearance with the foibles of others, gentleness of temper, a forgiving spirit, avoidance of unnecessary enmities, avoidance of anger and of all excess of emotion (*échauffements*), moderation in all things—these are its ever recurring demands. The ideal of life of a Hillel, a Gamaliel, a Yochanan ben Zakkai, is paraphrased in these words.—Wilhelm Bousset, *Die Religion d. Judentums*, pp. 486-488. (In appended notes, quotations from the Jewish-Palestinian Apocrypha and from Talmudical literature are given which establish and prove the foregoing opinion.)

2: It is not sufficient for *Yahveh* that He and He only simply be worshiped; all depends on the manner in which He is worshiped; *Yahveh* is the God of righteousness, of morality; His supreme, indeed, His single, indispensable requirement from His servants is righteousness, is morality.—Karl Budde, *Die Religion d. Volkes Israel*, p. 119.

3: If it be the last and highest task of religion to make us better human beings and to kindle in our hearts love toward God and our fellows, and if the measure of a religion's value lies in the extent to which it succeeds in carrying out this highest task, then Israel's religion has certainly no cause to shrink from such a test. At a time when all the rest of mankind was still covered by the darkest night of uncharitableness and inhumanity, even then the religion of Israel breathed a spirit of true humanity, which must fill even the outsider with reverence and admiration if he be but willing to admit it.—Heinrich Cornill, *Das A. T. u. d. Humanität*, p. 23.

4: Our formula is, "Act according to God's law," and in this connection the concept of God's law has been more fully explained above. On the basis of this formula it is a matter of course that the maxim of my action can always serve at the same time as the principle of a general legislation, for the two coincide here completely; but, furthermore, there are no longer various maxims, various principles of a general legislation such as the Kantian formula makes appear as possible; there is only one, great, general maxim that represents the single principle of a general legislation, namely, God's law. It is evident that in their ethics the ancient Jews were a goodly stretch in advance of Immanuel Kant.—Hugo Dingler, *Die Kultur d. Juden*, pp. 100-101.

5: "But *Yahveh* is a moral Being and desires only a meek spirit and moral conduct, and both demands are as easy to fulfill as to know" (The thoughts of Micah). Micah, therefore, and Amos raise religion from the sphere of nature *into that of morality*. From then on it is free to develop higher.—Bernhard Duhm, *Die Theol. d. Propheten*, p. 103.

6: Behind these holy ordinances and customs, the holy priests who protected them, the holy books which expounded them in writing, the infinitely holy place in which they were upheld—behind all this visible sanctity stood something holy in itself, of the loftiest meaning, the true religion, with its eternal verities and its loftiest hopes and strivings (which at that time had been already at their utmost tension), but also with its austere demands and moral code.— Heinrich Ewald, *The History of Israel* (tr. by J. E. Carpenter, 2d ed., London, Longmans, Green & Co., 1880), V, p. 62.   (Revised by Tr.)

7: But the ancient community of Israel had also much to offer to the better and wiser [class of] Greeks, which they, it seems, if we correctly interpret one of the leading endeavors of their philosophy, had for centuries been seeking, but had not yet discovered in actual national life, namely, the truths of a religion aspiring after the highest perfection, and the actual beginning of their realisation in a nation's life.— Heinrich Ewald, *l. c.,* p. 246.

8: The Israelitish religion is an earnest, holy religion. "Woe is me! for I am undone; Because I am a man of unclean lips; For mine eyes have seen the King, The LORD of hosts" (Isaiah vi. 5). Of this strength of feeling of the Israelitish people and its religion we would wish a portion for our people and its religion.—Hermann Gunkel, *Was bleibt vom A. T.?* p. 29.

9: The Israelitish prophets discovered, prior to the philosophers of Greece, the law of moral causality that governs the world uniformly. By clearly formulating the thought of the unity of God, and the thought of the moral meaning of cosmic events, particularly that of history, they [the Israelitish prophets] raised the religion of cult to a religion of morality, natural religion to a historical religion.—Gustav Hölscher, *Die Propheten*, p. 188.

10: Righteousness and mercifulness are essentially moral attributes. If these were the motives of the election and salvation of Israel, then the religion also that sprang from them bore fundamentally a moral character in an entirely different sense from any that would ever have been conceivable in the case of a purely national religion.—Emil Kautzsch, *Biblische Theologie d. A. T.*, p. 64.

11: We should be guilty of an unjustified restriction if we tried to base our estimate of the significance of the Old Testament as a rich treasury of moral instruction only upon single, isolated narratives. On the contrary, it is of the highest importance that despite certain imperfections of moral judgment, its whole general view of life (*Weltanschauung*) is characterized by the most profound moral earnestness. The reason lies, as everywhere, in the nature of the religious root out of which the Old Testament morality grew, above all in the vital faith in the unconditional holiness and righteousness of God, and in the fear of God which rests upon that faith. As the whole law and the prophets are included, according to the word of the master, in the commandment "Love thy neighbor as thyself," so also according to the word of the Old Testament sage, all knowledge is included in the fear of God—it is the beginning of wisdom.—Emil Kautzsch, *Die bleibende Bedeutung des A. T.*, p. 26.

12: In recent times especially, the religion of the

Old Testament and of the people of Israel has often been undervalued. In reality, their religion is not only the equal of all other religions of antiquity, but in itself represents *the flower* of them all; it far surpasses all of them.—Rudolf Kittel, *Das Alte Testament und das "deutsche Christentum"* (in *"Allgemeine Evangelisch-lutherische Kirchenzeitung,"* 55 Jahrg., Nr. 17), pp. 260-261.

13: Ethical precepts are in closest relation to the basic religious demand. Because Israel belongs to *Yahveh,* i. e. is in itself holy, it must attain to a corresponding perfection in respect to moral action. In Leviticus xix.ff. the transgression of moral commands, e. g. of love of parents, of love of fellow countrymen, of chastity, etc. (Leviticus xix. 3, 9, 11-18, 29, 32, 34-36), appears unquestionably as a crime against the *sanctity* of God (see Leviticus xix. 2). If the decalogue, as in general every Israelitish code of law, brought moral requirement into close connection with religious requirement, the so-called law of holiness brings it even closer.   That *failure in duty* toward one's neighbor, indeed even toward one's own person, is *"sin,"* a *religious transgression* in the strictest sense of the word, cannot be more strikingly emphasized than is done there.—Justus Köberle, *Sünde und Gnade,* pp. 230-231.

14: They [the demands of the covenant] bear in the first place a *religious-ethical character.* The requirement of devotion, of piety, and of morality rooted therein stands ever, according to the prophet guardians of the Israelitish religion, in the *foreground* of the divine demand.—Eduard König, *Prophetenideal, Judentum u. Christentum,* p. 4.

15: Accordingly, it is of the essence of the prophetic religion that religion and ethics are not separable. True religion leads to ethical conduct. The sincerely religious person can express his religion only in the practice of a moral life.—Karl Marti, *Die Religion d. A. T.*, p. 50.

16: "Know, therefore, my children, that two spirits wait upon man—the spirit of truth and the spirit of deceit. And in the midst is the spirit of understanding of the mind, to which it belongeth to turn whithersoever it will. And the works of truth and the works of deceit are written upon the hearts of men, and each one of them the Lord knoweth. And there is no time at which the works of men can be hid; for on the heart itself have they been written down before the Lord. And the spirit of truth testifieth all things, and accuseth all; and the sinner is burnt up by his own heart, and can not raise his face to the judge."—*Testaments of the Twelve Patriarchs*, IV, 20; [see pp. 135-136, II a 1]. These words may be considered a program and the substance of all subsequent development. At the same time, they show how the moral sensibility of the Psalms and the Book of Job continues to exist in these circles as the inner matrix of religion, and how that moral sensibility deepens religion and renders it completely ethical, by making its reality depend entirely on the inner core of every human being.—Eduard Meyer, *Ursprung und Anfänge des Christentums*, II, p. 106.

17: In fact, in Israel moral and religious perfection cannot be separated, even though the emphasis may lie now on the one, now on the other aspect.—

Friedrich Nötscher, *Die Gerechtigkeit Gottes b. d. vorexil. Propheten,* p. 8.

18: Knowledge of God, as the prophets understood it, is practical application of the Divine will; to exercise justice and forbearance toward the poor and the needy, that is to know *Yahveh* (Jeremiah xxii. 16; also ix. 23).—Friedrich Nötscher, *l. c.,* pp. 51-52.

19: Even at that early time in ancient Israel the conception of *Yahveh's* holiness was connected with the thought of *moral* sublimity and purity, not merely with the idea of physical inaccessibility. Moreover, in the preëxilic prophets, holiness does not express a condition or state appertaining exclusively to *Yahveh;* but is already applied to man, as in Isaiah where the "holy remnant" is spoken of, which is to emerge from the chastening judgment. Only an *ethical* holiness and purity can be intended (vi. 13; iv. 3) ; for only such can form the contrast required to the filth (iv. 4) and to the dross (i. 25) of sin which are to be removed at the judgment. The holiness of *Yahveh* is for Isaiah something far more overwhelming than physical majesty. When the "Holy One of Israel" revealed Himself to him in a sublime and stupendous vision he realised that *moral* impurity is repugnant to Divine holiness, otherwise the consciousness of his own moral imperfection would not have filled him with fear and trembling (vi. 5). He apprehends, therefore, in *Yahveh,* the Holy One, the morally Pure and Perfect Being, Who cannot tolerate any impurity. The name "The Holy One of Israel," accordingly, designates *Yahveh,* not only as the God venerated by Israel but as the morally sublime God, Who is offended by sin.—Friedrich Nötscher, *ibid.*, pp. 100-101.

20: Here (Micah vi. 8) then the fulfillment of moral duties and the love of all mankind and awe and reverence towards God are declared to be the quintessence of religion and morality. Love toward one's fellow men and awe towards the Divinity: how could one better express the character of a religion that is ethical through and through!—Paul Pflüger, *Der Sozialismus d. isr. Propheten*, p. 3.

21: In the religion of the Old Testament, moral perfection is the principal thought in the conception of God. The whole of human life, the whole outlook on life and the world are morally determined from the standpoint of God-consciousness; all individual moral tasks and laws of life have their unity in God's holy will and in their relation to their highest end, namely, personal relationship to God and the realization of His kingdom upon earth.—Eduard Riehm, *Alttestamentliche Theologie*, pp. 23-24.

22: The code of Hammurabi only regulates the whole of civil life, while the oldest Mosaic law also regulates the moral and religious life, consequently it is the expression of a uniform Divine will encompassing the whole of life.—Ernst Sellin, *Der alttestamentliche Prophetismus*, p. 224.

23: To be moral means, henceforth, to satisfy the requirements of a law superior to Israel, and this law is the expression of the good and perfect will of the most high God. The conception has been formed of moral laws that are eternal and immutable

because they flow from the nature of God Himself.—
Bernhard Stade, *Gesch. d. Volkes Israel,* II, p.
264.

24: As a matter of principle, in the religion of
Israel, to conform with its belief in election, every
form of naturalism is excluded from the outset.
YHVH does not exist in nature, but as Creator of
nature.   He is not the living sum-total or abstract
totality of nature, but a being in whom the spiritual
and the moral are combined. He is *moral personality,*
possessing the utmost power of will. His moral will
is the highest summit from which to view Israel's life
in history.—W. Staerk, *Das Werk Moses u. seine
Geschichte* (*"Neue Jüdische Monatshefte,"* III.
Jahrg., Heft 9-12), pp. 200ff.

25: That God is, and that He alone in the world
is active for the carrying out of the highest *moral*
ends—this has been the foundation of Jewish religious
life of every sort and kind. And this One and Only
God demands of His followers the fruits of *inner*
righteousness, a pure heart, and pure hands. This
demand of the Prophets has never been forgotten,
even if scrupulous observance of the law and the
striving for reward has often caused the more difficult
part of the law of God, morality in all relations of
life, to lag behind. This religious strength carried the
Jewish belief in God through all dangers from without and from within during the centuries after Ezekiel.
It also sustained it in the hard struggle with early
Christianity, in the mysticism and enthusiastic other-
wordliness of which other primary forces of religion
found expression. In the preservation and contin-
uance of this religious strength lies the guarantee for

the distinctive value of the Jewish religion among all the monotheistic religions of the world.—W. Staerk, *l. c.*, p. 218-f.

See also:

K. CH. BÄHR, *Symbolik d. mos. Kultus*, I, 1837, p. 37.

A. BERTHOLET, *Die Stellg. d. Israeliten u. d. Juden z. d. Fremden*, 1896, p. 95.

WILHELM BOUSSET, *Die Religion d. Judentums*, 1906, pp. 154, 471, 483, 488, 498f.

KARL BUDDE, *Die Religion d. Volkes Israel*, 1905, p. 31.

(BISHOP) CHRYSANTH, *Die Religionen d. alten Welt in ihrer Beziehung zum Christentum*, III, 1878, pp. 161, 241.

HEINRICH CORNILL, *Das Buch Jeremia*, 1905, p. 154.

————, *Das A. T. u. d. Humanität*, 1895, pp. 19f.

————, *Der isr. Prophetisme*, 1900, pp. 8-10, 25f., 42f.

BERNHARD DUHM, *Das Buch Jeremia*, 1901, p. 285.

————, *Die Theologie d. Propheten*, 1875, pp. 10ff, 105, 113, 178, 187, 215, 243.

———— *Israels Propheten*, 1875, pp. 135, 140, 142f, 269f, 280.

HEINRICH EWALD, *Gesch. d. Volkes Israel*, I, 1864, p. 464; IV, 1864, p. 320; V, 1867, p. 125f., 129.

———— *Die Propheten d. Alten Bundes*, I, 1867, p. 274.

FRANZ FELDMANN, *Israels Religion, Sitte u. Kultur in d. vormos. Zeit*, 1917, p. 21.

FRANCKH, *Die Prophetie i. d. Zeit vor Amos*, 1905, p. 82.

FRIEDRICH GIESEBRECHT, *Die Geschichtlichkeit d. Sinaibundes*, 1900, p. 8, n.

———— *Die Grundzüge d. isr. Religionsgesch.*, 1908, p. 100.

HUGO GRESSMANN, *Mose u. seine Zeit*, 1913, pp. 470f.

MAX HALLER, *Recht u. Sitte i. d. Genesissagen*, 1905, p. 88.

GUSTAV HÖLSCHER, *Die Propheten*, 1914, p. 187.

EMIL KAUTZSCH, *Die Bibl. Theologie d. A. T.*, 1911, pp. 68f., 122, 154, 201, 364, 374.

RUDOLF KITTEL, *Judenfeindschaft oder Gotteslästerung?* 1914, p. 38.

PAUL KLEINERT, *Die Propheten Israels in soz. Beziehg.*, 1905, p. 14.

AUGUST KLOSTERMANN, *Gesch. d. Volkes Israel*, 1896, pp. 11, 23, 27, 83f., 89f., 106, 200, 237.

JUSTUS KÖBERLE, *Sünde u. Gnade*, 1905, pp. 32, 90, 119, 123f., 138, 152, 306f., 327ff., 328f., 331f., 335f., 339ff., 354ff., 371, 385, 436f., 448f., 452, 456, 496f., 504, 533, 551, 581f., 602f.

EDUARD KÖNIG, *Gesch. d. alttest. Religion*, 1912, pp. 137f., 222, 462.

────── *Gesch. d. Reiches Gottes*, 1908, p. 273.

────── *Prophetenideal, Judentum u. Christentum*, 1906, pp. 6, 81ff.

A. KUENEN, *Volksreligion u. Weltreligion*, 1883, pp. 125, 131, 141.

KÜPER, *Die Propheten d. Alten Bundes*, 1870, p. 67.

MAX LÖHR, *Gesch. d. Volkes Israel*, 1900, p. 146.

KARL MARTI, *Die Religion d. A. T.*, 1906, pp. 22, 37f., 47, 50, 54, 56f., 62, 81ff.

────── *Gesch. d. isr. Religion*, 1900, pp. 70, 75f., 85, 111f., 144, 156, 188, 193, 198ff., 287.

MEINHOLD, *Die Propheten in Israel von Moses b. a. Jesus*, 1909, pp. 40, 112.

FRIEDRICH NÖTSCHER, *Die Gerechtigkeit Gottes bei den vorexil. Propheten*, 1915, p. 8.

WILHELM NOWACK, *Entstehung d. isr. Religion*, 1896, p. 26.

FREDERIC W. PERKINS, *The Attitude of the Liberal Christian toward the Jew. In "Proc. Fifth Intern. Congress of Free Christianity and Religious Progress,"* 1911, pp. 371-378.

PAUL PFLÜGER, *Der Sozialismus d. isr. Propheten*, 1914, p. 7.

ERNEST RENAN, *Histoire des origines du Christianisme*, 1866, II, p. 106.

EDUARD RIEHM, *Alttest. Theologie*, 1889, pp. 23, 34, 70f., 72f.

ERNST SELLIN, *Der alttest. Prophetismus*, 1912, p. 223.

────── *Die alttest. Religion*, 1908, pp. 26, 78.

RUDOLF SMEND, *Lehrb. d. alttest. Religionsgesch.*, 1899, pp. VI, 10, 322, 413f., 491.

BERNHARD STADE, *Gesch. d. Volkes Israel*, I, 1887, pp. 5, 516, 573, II, 1888, pp. 217, 431.

GEORG STERNBERG, *Die Ethik d. Deuteronomiums*, 1908, pp. 26f., 37.

PAUL VOLZ, *Mose*, 1907, pp. 9, 80ff., 93.

JULIUS WELLHAUSEN, *Israelitische u. jüd. Gesch.*, 1907, pp. 210ff.

II

FUNDAMENTAL VIEWS OF
MORALITY

I. DOING AND BELIEVING

Introduction by Dr. Ismar Elbogen

"The requirement of morality, as a principle of religion, is the core and backbone of Judaism." (See above, p. 17.) This means that what is perceived as good, what is taught as divine command, must be converted into *deed*. The teaching of Judaism is not a theoretical discussion of ethical tenets but a religion of action, and its moral demands are to be fulfilled in life. "To know God does not mean to understand the nature of His Being, but to walk in the righteousness which God has shown." *Belief* is not the central *motif* of the Jewish religion. The Hebrew word *Emunah* signifies "trust." Luther's translation of the Bible put "belief" in its place. In Biblical and Rabbinic literature this trust in God is presupposed as the foundation of a religious-moral character, but not as a result of thinking or of willing like a dogma. Only where reflection intervened, as in the Alexandrian and medieval Jewish philosophy of religion, did the conception of belief in God develop into the

51

position that it is a conviction reached through intellectual efforts; the principal theses of Judaism, frequently stated (*Ikkarim*), were thought of not as articles of faith, but as primary truths. In Judaism blind faith was not demanded, nor was freedom of thought suppressed. In Judaism, moreover, the view has never been held that piety was based solely upon faith, and never has redemption for the soul without the moral deed been regarded as possible. Paul's one-sided and dangerous valuation of faith, which met with opposition even among the early Christians (see e. g. James ii. 14-18), never found acceptance in Judaism. Now and then tendencies to transfer the climax of religious experience into the realm of speculation and intuitive mystical vision arose, but none of these disputed the urgent importance of the moral deed. On this point, only one opinion prevails throughout the entire post-Biblical literature, namely, that religion must justify itself through the moral action.

BIBLE

I,   1: Ye shall therefore keep My statutes, and Mine ordinances, which if a man do, he shall live by them: I am the LORD.—Leviticus xviii. 5.

2: And Moses called unto all Israel, and said unto them: Hear, O Israel, the statutes and the ordinances which I speak in your ears this day, that ye may learn them, and observe to do them.—Deuteronomy v. 1.

3: Thus saith the LORD of hosts, the God of Israel: Amend your ways and your doings, and I will cause you to dwell in this place. Trust ye not in lying words, saying: 'The temple of the LORD, the temple of the LORD, the temple of the LORD, are these.' Nay, but if ye thoroughly amend your ways and your doings; if ye thoroughly execute justice between a man and his neighbor; if ye oppress not the stranger, the fatherless, and the widow, and shed not innocent blood in this place, neither walk after other gods to your hurt; then will I cause you to dwell in this place, in the land that I gave to your fathers, for ever and ever.—Jeremiah vii. 3-7.

4: Seek good, and not evil, that ye may live; and so the LORD, the God of hosts, will be with you, as ye say. Hate the evil and love the good, and establish justice in the gate.—Amos v. 14-15.

5: Come, ye children, hearken unto me; I will teach you the fear of the LORD. Who is the man that desireth life, and loveth days, that he may see good therein? Keep thy tongue from evil, and thy lips from speaking guile. Depart from evil, and do good; seek peace and pursue it.—Psalms xxxiv. 12-15.

6: Depart from evil, and do good; and dwell for evermore.—Psalms xxxvii. 27.

JEWISH-HELLENISTIC LITERATURE

III,   1: And the reason why our lawgiver in his legislation far exceeded all other legislators in utility to all men, is that he did not make religion a part of virtue, but had the insight to make the various virtues parts of religion; I mean justice, and fortitude, and self-control, and mutual harmony in all things among the members of the community. For all our actions and studies and words have a connection with piety towards God.—Josephus, *Against Apion,* II. 17 (Whiston-Shilleto, *l. c.*).   (Revised by Tr.)

TALMUDICAL LITERATURE

V,   1: And not study is the chief thing but action. —*Ethics of the Fathers,* I, 17 (Herford, in Charles, *l. c.,* II).

2: Every one whose deeds are more than his wisdom, his wisdom endures. And every one whose wisdom is more than his deeds, his wisdom does not endure.—*Ethics of the Fathers,* III, 12 (Herford, *ibid.*).

3: Every one whose wisdom is greater than his deeds, to what is he like? To a tree whose branches are many and its roots few; and the wind comes and. roots it up and turns it over on its face, as it is said, 'For he shall be like a tamarisk in the desert, and he' shall not see when good cometh; but shall inhabit the parched places in the wilderness, a salt land undwelt in.' But every one whose deeds are more than his wisdom, to what is he like? To a tree whose branches are few and its roots many, which if all the winds that are in the world come and blow upon it, they move it not from its place; as it is said, 'For he shall be as a tree planted by the waters; and that sendeth out its roots by the river, and shall not perceive when heat cometh, but his leaf shall be green; and in the year of drought he shall not be anxious, neither shall cease from yielding fruit' (Jeremiah xvii. 6-8).— *Ethics of the Fathers,* III, 22 (Herford, *ibid.*).

4: Perform more than thou hast learned.—*Ethics of the Fathers*, vi. 5 (Herford, *ibid*.).

5: He who *only studies* Torah, has, so to say, no God.—*Abodah Zarah* 17 b.

6: Doing is more important than learning [studying].—*Yer. Pesachim* III, 7.   [See Berachot 7 b, "greater is the service of Torah than its study." —Rev. A. Cohen, *l. c.*, p. 43.—Tr.]

7: One day Rabbi Tarfon and the elders were sitting together on the balcony of the house Nitza in Lud and there the question was laid before them: "Is learning [studying] more important, or doing?" Rabbi Tarfon was of the opinion that doing was more important; but Rabbi Akiba thought that learning was of greater importance. They finally agreed that learning was more important by reason of the fact that it leads to doing.—*Kiddushin* 40 b (see *Sifre*, section *Ekeb*.).

8: "If ye walk in My statutes, and keep My commandments, and do them" (Leviticus xxvi. 3). In connection with this passage, Rabbi Chiyya taught: He who studies the Torah, shall study it in order to do its commandments, but he who studies the Torah and does not do its commandments, it were better for him had he never been born.—*Vayyikra Rabbah*, c. 35.

9: "The fear of the LORD is the beginning of wisdom; a good understanding have all they that do thereafter" (Psalms cxi. 10). All those that *do*, but not those who *only study it*.—Yalkut, *ad loc*.

10: "Who is the man that desireth life, and loveth days, that he may see good therein? Keep thy tongue

from evil, and thy lips from speaking guile. Depart
from evil, and do good" (Psalms xxxiv. 13-15).
Were you to think I might attain it while sleeping,
remember that it is written, "Do good."—*Yalkut,
ad loc.*, §720.

11: He who studies the words of the Torah and
does not follow them, his punishment is more griev-
ous than if he had not studied them at all.—*Debarim
Rabbah*, c. 7.

12: He who knows the Torah and does not practice it, it were better had he never been born.—*Shemot
Rabbah*, c. 40.

MIDDLE AGES

VI,   I: It is evident that God's benevolence is more
valuable for human beings through this procedure
[namely, commandments and prohibitions] than if
He had removed all difficulties from their path. In
clarification of the question, let it be remarked that it
is better that the attainment of the permanently good
should be founded as God has arranged it upon a
demand for the exertion from human beings needed
in the fulfilling of the commandments. Reason likewise teaches that the good attained by him who
strives earnestly to get it by doing his utmost is twice
as precious as that good to the possession of which
one comes out of mere grace without the slightest
self-exertion.—Saadyah, *Emunot ve-Deot* (Teachings of Revelation and Reason), III, 1.

2: How can one attain and strengthen in himself
such a mode of thought? He shall *always act accord-*

ingly, and do so once, twice, and thrice, and constantly practice it, until it becomes easy for him to act thus. *Then this will become in him a firm disposition.* That is the way of God. This way He taught our ancestor Abraham and his successors, and he who walks on this way, carries home blessings.—Maimonides, *Mishneh Torah Hilchot Deot* (on Ethics), I, 7.

3: Occupy yourself as often as you can with the divine teaching, and do that in order to practice it. When you close the book, see whether there is something in what you learned that you can do. Scrutinize your actions every evening and every morning, then your whole life will be on the ascent to God.—Rabbi Moses of Evreux, in *Kol Bo* (Compendium), §66.

4: Right belief leads to the true eternal happiness of the human being, namely, belief in God and in His teaching.—Nevertheless we must be mindful of the fact that belief does not in itself bring true happiness under all circumstances. If a human being believes in something that is impossible, then this does not lead to the way of what is moral. No human being can doubt that. *Only that faith which elevates the moral significance of the human being is the true faith, that is, only the faith in moral truths.* Therefore the human being shall not believe everything outright but shall investigate thoroughly and scrutinize the content of this faith and whence originates that which he believes, and whatever is not worthy of credence, he shall relinquish.—Joseph Albo, *Ikkarim* (Book of Principles), I, 21.

5: In all that thou doest, let the thought of God lead thee, for God requires the heart, and He sees everything.—The smaller *Sepher Chassidim* (Book of the Pious), quoted by Güdemann, *Gesch. d. Erziehungswesens u. d. Kultur d. Abendländ. Juden*, III, pp. 214-215. [This passage is cited in English in M. Joseph's *Judaism as Creed and Life*, London, 1919, 3d ed., p. 360—Tr.]

MODERN JEWISH LITERATURE

VII,   1: While in the Christian church religious mysteries are embodied in visible symbols and so are ensnarled in the tangible in the sacrament, in Judaism they remain ideal, intangible. In Judaism they denote the inscrutable, that which is of God and not of man, that which can only be conceived dimly. The darkness of distance through which no mortal can see spreads before the Being of God, and only devotion with its meditation and its silence can approach it. Here, *commandments* enter into the world of the human being for his assistance; to do the good is also the beginning of all wisdom (apprehension of the divine). Moral duty comes before knowledge of God, which itself has less the meaning of possessing than of seeking and of searching.

God's requirements of man constitute the sphere of man's life in which He placed him. These requirements are for man the given, definite factors. The "Principles of the Torah" are therefore, as the Talmud says, the principles of pious action. They are fixed in a religious sense, and response to them must be definite. On the other hand, the teaching concerning faith is in many respects quite provisional, it foregoes definitive conclusions and binding decisions arrived at once and forever.—Leo Baeck, *Das Wesen des Judentums* (2d ed.), pp. 5-6.

2: Wise is he who walks in the ways of God; he who does what is good. This conviction constantly recurs in Judaism through all the centuries; even the mystics utter it. *Religion* and *life* are thus most intimately connected; a religion which shall be proved through life and a life which shall be fulfilled through religion. The one is brought down to earth, the other raised to a divine level. All room for the least division between believing and doing is taken away. No piety exists beyond that proved true by the conduct of a person's life, no conduct can have any value except that in which religion finds realization.—Leo Baeck, *l. c.*, pp. 31-32.

3: Judaism is a religion that seeks its verification in *life* and finds its fulfillment in the connection established between life and God.—Leo Baeck, *ibid.*, p. 39.

4: Men must beware of looking upon religion as an ideal *to be yearned for*, it should be an ideal *to be applied* directly, day by day, to practical contingencies. In "Mosaism," so-called, the religious and the ethical are intimately interwoven with the social and the political. The chief dogmas of creed are stated as principles shaping practical life. . . . The Mosaic law is a "propaganda by deed." Everywhere it demands *active*, more than passive, morality.—Simon Dubnow, *Jüd. Geschichte*, pp. 25-26 [S. M. Dubnow, *Jewish History, An Essay in the Philosophy of History* (tr. into English by H. S., The Jewish Publication Society of America, Philadelphia, 1903), pp. 54-55].

5: Practicing religion, or practical Judaism, shall of necessity express itself unmistakably in moral action, but it extends to all relations of life. Nothing is so insignificant that it may not be ennobled by receiving the stamp of religion, and become a means of drawing us near to God. That is the fundamental conception which runs through practical Judaism and the portions of the Talmud devoted to its presentation.—M. Güdemann, *Das Judentum in s. Grundzügen*, p. 81.

6: There exists, therefore, an *external* measure for the *deeds* of men, namely, correspondence to the will of God and an *internal* measure for the *greatness* of men, namely, not the magnitude of the powers conferred, not the amount of results achieved, but the *proportion* between the fulfillment of the divine will and the powers possessed. Life, therefore, may be an utter failure in spite of the purest sentiments, if the deeds done be not right; or may, on the other hand, be most sublime despite infinitesimal results, if the powers conferred do not suffice for more. Happiness and perfection, therefore, are nothing but the outcome of the greatest plenitude of external and internal possessions *employed in accordance with the will of God*, which constitutes the greatness of man.—S. R. Hirsch, *The Nineteen Letters of Ben Uziel, Being a Spiritual Presentation of the Principles of Judaism*[1] (tr. by the Rev. Dr. Bernard Drachman, Funk & Wagnalls Company, New York and London, 1899), pp. 35-36. (Revised by Tr.)

7: But a life of seclusion devoted only to medita-

[1] This fine book is well worth reading today by both Jews and Gentiles.—Tr.

tion and prayer is not Judaism. Study and worship
are but paths which lead to work [action]. *Talmud
gadol she-mebi lijde maasse*—"Great is study, for it
leads to practical fulfillment of the precepts"—is a
saying of our sages, and the flower and fruit of our
devotions should be the resolve to lead a life of
activity, pervaded with the spirit of God. Such a life
is the only and universal goal.—S. R. Hirsch, *l. c.,*
p. 150.

8: In the whole realm of the Divine Law, not
one single truth is revealed to us which is only of
theoretical interest, not a single one that enriches our
knowledge only, and is incapable of exerting influence upon our moral behavior.—S. R. Hirsch, *Ges.
Schriften*, III, p. 372.

9: The commandment, "Thou shalt become a
blessing," which according to very ancient tradition
God gave to our ancestor Abraham, turns out to be,
if one brings its content and its exceedingly abundant
fruitfulness clearly before one's consciousness, the
most important fundamental principle, the shortest
primary formula, and also the one fraught with the
most meaning in either *Jewish* or *universal human*
ethics. The commandment is preëminently Jewish
through and through, and comprises within itself all
the principles on which the ethical efforts of Judaism
recorded in our literature are based. The command is
not ascetic and highly in favor of renunciation but,
like all that is genuinely Jewish, has its face turned
toward life. Moreover it in no wise excludes the
natural and wholly justifiable claims of the instinct
of self-preservation. On the contrary, it requires that

everyone shall so order his life that the lives of others also shall be thereby vigorously speeded on and made happy. The commandment stimulates to strenuous activity and gives the energetic will clear guidance and concrete aims whose object is steady progress in life. But the commandment also tells me clearly that I am not alone in the world, that my life is destined to make the lives of other human beings easier, and that my actions and aspirations fulfill their purpose only if through them the lives of others and the life of all the world are vigourously aided.—Wilhelm Jerusalem, *"Du sollst zum Segen werden"* (*Gemeindeblatt*, XI, p. 2, 1921).

10: The study which above all else the Talmudists have at heart is that which has to do with the establishing of the Halachah. This they carry on with ardor and wrestling and disputation; it is this which they most highly praise. Only a mere theory, a hollow and empty theory, one that would not be an incentive to practice, is rejected by the Rabbins.— M. Lazarus, *Die Ethik d. Judentums*, I, p. 422.

11: Mere abstaining from evil does not suffice, but positive moral action is demanded—free initiative moral in basis and motive. See *Abodah Zarah*, 19 b: Should a man perchance say: Because I guarded my tongue and lips from speaking guile I will go and give myself over to sleep, remember, it is written, "Depart from evil and do good" (Psalms xxxiv. 15). *Positive energy* and initiative is demanded. *To intervene for the good*, to come forward as a witness, to set himself up for a rescuer.—M. Lazarus, *l. c.*, II, pp. 53-54.

12: Although this divine book which we have received through Moses is truly said to be a code of law and to contain ordinances and precepts, and rules of conduct, nevertheless included in it, also, as is known too, is an unfathomable treasure of truths founded on reason, as well as of religious teachings which are so very intimately connected with the laws that they constitute but one doctrine. However, all these excellent doctrines are presented to the intellect, are laid before reason, without being obtruded, be it observed, upon faith. Among all the precepts and ordinances of the Mosaic law not a single one reads, *"Thou shalt believe,"* or *"Thou shalt not believe";* instead, they all read, *"Thou shalt do,"* or, *"Thou shalt not do!"* To believe, no commands are given; for faith receives only such orders as take the route of conviction in coming to it. All commands of the Divine Law are addressed to the will, to the energy of man.—Moses Mendelssohn, *Jerusalem,* pp. 174-175.

13: The great maxim of this constitution appears to have been, *"To action, man must be driven; to meditation, it suffices that inducement be given him."* Hence, every one of these prescribed actions, every custom, every ceremony had its meaning, its inner significance, and the connection was close between that meaning and the knowledge of religion and of ethics obtained through speculation, and to the seeker after truth it served as an inducement to meditate upon those hallowed things or to procure instruction concerning them from wise men.—Moses Mendelssohn, *l. c.,* p. 191.

14: The conception of *Maassim tobim,* of *"good*

deeds," on the whole plays the largest rôle in Jewish ethics and has never been crowded into the background, as it was in Christianity through the conception of "faith."—Felix Perles, *Bousset's "Religion d. Judentums,"* p. 65.

15: Beginning with the prophets down to the treatises on ethics of the middle ages (see on these Zunz, *Zur Geschichte und Literatur,* 122-157 [*Ges. Schr.,* I, p. 60-85]) there breathes a heroic spirit; not only through the moral *teachings,* but what is of very much greater consequence and most convincing, also through moral *life.* The same earnestness, the same inexorability with which the moral command was pronounced appear also in the emphasis on its practical fulfillment. What the leaders of the people taught, what their lives also exemplified to the people, that did not remain merely words spoken and written, but passed over into the consciousness of all the people, and was complied with even under the most trying external circumstances. Just that is the characteristic feature in Jewish fulfillment of duty. Duty was never taken by the Jew in lukewarm fashion, performed only halfway or only for show, but he drew out unhesitatingly all the consequences involved and then did not shrink from any sacrifice required of him to fulfill *all* demands of religion truly in their full scope and under all circumstances (see on that, e. g. H. Steinthal, *Jahrb. f. jüd. Gesch. u. Lit.,* 1901, pp. 59, 61).—Felix Perles, *l. c.,* pp. 66-67.

16: That alone is the meaning of the conception, taken very seriously in Judaism to the present day, of *Kiddush ha-Shem* (hallowing of the Divine Name).

Every noble action is a victory of the God-idea and hence a hallowing of God before all human beings, while every evil mode of action signifies a defeat of the God-idea, a profanation of God before all human beings.—Felix Perles, *ibid.*, pp. 69-70.

17: The desire to realize ideals must never be lost from among us and must ever inspire us, for it forms the necessary transition point in passing from the idea to the will. We must ever wish, e. g. to practice benevolence and love, in order that we should be willing and ready, as often as opportunity presents itself, to practice them. Then when we behold the needy, the hazy general desire to help *must* lead to the definite deed.—H. Steinthal, *Zu Bibel u. Religionsphil.*, II, p. 204.

See also:

MARTIN BUBER, *Vom Geist des Judentums*, 1916, pp. 32f.

HERMANN COHEN, *Streiflichter üb. jüd. Rel. u. Wissenschaft,* (*Der Tag der Versöhnung.*) "*Neue jüdische Monatshefte*," 1917, Nr. 10, p. 702.

MAX DIENEMANN, *Die jüd. Wertung d. Gesetzes u. d. Gerechtigkeit* (*Korresp. d. V. d. D. J.*, Nr. 14, Juni 1914), pp. 6ff.

I. ELBOGEN, *Die Religionsanschauungen d. Pharisäer,* 1904, p. 41.

FEUCHTWANG, *Kohlers Grundr. e. syst. Theologie d. Judentums,* Dr. Bloch's Österr. Wochenschrift," Nr. 21, Wien, 1910.

M. GÜDEMANN, *Das Judentum in s. Grundzügen,* 1902, p. 14.

S. R. HIRSCH, *Choreb,* 1837, c. 72 §485; c. 80 §525.

——— *Ges. Schr.*, II, 1904, p. 53; III, 1906, p. 136; IV, 1908, p. 136.

KAUFMANN KOHLER, *Grundr. e. syst. Theologie d. Judentums,* 1910, pp. 14f.

L. LAZARUS, *Zur Charakteristik d. talmudischen Ethik,* 1877, p. 18.

M. LAZARUS, *Die Ethik d. Judentums,* I, 1899, pp. 21f., 24f., II 1911, pp. 96ff., 109.
MARX, *Ethik u. Religion,* "Strassburger Israel. Wochenscrift," Gebweiler i. Els., Nr. 18, 1910.
MOSES MENDELSSOHN, *Jerusalem,* 1783, pp. 174f.
FELIX PERLES, *Bousset's "Religion d. Judentums,"* 1903, pp. 65ff., 87.
R. SELIGMANN, *Vom Wesen d. jüd. Moral,* "Gemeindeblatt," Nr. 12, Berlin, 1916, pp. 139ff.
H. STEINTHAL, *Zu Bibel u. Religionsphil.,* 1895, II, pp. 1, 155, 204.
MAX WIENER, *Die Anschauungen d. Propheten v. d. Sittlichkeit,* 1909, pp. 15f.

CHRISTIAN AUTHORS

VIII,   1: Judaism is, in its character, preponderatingly *a religion of practice and of action.* All reflection concerning faith retreats before the emphasis on simple practice.—Wilhelm Bousset, *Die Religion d. Judentums,* p. 220.

2: In these circles [of the teachers of the Law] the extermination of a *one-sided intellectualism* was vigorously striven for. Thoroughgoing fulfillment and performance are emphasized with the utmost energy in very many passages as the final aim of Torah-study.—Wilhelm Bousset, *l. c.,* p. 494.

3: The prophets struggled with their fellow countrymen over the question, *"Wherein does the true service of God consist?"* The notion which they combated was the notion general in antiquity, namely, that the Deity should be honored by all sorts of pious homage, in the form of sacrifices and ceremonies. In opposition to that view of the matter, the prophets achieved a fundamentally new conception of religion.

God does not require that one shall pay Him pious homage occasionally; He demands the whole life; an active, practical form of holiness expressed in moral action.—Hermann Gunkel, *Was bleibt vom A. T.*, p. 20.

4: Since the Old Testament religion is the religion of *deed*, since it is the religion characterized not by pious speculation and not by the observance of a cult, but by *the moral demand of God Who is revealed as the highest moral personality*, then indeed it can be no cause of surprise to find that everywhere in the religious documents of Israelitism a conspicuous stand is taken, if we may so express it, on social-ethical problems.—J. Herrmann, *Die soziale Predigt d. Propheten*, pp. 3-4.

5: With all that, the prophets enter the sphere of social activity. Those men became and remain guides for the future, not only through the manner in which their lives set an example to their generation of what the religion of God is like, but also through their insight into the drift of current events. The essential reason for that is partly to be found in the uncompromising energy with which they vindicated the moral forces of religion as directing, purifying, and regenerating powers in the community life of the people—in their emphasis on their social efficacy.— Paul Kleinert, *Die Propheten Israels in soz. Beziehung*, pp. 1-2.

6: To be sure, the consciousness ever remained alive that erudition and practical fulfillment of the Law belong together. The ideal is for one to teach finely and act nobly, *Yer. Chag.*, II, 1, 7 a (to the text compare Bacher, *Tann.*, 2d ed., I, 70, note 5; see also *Yeb.* 63b), and if occasionally study is placed before practice, it is, after all, only because study alone is capable of discovering the way to right practice. Compare Bacher, *Pal. Amor.*, II, 107; see also *b. Kidd.*, 40 b; *Yer. Pes.*, III, 7, 21 b (slightly otherwise with Jose the Galilean, Bacher, *Tann.*, 2d ed., I, 359); see also *b. Ber.*, 17 a: "The final purpose of wisdom is repentance and good works," etc.—Justus Köberle, *Sünde u. Gnade,* p. 508.

See also:

WILHELM BOUSSET, *Die Religion d. Judentums*, 1906, pp. 220, 493.
BERNHARD DUHM, *Das Buch Jeremia*, 1901, pp. 253f.
HERMANN GUNKEL, *Was bleibt vom A. T.?*, 1916, p. 20.
R. TRAVERS HERFORD, *Pharisaism, Its Aim and Its Method*, 1912, pp. 64f.
PAUL KLEINERT, *Die Propheten Israels in soz. Bezhg.*, 1905, pp. 1f.
AUGUST KLOSTERMANN, *Gesch. d. Volkes Israel*, 1896, p. 237.
JUSTUS KÖBERLE, *Sünde u. Gnade*, 1905, pp. 136f., 180, 307f., 339ff., 347f., 501f., 508, 514, 526f.
MAX LÖHR, *Gesch. d. Volkes Israel*, 1900, p. 17.
ERNEST RENAN, *Histoire du peuple d'Israel*, 1887, I, p. XXVIII, Preface.
EDUARD RIEHM, *Alttest. Theol.*, 1889, pp. 295f.
ERNST SELLIN, *Alttest. Religion*, 1908, p. 78.
HANS SCHMIDT, *Der Prophet Amos*, 1917, pp. 76f.
BERNHARD STADE, *Gesch. d. Volkes Israel*, I, 1887, p. 509, II, 1888, p. 264.
W. STAERK, *Neutest. Zeitgesch.*, II, 1907, pp. 39, 56.
GEORG STERNBERG, *Die Ethik d. Deuteronomiums*, 1908, pp. 36, 38.
P. VALETON, JR., *Amos u. Hosea*, 1898, p. 107.
FERDINAND WEBER, *Jüd. Theol. auf Grund d. Talmud*, 1897, pp. 286, 315.

[R. Travers Herford, *The Pharisees* (New York, Macmillan, 1924), Chap. V, A, pp. 107-123 (The Halachah as a Moral Discipline); Chap. V. C. pp. 135-138 (The Relation of Pharisaism to the Teaching of the Prophets); Chap. V, D. pp. 138-146 (The Torah and the Moral Law). This truly epochal work merits not only attentive and repeated perusal, but also serious and diligent study by both Christians and Jews.—Tr.]

2. MORAL-MINDEDNESS

Introduction by Prof. Dr. Ismar Elbogen

The deed that Judaism demands is the *moral* deed. It acquires moral quality and exerts moral influences according to the intention on which it is based. Judaism does not esteem the deed as such, but prizes exclusively the moral-mindedness, the moral disposition, and intent back of it. Judaism does not fail to recognize differences of value between religious commandments. It distinguishes duties of the heart from duties of the hands (see below pp. 75-76, VI, 1); nor does it become so engrossed in the many individual commands as to overlook the one all-inclusive command, "to love God with one's whole heart, with one's whole soul, and with one's whole might." It requires a pure heart and a clean mind, performance of the good for the sake of the good; it rejects as sinful not only the impure deed, but likewise the impure thought. To the danger of sanctimoniousness, from which no human community remains permanently free, persons professing Judaism have also succumbed. As everywhere else in the world, there have been dissemblers also in Jewish circles. Jewish teaching, however, should not bear the blame for these instances of aberration from the moral code. On the contrary, Jewish teaching has been fighting from the remotest times against the externalization of religion, against the formal action divorced from moral disposition and intent. Israel's prophets are the leaders of mankind in enjoining the service of God in inwardness and piety of heart. Their fight against lip-service and formal compliance with the law has been continued by the teachers of Judaism at all times. As the Talmud demands that every act of every human being shall be done for the sake of God, that his whole life shall be "a sanctification of the Divine Name," so the Rabbis of the middle ages as well as of modern times teach that "no human deed possesses religious value without an inner impulse of the soul," and that "true and false in the religious sense refer to true or false intent." It is misleading and fallacious to characterize Judaism as a mere "legalistic religion." The use of "law" as a designation for the Jewish religion has been chiefly due to the old Greek translation of the Bible, in which the word "Torah" was translated as *nomos*="law," whereas in truth it means "teaching." This error was taken advantage of in the early days of the Church for the purpose of disparaging Judaism as a religion of law in contrast to Christianity as a religion of the heart. Although that prejudice has continued its mischief-making to the present time, even in Christian theological circles the knowledge is now spreading more and more that the insistence of the prophets upon moral-mindedness, morality of the heart, moral disposition and intent has through the centuries remained a living possession of Judaism.

BIBLE

I,   1: Walk before Me, and be thou whole-hearted. —Genesis xvii. 1.

2: Thou shalt be whole-hearted with the LORD thy God.—Deuteronomy xviii. 13.

3: After those days, saith the LORD, I will put My law in their inward parts, and in their heart will I write it.—Jeremiah xxxi. 33.

4: Cast away from you all your transgressions, wherein ye have transgressed; and make you a new heart and a new spirit.—Ezekiel xviii. 31; compare also Ezekiel xxxvi. 26.

5: Who shall ascend into the mountain of the LORD? and who shall stand in His holy place? he that hath clean hands, and a pure heart; who hath not taken My name in vain, and hath not sworn deceitfully—Psalms xxiv. 3-4.

6: Create me a clean heart, O God; and renew a stedfast spirit within me.—Psalms li. 12.

7: Surely God is good to Israel, even to such as are pure in heart.—Psalms lxxiii. 1.

PALESTINIAN APOCRYPHA

IIa,   1: He that is just and humble is ashamed to do what is unjust, being reproved not of another but of his own heart.—*The Testaments of the Twelve Patriarchs* IX. 5, 3 (Charles) in Charles, *l. c.*, II).

2: And let your mind be unto good . .; for he that hath his mind right seeth all things rightly. Fear ye the Lord, and love your neighbor.—*Ibid.,* XII. 3, 2 (Charles, *ibid*).

3: In everything which he [man] doeth, or speaketh, or seeth, he knoweth that the Lord looketh on his soul. And he cleanseth his mind that he may not be condemned by men as well as by God.—*Ibid.,* XII. 6, 6-7 (Charles, *ibid.*).

JEWISH-HELLENISTIC LITERATURE

III,   1: For when such the words are, such also is the mind; and when such the thoughts are, such likewise are the actions; then life is worth living and perfect.—Philo, *On Virtues, On Repentance* (M. II, 406; C.-W. 184).

2: It is proper to lay up the precepts of justice in one's heart, says the Law.—Philo, *On Special Laws,* IV, *On Justice* (M. II, 358; C.-W. 137).

PRAYERS

IV,   1: Unite our hearts to love and fear Thy name.—Daily Prayer.

2: Sanctify us by Thy commandments . . . purify our hearts to serve Thee in truth.—In the Service for Sabbaths and Festivals.

TALMUDICAL LITERATURE

V,   1: "Thou shalt be whole-hearted with the LORD thy God" (Deuteronomy xviii. 13). Only if thou art whole-hearted with the Eternal, thy God, is He thy portion.—*Sifre, ad loc.*

2: Qualify thyself for the study of the Torah,' since the knowledge of it is not thine by inheritance, and let all thy deeds be done for the sake of Heaven. —*Ethics of the Fathers*, II, 17 (Singer's *Prayerbook*, p. 277).

3: Run to do even a slight precept [pious deed, good deed] and flee from sin; for precept leads to precept [one good deed draws another], and sin leads to sin; for the recompense of a good deed is a good deed,[1] and the reward of a sin is a sin.[2]—*Ethics of the Fathers*. IV, 2.

4: Rabbi Zadok said, Make not of the Torah a crown wherewith to aggrandize thyself, nor a spade wherewith to dig. So also used Hillel to say, He who makes a worldly use of the crown of the Torah shall waste away. Hence thou mayest infer, that whosoever derives a profit for himself from the words of the Torah is helping on his own destruction.—*Ethics of the Fathers*, IV, 7 (Singer's *Prayerbook*, pp. 283-284).

5: Our Torah teaches that the human being shall comply with the Divine commandment with a joyous heart.—*Vayyikra Rabbah*, c. 34.

6: For all commandments that a man does in this world and does not do them in love and fear of God, he will receive no reward in the world to come.

[1] "In the Rabbinical view, a precept (*mitzvah*) was simply an opportunity offered of doing the will of God; there could be no greater reward than a further opportunity. A *mitzvah* was never regarded as a burden" (Herford).—Tr.

[2] "The just retribution for sin is a further temptation. This is one of the great sayings of the book" (Herford).—Tr.

—*Otiyyot de R. Akiba* (2d rev.), Letter *Gimmel* (*Bet ha-Midrash*, ed. Jellinek, I, p. 23).

7: As for him who does not do the good for the sake of the good, it were better had he never been created.—*Berachot* 17 a.

8: It matters not whether one does much or little, if only he direct his heart to Heaven.—*Berachot* 5 b and 17 a (Rev. A. Cohen, *l. c.*, p. 111).

9: Rab Yehudah said in the name of Rab [Abba Areka]: It is good that the human being occupy himself with the Torah and with pious works even though it were not for their own sakes, for thereby he will arrive at doing them for their own sakes.—*Nazir* 23 b. (and elsewhere; see also *Echah Rabbati*, Introd., p. 2).

10: "And thou shalt love the LORD thy God" (Deuteronomy vi. 5).—Do everything out of love! —The Scripture makes a difference between him who does [everything] out of love and him who does it merely out of fear.—*Sifre, ad loc.* §32.

11: He who fulfills [the commandments] out of love to God, is greater than he who fulfills them only out of fear.—*Sotah* 31 a.

12: "And these words, which I command thee this day, shall be upon thy heart" (Deuteronomy vi. 6).—Lay the words upon thy heart, for thereby thou comest to the knowledge of the Holy One, blessed be He, and departest not from His ways.—*Sifre, ad loc.,* §33.

13: What ye do, ye shall do solely out of love.—*Sifre to* Deuteronomy xi. 13, §41; see also *Nedarim* 62 a.

14: One shall not indulge in sinful thoughts, for out of that follows the sinful deed.—*Derech Eretz Zuta*, c. 10.

15: Sinful thoughts are worse than sin itself.—*Yoma* 29 a.

16: A scholar unversed in the Torah spoke to me: I occupy myself with the Torah and long for her and wish and wait in expectation that she become mine, but she would not become mine. Thereupon I said to him: My son, the Torah does not become the possession of anyone who does not with body and soul give himself over to her for the sake of Heaven.—*Tanna Debe Elijahu* 22, 23.

17: [It is written in Lamentations iii. 41]: "Let us lift up our heart with our hands unto God in the Heavens." Is it possible that a man take his heart and lay it upon his hand? No, the words are to be understood thus: Let us direct our heart to that which is in our hands, and then pray to God in heaven; for if a man has an abomination in his hand, even though he immerse himself in all the waters of the earth, yet he will not become clean, but if he throws it away, he will be clean immediately.—*Yer. Taanit* II, 1 (ed. Shitomir, 7 b).

MIDDLE AGES

VI, 1: Moreover, it has also become clear and explicit to me that even duties are not perfectly fulfilled if the heart has not the will, and the soul the desire, to fulfill them. And if we should admit the thought that it is not the duty of our heart to choose the service of

God and to yearn for it, then even for our hands every obligation would vanish, since no deed is perfect without the impulse of the soul.—Bachya ibn Pakuda, *Chobot ha-Lebabot* (Duties of the Heart), Introd., p. 6.

2: The inner service of God consists in these duties of the heart: to comprehend God's unity with the heart, to believe in Him and His teaching, to give ourselves over to His service, to fear Him and to be filled with awe before Him, to be meek before Him, to love Him, to trust in Him, to sacrifice our life for Him, to keep ourselves far away from everything that is hateful to Him, to consecrate our whole conduct to His name. . .—Bachya ibn Pakuda, *l. c.*, Introd., p. 6.

3: It has become clear to me that the root of all actions in honor of God must be cleanness of heart and purity of the mind, and if the mind is not quite pure, the actions cannot be acceptable either, be they ever so numerous or be they performed ever so often.—Bachya ibn Pakuda, *ibid.*, Introd., p. 17.

4: Piety is solely a matter of the heart, of the mind, and of the thoughts.—Bachya ibn Pakuda, *ibid.*, V, p. 286.

5: If we would consecrate our conduct to God, no other thought must guide us except this, that it be done for the sake of His great Name, not from passion for fame, nor for hope in men nor fear of them, nor from regard for benefit or injury in this world and in the next.—Bachya ibn Pakuda, *ibid.*, VIII, p. 357.

6: Proof of the divine Influence is not found in well-chosen words, in raising the eyebrows, closing the eyes during prayers, contrition, gesture, and talk which are backed up by no deeds; but a pure mind, expressed in corresponding actions which, by their very nature, are difficult to perform, and are yet performed with the utmost zeal and love.—Yehudah ha-Levi, *Kuzari*, II, 56 [Judah Hallevi's *Kitab al Khazari* (tr. from the Arabic by H. Hirschfeld, New York, Dutton, 1905)].   (Revised by Tr.)

7:   . . . Let no one serve his Creator out of hope for paradise, but out of pure love to Him and to His commandments.—*Book of the Pious* (quoted by Zunz, *Zur Geschichte und Literatur*, p. 135).

8: If anyone regrets his pious actions and thinks in himself, "What benefit have I therefrom? would that I had rather not done it," with that he has nullified everything.—Maimonides, *Mishneh Torah Hilchot Teshubah* (Return to God), III, 3.

9: Perform the commandments out of pure love, neither for the sake of men, nor for the sake of reward. —From the *Book of Morality* (quoted by Zunz, *l. c.*, p. 153).

10: The Divine Law surpasses the law of the state in manifold ways: thus the human law purposes in the first place the welfare of human society, but not the ennobling of the mind of the individuals composing it.   The law of the state at its best has no occasion to occupy itself with the immortality of the soul, for it commands only the lawful deed and forbids wrongdoing without concerning itself about the mind.   The Divine Law, on the other hand, while it has in view all that the law of the state demands, puts the principal emphasis on the good intent.   Good and bad in the religious sense do not mean, to act in a good and bad way, but good and bad intent. Likewise, true and false in the religious sense refer to true and false intent.—Joseph Albo, *Ikkarim* (Book of Principles), I, 8.

11: However, in all that you do, let the thought of God lead you, for God requires the heart, and He sees everything. Therefore be chaste in private even as you are in the street and in the marketplace, for wood and stone in the walls of your room are the two witnesses that will appear against you. Guard yourself against the evil instinct of the heart. It is, as it were, the thief within doors, against whom, as the parable writers say, one can guard oneself only with the greatest difficulty. Therefore thwart it resolutely. —Moses Cohen b. Eleasar, the smaller *Book of the Pious*, p. 2.

MODERN JEWISH WRITINGS

VII,   1: Not by external fulfillment of duty without inward participation shall the commandments be performed, rather *Kavvanah*, devotion of the heart, is required. In living connection with revelation shall the human being live. "Thou shalt take these words to heart," they shall be unto you as an ever new *ordinance* (*Sifre* on Deuteronomy, §33 [p. 74a], they shall be dear and precious unto you as if you had just received them [*ibid.*, 58 p. 87 a]. Therefore not the measure, the extent of the performance is decisive, but only the intent, the submissiveness to the will of God, which are therein manifested. "It is all the same whether one does much or little, it suffices that he keep his *heart* directed to *God.*"—I. Elbogen, *Die Religionsanschauungen d. Pharisäer*, p. 26.

2: *To love with one's whole heart*, with *mind and heart;* for to strive after God *with the mind* means this—to employ all the mental power granted you only to know Him [God], to ascertain His will in His Torah and to know His World, in order that you may know how to fulfill His will in that world. To strive after God *with the heart* means that you fight to a conclusion the battle that God would have you wage between the tendency that leads you upward and the tendency that drags you downward, that you make peace between the animal and the man in you; that you elevate the animal to the moral dignity of man and that both tendencies respond only to one and the same demand, namely, to serve God, to call good and beautiful only that which God calls good and beautiful, to avoid that which He would have shunned, that your heart feel only one attraction—to your Father in Heaven.—S. R. Hirsch, *Choreb*, c. 9, §54.

3: This fitness, however, does not rest so much in the possession of external means; not in the possession of knowledge, nor in the possession of technical skill; it rests preëminently in purity of heart, in ingenuousness of character and in holiness of aim. It depends preëminently on the heart and mind being free of everything that might come between you and your calling, and on being equipped with all the strength of consecration to life which your calling requires.—S. R. Hirsch, *l. c.*, c. 14, §106.

4: Judaism is based upon acceptance of the unity of God and of a divine revelation, without which no moral law could exist in the sense in which the term is used in Jewish ethics. But the dogmas of Judaism, largely because of the prevailing legal tendency of the Torah, were never fully and clearly systematized. To brand Judaism as a religion of legalism, however, is to misinterpret its nature and character. It is never the *deed,* but the *intent* upon which all stress is laid. The pure *heart* alone has value before the holy God. —Kaufmann Kohler, *Grundr. e. Syst. Theol. d. Judentums,* p. 2.

5: *Not for the sake of attaining bliss* shall we love God and practice virtue and truth, *but to love God and practice virtue is in itself true bliss.* This is the nearness of God referred to by the Psalmist and declared to be man's *highest good* (Psalms lxxiii. 28). There is no need of any other reward, and there is no greater punishment than to be deprived of this boon forever.—Kaufmann Kohler, *Jewish Theology,* pp. 308-309.

6: The demand constantly recurs in the Talmudic writings that each of man's acts and therefore his whole conduct shall be "in the name or for the honor of Heaven" (*le-shem shamajim,* as in *Aboth* 2:2 and 17). Now, whether Heaven be taken as a figure of speech for God, or for the sphere of the sublime above and beyond the earthly, the thought conveyed is that the motive of morality, so far from being anything external or base, should be nothing less than man's elevation to a higher dignity.—M. Lazarus, *Die Ethik des Judentums,* I, p. 109 (Szold, *l. c.,* I, p. 142). (Revised by Tr.)

7: The whole view of life in the Talmud (as was true of the Prophets) is permeated by the thought that no mere deed as such but only the disposition, the intent, makes the prescribed action a moral one. *Rachmana libba ba'i,* one thing the All-merciful (God) requires above all—the heart; and even in the case of charity, for all its yield of benefit to him who receives it, it is valued only according to the measure of love, of the benevolent heart, of the kind disposition and intent which prompted it.—M. Lazarus *l. c.,* II, p. 51.

8: Among the people of Israel, however, its poets and prophets had from time immemorial, with incessant emphasis and untiring impressiveness, repeated the admonition that action in obedience to the law was, to be sure, necessary, but that it was null and void without the inner disposition and intent, without the consent of the heart; that for the finite and corporeal man a fixed external form and manner of life was requisite, but that only the inner impulse of the heart, the inner content of the spirit and mind, the inner source of the complexion, which is imprinted upon an action, gives it real worth, dignity, and consecration. Now, if the Talmudical sages have felt compelled to strengthen the ordinances still more, they have also laid more and more ardent stress on the pure heart, disposition, and intent, out of which the fulfillment of them must arise.—L. Lazarus, *Zur Charakteristik d. talmudischen Ethik,* pp. 24-25.

9: Talmudical ethics demands therefore not merely holiness of works, but purity and uprightness of disposition; consequently even the culpable thought is stigmatized, though the deed contain no transgression.—L. Lazarus, *ibid.*, p. 28.

10: Give Him your whole heart! Serve Him with pure intention free from every secondary thought; serve not two masters; do not pay attention to man-made statutes which you had to acquire by learning; let your whole heart be consecrated to Him!—Moses Chayim Luzzatto, *Mesillat Yesharim* (The Path of the Pious), Preface.

11: We call that man clean and pure who keeps himself completely free from every bad quality, from every sin. It suffices not for him to remain free from a quite clear and recognizable sin; but every impulse of his inner self must be eliminated which deems anything permissible which will not stand the test of a real examination, or that sincere scrutiny perceives is an effluence of passion from which the heart has not yet been entirely cleansed. . . .—Moses Chayim Luzzatto, *l. c.*, c. 10.

12: It does not suffice God that the *Mitzvah* [the Divine command] is performed; the thing most important to Him is that the heart be pure and clean and that it be directed in its innermost stirrings to the right service of God.—Moses Chayim Luzzatto, *ibid.*, c. 16.

13: If we investigate more thoroughly, we find that to humility two things are essential, namely, *to think of oneself modestly and to conduct oneself modestly. Humble-mindedness* must first be present, after that *modest behavior* is able to follow. *Whoever is not humble-minded and still desires to bring in his*

*actions humility into prominence, belongs to those
conceited, sorry representatives of humility,* of whom
we have already spoken, he is, indeed, a downright
hypocrite.   And is there anything in the world that
is worse than a hypocrite?—Moses Chayim Luzzatto,
ibid., c. 22

14: Obedience is only the *effect* of religion.   Not
the mere observance of religious precepts, but the
heart, the disposition and intent, which leads to their
observance, constitute the essence of religion.—Felix
Perles, *Bousset's "Religion des Judentums,"* p. 126.

15: Not what a man does, but how he does it, is
profane or holy.—H. Steinthal, *Über Juden u. Judentum,* p. 29.

16: Whether it be of laws of the state or of religion or of morality, of them all the same principle
holds true: it is solely the heart, the disposition and
intent, that give value to the deed.—H. Steinthal, *l. c.,*
p. 30.

17: Even obligatory conduct, if it aims merely at
the favor, the protection, and the beneficence of God,
or at the respect and honor of men, is just as immoral
as the insincere devotional exercise.   If devotion needs
for its complement the moral deed, then, vice versa,
the moral deed lacking in devotion is lacking in essence.—H. Steinthal, *Zu Bibel u. Religionsphilosophie* I, pp. 155-156.

See also:

M. BLOCH, *Die Ethik i. d. Halacha,* 1886, pp. 2ff, 70.
MARTIN BUBER, *Vom Geist d. Judentums,* 1916, pp. 66f.
HERMANN COHEN, *Gesinnung, "Korrespondenzblatt d. Verb. d.
   Deutschen Juden,"* Nr. 7, pp. 1ff.

———— *Innere Bezhg. d. Kant. Philos. z. Judentum*, 1910, pp. 47ff.

M. DIENEMANN, *Judentum u. Christentum*, 1914, pp. 30, 51.

I. ELBOGEN, *Die Religionsanschauungen d. Pharisäer*, 1904, p. 27.

M. GÜDEMANN, *Das Judentum in s. Grundzügen*, 1902, pp. 14, 86ff.

S. R. HIRSCH, *Choreb*, 1837, c. 14, §108; c. 24, §180; c. 33, §244; c. 75, §493; c. 98, §617.

KAUFMANN KOHLER, *Grundr. e. syst. Theol. d. Judentums*, 1910, p. 181.

L. LAZARUS, *Zur Charakteristik d. talmudischen Ethik*, 1877, pp. 13, 20f., 27ff., 33.

M. LAZARUS, *Die Ethik d. Judentums*, I, 1899, pp. 67, 93f., 108ff., 126f., 160, 203f., 221, 228, 230f., 238; II, 1911, pp. 51f., 91.

MOSES CHAYIM LUZZATTO, *Mesillat Yesharim*, c. 11, c. 16.

SALOMON MAIMON, *Lebensgeschichte*, 1792, pp. 76ff.

FELIX PERLES, *Bousset's "Religion d. Judentums,"* 1903, pp. 104f., 129.

H. STEINTHAL, *Über Juden u. Judentum*, 1906, pp. 29f.

[Nathan Isaacs, "Is Judaism Legalistic?" in *The Menorah Journal*, December, 1921, pp. 259-268.—Tr.]

CHRISTIAN AUTHORS

VIII,   1: Moreover, in Hillel's circle it was not wholly forgotten that in ethical action what is of consequence is a totality, of which, the heart, the disposition and intent form part, and not the deed by itself. Rabbi Elieser (about 100) was asked by his disciples upon his deathbed: "Master, teach us the ways of life so that through them we may be deemed worthy of the life of the future world" (Berachot, 28 b; Wünsche, I, 45). The "Rabbins in Yabne" are reported to have said: "It is all the same whether a person does much or little, if one only directs his

heart [his thoughts] to Heaven [God] (Berachot.
17 a; Goldschmidt, I, 61). Indeed, instances are not
wholly wanting in which this consciousness that religion and morality lay stress on a living purpose per-
meating the whole transaction, turns critically against
the casuistry of the ceremonial law. The following
saying of Simeon ben Menasja (second century) has
been handed down: "The Sabbath is committed to
you, but not you to the Sabbath" (*Mechilta* to Exodus xxxi. 14; Ugolini, XIV, 575; Hamburger, II,
406; Derenbourg, I, 144). Moreover, teachers like
Eleasar ben Asarja, Ishmael, Akiba taught that one
might break the Sabbath in order to save a human life
in jeopardy, indeed, that many kinds of need [the
cares of subsistence] often annul the whole commandment. The point is stressed, for example, in the Testaments. Benjamin, 3: "Your mind shall be directed
to the good." Compare Benjamin, 5, Gad, 5: "The
righteous and the meek shrinks from doing wrong
. . . before his own heart." It is reported of
Yochanan ben Zakkai that he had asked his disciples:
"Do tell me which is the best way for a man to
choose?" and that he had preferred Eleazar's reply,
"a good heart," to all the others [*Pirke Aboth* II, 9
(13); compare also *Ps.—Arist.*, §133 and 189].—
Wilhelm Bousset, *Die Religion des Judentums*, pp.
159-160.

2: However, despite the manifold motives of
moral action that we meet with, one thing more belongs to the inalienable original stock of ethics: *the
religious orientation of the moral requirements.*
Whether the more immanent justification of moral re-

quirements prevails, characteristic of the Wisdom literature, or whether the thought is fixed upon recompense in this world or the next, at bottom, the thought of God always stands behind all the more immediate motives. In this intimate union of religion and ethics —despite all encumbrances of the two with external things—later Judaism also safeguarded its ancestral heritage. In summarizing, one can rightly maintain that *moral action is an action initiated by the fear of God*. Even the proverb-wisdom given to the more immanent mode of contemplation puts forward as its first and foremost principle the thought that the fear of God is the beginning and root of all wisdom (*Sir.* I. 20).—Wilhelm Bousset, *l. c.*, p. 476.

3: Still more can be said, however. The consciousness is not wholly wanting that in the end all ethical requirements and all ethical actions form a unity. They perceive the *unity running through a good heart, of a good disposition and intent*, and the action to which it leads. To that we have already referred above (compare pp. 158f.). The greatest value is attached by Ben-Sira to unadulterated ethical-mindedness.—Wilhelm Bousset, *ibid.*, p. 480.

4: Consequently, it is morality in itself that *Yahveh* requires, immorality in itself that He punishes; with that the barriers of particularism, of the merely national religion are, in principle, broken through. Out of that, in the long run, universalism and individual religion must grow up.—Karl Budde, *Die Religion des Volkes Israel*, p. 120.

5: It became evident from what has been said until now that Jewish ethics in its highest perfection has developed into an ethics of the heart, pure and simple. We are to follow the law of the Lord, to be sure, but this is not known to anyone completely; rather, therefore, is a general attitude, a disposition, namely, "the fear of the Lord," the last wisdom, or the "delight in the law of the Lord," as the first psalm expresses it.—Hugo Dingler, *Die Kultur der Juden,* p. 106.

6: It [the Torah] turns its back on covetousness, the evil desire, which is the source and the focus of all violations of the law; it [the Torah] combats natural self-seeking, to which [in the Hammurabi code] bounds are set only when it encroaches upon the rights of one's fellowmen; it [the Torah] sets up the postulate of love of fellowmen. A law like Exodus xx. 14 (Deuteronomy v. 18), "Thou shalt not covet," even if it were to be understood first of all as a commandment of morality, and not as a punitive rule, places the decalogue above all laws of the world, which are incapable of preventing or effectively dealing with acts of the mind prior to the positive manifestation of criminal intent in a punishable offense.— Johannes Jeremias, *Moses und Hammurabi,* p. 54.

7: The prophet who prophecies of the new covenant where the law would be laid in their inward parts and written in their hearts, or who demands a circumcision of the lips and hearts, a rending of hearts and not of clothes; the psalmist who recognizes only a broken spirit, a contrite and penitent heart as "genuine sacrifices to God," have a deep comprehension of the worship of God in the spirit and of truth, a deep understanding of this point that in comparison with such worship the divine service of the Old Testament [the sacrificial cult only is meant] is only an imperfect fragment. And we say once more that, where such knowledge gets circulated, there is God's spirit and word, there we stand in the presence of something that is permanent, imperishable already in the Old Testament.—Emil Kautzsch, *Die bleibende Bedeutung d. A. T.*, pp. 17-18.

8: It is the disposition which a person adds to God's *word of promise* which converts it into a *reality* for him. That this is what gives firmness and strength to it for the overcoming of affliction, has been confirmed by the exile.—Justus Köberle, *Sünde u. Gnade*, p. 211.

9: Nothing less indeed was required by God than is expressed in the command to Abraham: Walk before me and be pious, that is, perfect, irreproachable (Genesis xvii. 1)! It is obvious that Judaism was not lacking in an inward conception, sustained by religious earnestness, of the divine requirement.—Justus Köberle, *l. c.*, pp. 328-329.

10: The moral requirements of the Law stand higher than the popular custom of ancient times; they take into consideration also the sphere of the heart, of the inner disposition, and the ideals thus set up stand upon the height of prophetic intuition.—Justus Köberle, *ibid.*, p. 337.

11: Moreover, in that, Ezekiel also is concerned with the outgrowth of morality from the right *disposition*. For he emphasized the necessity of the regeneration of the *inner* man. Indeed, he several times demanded the replacement of the unfeeling and unresponsive heart by a sensitive and willing *heart* (xi. 19; xviii. 31; xxxvi. 26-27), and he also characterized strangers first of all as the "uncircumcised in *heart*" (xliv. 9).—Eduard König, *Geschichte der alttestamentlichen Religion*, p. 395.

12: The duties that this regulation imposes (namely, Deuteronomy) are not to be performed out of fear of consequences, but obedience to them shall be the immediate effluence of a community of heart between the pious and *Yahveh*, their God, Who is the God of gods and the Lord of lords, the great, mighty, and fearful God. The love of God as a fundamental governing motive in human action is a characteristic thought of the "Book of the Torah."—Max Löhr, *Geschichte des Volkes Israel*, p. 125.

13: *Yahveh* is a living God and is not content with only an external performance of His commandments; He tries heart and reins *and looks at the disposition and the intent.*—Karl Marti, *Geschichte der israelitischen Religion*, p. 186.

14: At the same time, however, the forbidding of evil desire bears witness that, in the kingdom of God, even the thoughts and aspirations of the heart that run counter to God's will are already accounted as transgressions of the Law.—Eduard Riehm, *Alttestamentliche Theologie*, p. 74.

15: Accordingly, in the prophetic conception of the Law, *those requirements growing out of the inward belonging* of the individual to *Yahveh*, stand apart from the multitude of the commandments relating to external action, as the *presupposition of all conduct that is pleasing in the sight of God.* The sum

of the whole Law is contained in the basic requirement
that Israel shall fear and love *Yahveh.*—Eduard
Riehm, *l. c.,* p. 239.

16: In consequence of the intensification of the
religious life, the *fulfillment of the religious-moral requirements of Yahveh,* as a condition of civic rights
in the community, had to be stressed far more than
mere national membership in Israel, and moreover,
the knowledge of those requirements had deepened.—
Eduard Riehm, *ibid.,* p. 249.

17: The presupposition of all worship that is
pleasing in the sight of God is a *sincerely pious disposition; a love of Yahveh which comprises within itself* honest striving after *righteousness and purity;
joy in His glory and grace* as these have become manifest; *gratitude for His demonstrations of mercy,*
coupled with humble *reverential awe before His holy
majesty.*—Eduard Riehm, *ibid.,* p. 312.

18: To him [to Jeremiah], in his own struggle
over matters of faith, prayer, and life, the inward possession of this God as the sole abiding good has become a certainty. He is his strength and his praise
(xvi. 19; xvii. 14-17). He realizes that this God
stands in a direct relation to each devout individual,
that He tries the hearts and reins, that is, the innermost parts (xi. 20; xii. 3; xvii. 10; xx. 12), and
that, on the other hand, humanity to its last member
can, in prayer, directly touch Him (xvii. 14-17).
Thus he perceived the heart as the real seat of religion;
speaking of the "return" he very characteristically
adds, "with their whole heart" (xxiv. 7); he demands

removal of the foreskin of the heart (iv. 4; ix. 25).—
Ernst Sellin, *Der alttest. Prophetismus*, p. 71.

See also:

WILHELM CASPARI, *Die israelitischen Propheten*, 1914, pp. 69f.

G. W. F. HEGEL, *Vorlesungen üb. d. Philos. d. Gesch.*, 1907, p. 411.

PAUL KLEINERT, *Die Propheten Israels in soz. Bezhg.*, 1905, p. 33.

JUSTUS KÖBERLE, *Sünde u. Gnade*, 1905, pp. 118, 175, 204, 211f., 226, 337ff., 353, 448f., 454f., 465f., 493f., 496f., 500, 504f.

EDUARD KÖNIG, *Geschichte d. alttest. Religion*, 1912, p. 41.

———— *Prophetenideal, Judentum u. Christentum*, 1906, pp. 6f.

———— *Geschichte d. Reiches Gottes*, 1908, pp. 244f., 257f., 326f.

KARL MARTI, *Geschichte d. israelitischen Religion*, 1900, pp. 188, 192f., 261.

JOHANNES NIKEL, *Das A. T. u. d. Nächstenliebe*, 1913, p· 38.

EDUARD RIEHM, *Alttest. Theol.*, 1889, pp. 241, 286ff.

ERNST SELLIN, *Alttest. Religion*, 1908, pp. 22f.

RUDOLF SMEND, *Lehrb. d. alttest. Religionsgeschichte*, 1899, pp. 177, 416.

FERDINAND WEBER, *Jüd. Theol. auf Grund d. Talmud*, 1897, pp. 284f.

JULIUS WELLHAUSEN, *Israelitische u. jüd. Geschichte*, 1907, p. 218.

R. T. HERFORD, *The Pharisees*, 1924, Chap. V. D. pp. 138-146 (The Torah and the Moral Law).—Tr.

GEORGE FOOT MOORE, *Judaism in the First Centuries of the Christian Era. The Age of the Tannaim*, 2 Vols., Harvard University Press, 1927.[1]—Tr.

---

[1] "A scholar of world wide reputation, he [Professor Moore] presents to us in this magnum opus the result of thirty years of painstaking research. He has consulted the entire literature bearing on the subject, has re-examined the sources and has given us a really dependable interpretation of Judaism. There is no space to praise adequately this profound work" (From a review by M. Jung).—Tr.

III

PURITY OF SOUL

Introduction by Dr. Abraham Loewenthal

"My God, the soul that Thou gavest me is pure."
That is the profession which the Jew makes in his
daily morning prayer before God. God has not created man sinful. The human being has been created
pure. God crowned him with glory and honor; he
is made but little lower than the angels (Psalms viii.) ;
he has been created in the image of God. Hence all
human beings carry within themselves a spark of divine fire; in some it is dimmed by sin, or through inherited depravity, or corruption, but the soul created
by God, through which man bears His image, was
pure at its creation. It is of his own free will that any
man becomes a sinner.

Here begins the Christian doctrine of sin. It teaches
that when the first man had committed a sin, it became his unconquerable natural disposition, and all
persons descending from him are afflicted with this in-
delible taint; they must all bear the damnation and
the punishment that befell them, too, when the first
man sinned of his own free choice. They are incapable by their own efforts of removing the sin, or es-
caping from the punishment; they can be freed there-

from only through another, through a "redeemer."

Judaism has also expounded the story of the disobedience of which Adam, the first man, became
guilty. But in Jewish literature, not even the slightest
trace can be found of any discussion of an original
sin that can no longer be overcome, nor, of course, is
there any mention whatsoever of a death that is alleged to have been affixed to it as a punishment. Judaism does not try to make more of this narrative than
what it proves itself to be. It has not sought in it,
nor drawn from it, a solution for the riddles of human nature.

Judaism attributes to man now as ever capacity
[out of free choice] to prefer the good and to do it,
and also imposes upon him the obligation to do so.
While it [Judaism] also takes cognizance of the inclination to sin present in sensuous man, nevertheless
it asserts that he can conquer it in himself, requires
this of him and also credits him with the strength required to efface the sinful disposition himself and to
make amends for the sin committed through his own
repentance. Thus Judaism is not wanting in a
method of redemption. Man finds redemption from
sin through his own manful return to the good and
the mercy of God (Psalms cxxx. 7-8).

He who cultivates his sensual nature instead of
letting his sense of God and of awe before Him control his conduct, and win the victory for his higher
nature, creates in himself, as the Talmud says, a
strange god; that is, he allows the natural impulse to
evil, which the religious man subdues through the good
deed, to grow ever stronger until finally it becomes

his master.   To be sure, man's heart is evil from his youth (Genesis viii. 21), that is, as our sages teach, evil example can even in childhood have a devastating effect upon the purity of the soul, but over against evil example education and good example stand as equally strong forces.   Thus Judaism does not believe in the depravity of human nature; it only asserts susceptibility to sin.

If the soul of man is pure, so is his body also; man's body as God's creation carries within itself, no natural uncleanness.   Nor is the evil inclination embedded in man's corporeal life.   The human being who sins acts out of moral perversity.   Over against all other views, Judaism holds firmly to the purity of the human being.

BIBLE

I,   1: And God created man in His own image, in the image of God created He him.—Genesis i. 27.

2: What is man, that Thou art mindful of him? and the son of man, that Thou thinkest of him?   Yet Thou hast made him but little lower than the angels, and hast crowned him with glory and honor.— Psalms viii. 5-6.

3: God made man upright.—Ecclesiastes vii. 29.

PRAYERS

IV,   1: O My God, the soul which Thou gavest me is pure.—Daily Prayer, Morning Service.

2: Thou hast distinguished man from the beginning, and hast recognized his privilege that he might

stand before Thee.—In the Conclusion Service for the
Day of Atonement (Singer's *Prayerbook*, p. 412).

TALMUDICAL LITERATURE

V,   1: Beloved [of God] is man, for he was created in the image of God; but it was by a special
love that it was *made known* to him that he was
created in the image of God, as it is said, "For in the
image of God made He man" (Genesis ix. 6).—
Ethics of the Fathers, III. 18 (Singer's *Prayerbook*,
p. 281).   (See below, p. 168, VII, 15.)

     2: You will have to return it [the soul] to Him;
as He has given it to you in purity, so give it back
to Him in purity.—*Shabbat* 152 b.

     3: [At birth the child is told]: you shall be a
righteous person and not a sinner . . . And know
that the Holy one, blessed be He, is pure and those
that serve Him are pure; the soul which He has given
you is pure—if you keep it in purity, it is well; but
if not, God will take it away from you.—*Niddah*
30 a.

     4: May your departure from the world be as
your entrance into it.   As your entrance into the
world is without sin, so may your departure also be
without sin.—*Baba Metzia* 107 a.

     5: "There shall not be in thee a foreign god"
(Psalms lxxxi. 10).   What is the foreign god in
the human being?   The evil impulse.—*Shabbat*
105 b.

     6: "For the inclination [in the English version:
"imagination"] of man's heart is evil from his

youth" (Genesis viii. 21). Should you say, however: Why has the Holy One, blessed be He, created the evil inclination, of which it is said: "For the inclination of man's heart is evil from his youth"— and who can change it into a good one? The Holy One, blessed be He, replies: "You yourself make it evil." "How?" "You were a child and did not sin, you have grown up and you sin."—*Abot de R. Natan*, c. 17; *Midrash Tanchuma, ad loc.*

MIDDLE AGES

VI,   1: We declare: In the whole body of the human being there is nothing that is morally impure; he is pure.—Saadyah, *Emunot ve-Deot* (Teachings of Revelation and Reason), vi, 17.

MODERN JEWISH LITERATURE

VII,   1: For Judaism the sin does not exist, but only the *sin of a human being, the sin of an individual*. Judaism does not know the myth of sin as a thing fastened upon man by fate—its prophets overcame whatever tendency there was to adopt such a theory. Judaism does not know original guilt or sin as a one-time event which has man as its effect and object. The fate attached to sin is a fate that the individual prepares for himself when he surrenders himself to it, voluntarily makes himself its object. He is not mixed in sin fixed upon him by fate but in a fate fixed upon him by sin. *"Thy sin," "thou hast sinned," "the soul that sins,"* such expressions indicate the Jewish view. In it there is no minimizing of the countless ways that evil impulse lays hold of man and draws its circles around him. Here as elsewhere the Jewish religion takes full account of human weakness, of the defects of man's nature and the mistakes to which he is prone. It says again and again that all good life is a refusal to follow these false leads; it is not unaware of temptation, of the "evil inclinations," of the "longing of sin" for man; it is acquainted with the relationships and complexities of life, of its inheritances and dependences, of everything of that kind which grows up out of the soil upon which man is placed, and awaits him on the threshold of his existence. It knows about habits, about the paths of evil, about how the heart may chill and stiffen, about "the sin that brings on sin." It can speak of "the guilt of the fathers" and of "the guilt of the land," but it knows nothing at all of an evil that is inevitably inherent in human nature. It does not admit the existence of any hereditary sin. The word sin is to it not a word relating to fate, but to judgment, judgment concerning an act of human authorship. It is a human being, who can be either for or against God, who himself sponsors the sin; it remains in the field of his own responsibility.— Leo Baeck, *Das Wesen des Judentums* (2d ed.), pp. 171-172.

2: "My God, the soul which Thou gavest me is pure." Purity, after all, is what makes the religious exercise of freedom possible. Purity of soul is what makes man the image of God. Man is not *holy*. Any claim to holiness on the part of man is looked upon by us as blasphemy. But at the start man is pure; his soul is pure. That purity puts the surest stamp of immortality upon man; at the same time, however, it is also the prototype of its freedom.—Hermann Cohen, *Innere Beziehungen der Kantischen Philosophie zum Judentum*, p. 56.

3: "From the hands of the Creator there originates nothing that is evil," says the oldest wisdom. "My God, the soul which Thou gavest me is pure," is a confession which that same wisdom teaches its pupils to utter from the cradle to the grave; "pure didst Thou breathe it into me, pure shall it return again to Thee." It knows nothing of an innate, hereditary sinfulness . . .—S. R. Hirsch, *Gesammelte Schriften*, IV, pp. 420-421.

4: Rabbinical Judaism never followed Philo so far in the footsteps of Plato as to consider the body or the flesh the source of impurity and sin, or "the prison house of the soul." This view is fundamental in the Paulinian system of other-worldiness. For the Rabbis the sensuous desire of the body (*yezer*) is a tendency toward sin, but *never a compulsion*. The weakness of the flesh may cause a straying from the right path, but man can turn the desires of the flesh into the service of the good.—Kaufmann Kohler, *Theol. d. Judentums*, p. 162 (*Jewish Theology*, p. 215).

5: Judaism rejects completely the belief in hereditary sin and in the corruption of the flesh. The Biblical verse, "God made man upright; but they have sought out many inventions" (Eccl. vii. 29), is explained in the Midrash: "Upright and just as is

God, He made man after His likeness in order that he might strive after righteousness, and unfold even more his god-like nature, but men in their dissensions have marred the divine image" (*Tanh. Yelamdenu* to Gen. iii. 22). With reference to another verse in Ecclesiastes (Eccl. xii. 7): "The dust returneth unto the earth as it was, and the spirit returneth unto God who gave it," the Rabbis teach "Pure as the soul is when entering upon its earthly career, so can man return it to his Maker" (*Shab.* 152 b). Therefore the pious Jew begins his daily prayers with the words: "My God, the soul which Thou hast given me is pure" (*Ber.* 80 a). The Rabbis did not hold the belief that the body is morally impure and therefore the seat of the *yezer ha ra*, as is stated by Weber, *Jüdische Theologie*, 228 f. See F. Ch. Porter: "The Yezer ha Ra" in *Biblical and Semitic Studies*, 98-107; Schechter, *Some Aspects of Rabbinic Theology*, New York, 1909, 242-292. It is also wrong to explain Ps. li, 7, "Behold I was brought forth in iniquity, and in sin did my mother conceive me," as a reference to inherited sinfulness, as Delitzsch and other Christian commentators have done, following Ibn Ezra, who makes this refer to Eve, the mother of all men. The correct interpretation is given by R. Ahha in *Lev. R.* XIV. 5; (comp. *Yoma* 69 b).—Kaufmann Kohler, *l. c.*, p. 169 (*Jewish Theology*, p. 223, and note). (Revised by Tr.)

6: Thus, God had separated man at creation already from the rest of creation, lifted him out from among the beings of nature; for in man there is a breath of the Divine, he is not a creature of the earth,

he is an image of God.   Moreover, God had chosen
him—not merely this man or that man, not this or
that people, not Ashur, not Egypt, and not Israel
either—but simply mortal, frail man.   And for what
did He choose and destine him?   And of what is he
recognized as worthy?   Solely for and of this: to
serve God.   The [eighth] psalm had emphasized the
sovereign dignity of man; here [in a prayer at the
conclusion of the Day of Atonement] it is the priestly
dignity of man that is looked upon as his destiny.   It
elevates him high *above* all nature, *within* which his
standing is exactly that of the animal.—H. Steinthal,
Zu Bibel und Religionsphilosophie, I, pp. 178-179.

CHRISTIAN AUTHORS

VIII,   1: The course of speculation about "the
evil inclination" shows how thoroughly convinced
pious Jewish students were of the insufficiency and
sinfulness of human nature.   In that same connection also, *two further consequences or by-roads* have
been *permanently avoided* within Palestinian Judaism.   In the first place, even this doctrine of the evil
inclination contains no distinct trace of the view that
sin, the evil inclination, is necessarily and of itself
connected with the bodily existence of man.   *The
evil inclination belongs, in the collective opinion, not
to the body,* but to the heart of man.   It is a question
in the last analysis not of natural disposition, but of
ethical perversity.   Moreover, it has been strikingly
proved recently that even later rabbinical theology
teaches on the subject of good and evil inclinations

that the good inclination does not belong to the soul and the evil inclination to the body of man, but both belong to the whole of human nature.—Wilhelm Bousset, *Die Religion des Judentums*, pp. 464-465.

2: To Judaism, the *universality of sin* was a certainty, a matter of course; compare Proverbs xx. 9; Eccles. vii. 20. It was not the spawn, however, of the material nature of man as such. The view that since the body is the material part of man, the seat of the senses, it defiles the soul, acts as a drag upon it and disturbs its freedom and purity, is not a Jewish view. Where it appears in later Judaism, it is an intruder from alien sources.—Justus Köberle, *Sünde und Gnade*, pp. 345-346.

3: This belief also exists from olden times, that Israel's nature on the whole is good. Every trace of the Christian view that humanity dwells under the dominion of sin and that each individual because he was born into the sequence of human development necessarily falls under the dominion of sin, is entirely absent.—Bernhard Stade, *Geschichte des Volkes Israel*, I, p. 511.

[See also: R. Travers Herford, *The Pharisees*, pp. 165-169, 155-157.—Tr.]

IV

FREEDOM OF THE WILL

Introduction by Dr. Simon Bernfeld

The fundamental condition anteceding morality is the freedom of the will, the self-determination of man as to what he will do or leave undone, the free choice to will the good and to do it, or to avoid the evil in thought and deed. Judaism teaches this freedom of the will. Upon it rests the moral responsibility by which man endowed with reason is obligated to be self-guided. Judaism does not know the doctrine of hereditary sin, of an invincibly sinful nature in man, nor the doctrine of the election of grace, nor that of inevitable fate.

The ancient teachers of Judaism clearly recognized, it is true, that this teaching concerning moral freedom is in many ways at variance with the phenomena and experiences of life. Just as the acts of the individual can exercise a more or less determining influence upon the destinies of human society for good as well as for evil, so the individual likewise is subject more or less to the determining influence of his surroundings, his national community and past tradition. The sins of the parents affect also their children and children's children, as, on the other hand, the virtu-

ous life of the parents may become a source of blessing to the children.   But according to the teaching
of Judaism this situation should not so paralyze the
moral will either of communities or individuals as
to lead them to abandon themselves indolently to
fate, but should serve as an incentive to moral and
righteous conduct, and all the more so, if their actions affect their contemporaries and posterity as well.
The consequences of your actions, Judaism proclaims
to all, are borne not only by yourselves, but also by
the community and by later generations.   Yet the
road to the good is neither barred to them nor does
the merit of their progenitors give them a license for
reprehensible conduct on their own part.   This
thought, momentous in its bearing for ethics, is vigorously emphasized, particularly by Ezekiel.

Post-Biblical Judaism was also very seriously concerned with the problem of moral freedom and man's
moral responsibility.   Even the Sadducees and the
Pharisees, the parties who, according to Josephus
were of different opinion on particular cases of man's
responsibility, concurred in the principle of the freedom of the will.   And this conviction remained dominant in Jewish religious philosophy and in the ethics
of the people, with few exceptions, until quite recently.

Under the influence of Islam, the Jewish philosophers of religion of the middle ages concerned themselves minutely with the question of how the freedom of will is to be harmonized with the dispensa-
tion of Divine Providence and with the idea of God's
omniscience.   And however difficult they found the

solution of the problem to be, they almost all concurred in the view that the freedom of the will does not undergo any limitation through Divine Providence.

BIBLE

I,   1: I call heaven and earth to witness against you this day, that I have set before thee life and death, the blessing and the curse; therefore choose life.—Deuteronomy xxx. 19.

2: At one instant I may speak concerning a nation, and concerning a kingdom, to pluck up and to break down and to destroy it; but if that nation turn from their evil, because of which I have spoken against it, I repent of the evil that I thought to do unto it.   And at one instant I may speak concerning a nation, and concerning a kingdom, to build and to plant it; but if it do evil in My sight, that it hearken not to My voice, then I repent of the good, wherewith I said I would benefit it.   Now therefore do thou speak to the men of Judah, and to the inhabitants of Jerusalem, saying: Thus saith the LORD: Behold, I frame evil against you, and devise a device against you; return ye now every one from his evil way, and amend your ways and your doings.—Jeremiah xviii. 7-11.

3: Therefore I will judge you, O house of Israel, every one according to his ways, saith the Lord GOD. Return ye, and turn yourselves from all your transgressions; so shall they not be a stumbling block of iniquity unto you.   Cast away from you all your transgressions, wherein ye have transgressed; and

make you a new heart and a new spirit: for why will
ye die, O house of Israel?   For I have no pleasure
in the death of him that dieth, saith the Lord GOD;
wherefore turn yourselves and live.—Ezekiel xviii.
30-32.

4: His own iniquities shall ensnare the wicked,
and he shall be holden with the cords of his sin.—
Proverbs v. 22.

PALESTINIAN APOCRYPHA

IIa,   1: Say not thou: "It is through the LORD
that I fell away;" for thou oughtest not to do the
things that He hateth.   Say not thou: "He hath
caused me to err;" for He hath no need of the sinful
man.   The LORD hateth all abomination; and they
that fear God love it not.   He Himself made man
from the beginning, and left him in the hand of his
own decision [free will].   If thou wilt, keep the
commandments, and perform acceptable faithfulness.
He hath set fire and water before thee: stretch forth
thy hand unto whichever thou wilt.   Before man
is life and death; and whichever he liketh shall be
given him.—*Ben-Sira* xv. 11-17.

2: He hath commanded no man to do wickedly,
neither hath He given any man license to sin.—*Ben-
Sira* xv. 20.

3: Sin has not been sent upon the earth, but
man of himself has created it.—*The Book of Enoch,*
98, 4 (Charles, in Charles, *l. c.,* II).

4: Woe to them who pervert the words of uprightness, and transgress the eternal law, and trans-

form themselves into what they were not, into sinners.—*Ibid.*, 99, 2 (Charles, *ibid.*).

5: Two ways hath God given to the sons of
men, and two inclinations, and two kinds of action,
and two modes (of action), and two issues. Therefore all things are by twos, one over against the
other. For there are two ways, of good and evil,
and with these are the two inclinations in our breasts
discriminating them. Therefore if the soul take
pleasure in the good (inclination), all its actions are
in righteousness; and if it sin it straightway repenteth.
For, having its thoughts set upon righteousness, and
casting away wickedness, it straightway overthroweth
the evil, and uprooteth the sin.—*The Testaments of
the Twelve Patriarchs* X. 1, 3-7 (Charles, *ibid.*).

6: Our actions ensue from the choice and will
of our soul; right and wrong is the work of our
hands.—*The Psalms of Solomon* IX. 4.

7: For though Adam first sinned and brought
untimely death upon all, yet of those who were born
from him, each one of them has prepared for his own
soul torment to come, and again each one of them
has chosen for himself glories to come. . . . Adam
is therefore not the cause, save only of his own soul,
but each of us has been the Adam of his own soul.—
The Syriac Apocalypse of Baruch, 54, 15 and 19
(Charles, in Charles, *l. c.*, II).

8: For out of their own free resolve [having received liberty] they despised the Most High; scorned
His Law, and forsook His ways.—For the Most High
willed not that men should come to destruction; but
they—his creatures—have themselves defiled the

Name of Him that *made* them, and have proved themselves ungrateful to Him who prepared life for
them.—*The Fourth Book of Ezra* VIII. 56, 60 (Box,
in Charles, *l. c.,* II).

9: If ye, then, will rule over your inclinations,
and will discipline your heart, ye shall be preserved
in life, and after death obtain mercy.—*The Fourth
Book of Ezra* XIV. 34 (and Box, *ibid.*).

JEWISH-HELLENISTIC LITERATURE

III,   1: . . . What is the highest form of government? . . . To rule oneself and not to be carried away by impulses.—*The Letter of Aristeas,* 221-
222 (Andrews, in Charles, *l. c.,* II).

2: Verily, when the Law orders us not to covet,
it should be taken, I think, as strong confirmation
of the argument that the Reason is capable of controlling covetous desires.—*The Fourth Book of Maccabees* II. 6 (Townshend, *ibid.*). (Revised by Tr.)

3: For the temperate mind is able, as I said, to
win the victory over the passions, modifying some,
while crushing others absolutely.—*The Fourth Book
of Maccabees* II. 18 (Townshend, *ibid.*).

4: For example, none of you is able to extirpate your natural desire, but the Reason can enable
him to escape being made a slave by desire. None
of you is able to extirpate anger from the soul, but
it is possible for the Reason to come to his aid against
anger. None of you can extirpate a malevolent disposition, but Reason can be his powerful ally against
being swayed by malevolence. Reason is not the ex-

tirpator of the passions, but their antagonist.—*The Fourth Book of Maccabees* III. 2-5 (Townshend, *ibid.*).

5: But as many as with their whole heart make righteousness their first thought, these alone are able to master the weakness of the flesh, believing that unto God they die not, as our patriarchs, Abraham and Isaac and Jacob, died not, but that they live unto God.—*Ibid.*, VII. 18-19 (Townshend, *ibid.*).

TALMUDICAL LITERATURE

V,   1: Everything is foreseen [by God], yet freedom of choice is given [to man].—Rabbi Akiba in *Ethics of the Fathers*, III, 19.

2: Who is mighty? He who subdues his passions, as it is said, "He that is slow to anger is better than the mighty, and he that ruleth over his spirit than he that taketh a city" (Proverbs xvi. 32).—*Ethics of the Fathers*, IV, 1 (Singer's. *Prayerbook*, p. 283).

3: He who yields to his inclinations is like an idolater, for it is said, "There shall no strange god be in thee" (Psalms lxxxi. 10)—that means, Thou shalt not let the strange god have dominion over thee.—*Yer. Nedarim* IX, 1 (compare above, p. 95).

4: At first the evil inclination in man is like a cobweb, but afterwards like strong thick ropes.—*Sukkah* 52 a.

5: Happy is he who proves himself to be valiant and represses his evil inclination.—*Abodah Zarah* 19 a.

6: When Israel occupies himself with the Torah and good works, he will become master of the evil inclination and not let the evil inclination become his master.—*Abodah Zarah* 5 b.

7: A man should always oppose the good impulse to the evil impulse.—*Berachot* 5 a (Cohen, *l. c.*, p. 19). (See also note thereto.—Tr.)

8: Keep thyself from trivial sin, that it may not lead thee to a grave one.—*Abot de R. Natan*, II, 1 (Michael L. Rodkinson, *The Babylonian Talmud*, tr. into English, Boston, 1901, Vol. IX, p. 13); *Tosefta Yebamot*, c. 4; *Chullin* 44 b.

9: Man shall never think and say: I am a sinner and have committed many sins and now what will it help me to perform the commandments—but if he has committed many sins, over against them he shall perform many pious works.—*Midrash Leolam*, VI (*Bet ha-Midrah*, ed. Jellinek, III, 112-113).

10: Everything is in the hand of Heaven except the fear of Heaven (i. e. God determines whether the person will be tall or short, rich or poor, etc.; but not whether he will be God-fearing or not. That is left to his own choice).—*Berachot* 33 b (Cohen, *ibid.*, p. 226 and note); *Megillah* 25 a.

11: At man's birth God determines whether he will be strong or weak, sensible or stupid, rich or poor, but not whether he will be pious or wicked.— *Niddah* 16 b.

12: The evil never comes from Me [from God]. —*Sifra*, section *Bechukkotaj*, Nr. 4; compare Bacher, *Die Agada der Tannaiten*, I, pp. 282, 325f., 415).

MIDDLE AGES

VI,   1: The Prophets teach us that God granted man the ability to serve Him, that He gave it to him and made him master over it, that He gave the freedom of the will into his power and bade him to choose the good.—Saadyah, *E m u n o t   v e - D e o t* (Teachings of Revelation and Reason), IV, 2.

2: Here I declare: The Creator exercises no influence upon the doings of men and compels them neither to service nor to disobedience.—Saadyah, *l. c.,* IV, 10.

3: The return of the sinner is impossible only if his inner self and his heart's deception restrain him from it; but if he has the will to draw nigh to God, the portal of return is not closed to him and nothing prevents him from reaching it; on the contrary, God opens for him the gate to virtue and in His grace and His kindness shows him the good way.—Bachya ibn Pakuda, *Chobot ha-Lebabot* (Duties of the Heart), VII, 342.

4: Man finds in himself this power of doing evil or avoiding it in matters which are in his own hand.—Yehudah ha-Levi, *Kuzari,* V, 20 (Hirschfeld, *l. c.*).

5: *Every human being is master of his actions, of what he does or leaves undone;* if he desires to set out upon the good way and be a righteous person, he is free to do so, and if he desires to set out upon the bad way and be a wicked person, he is free to do so. That is the meaning of the Biblical words, "The man is become as one of us, to know good and evil" (Genesis iii. 22). Man is the only being in crea-

tion—and no second one resembles him therein—
who by himself and through his own discernment
and his thinking differentiates the good and the evil,
and can do everything that he desires; and no one
prevents him from doing the good or the evil. Do
not listen to the idle talk of the fools among the
heathen and of the stupid among the Israelites, that
God decrees for man before he is born whether he
shall act rightly or wrongly. That is not so. On
the contrary, every man has it in his power to become
a righteous person like our teacher Moses, or a wicked
person like Jeroboam, either a wise man, or a fool,
either compassionate, or cruel, either avaricious, or
generous. And so it is with all the attributes of
character. No one can compel him, dictate to him,
draw him to one of the two ways, but he enters of
his own will upon whichever way he desires—according to his discernment. That is a very important principle, a foundation pillar of the Torah and
of the divine commandments.—Maimonides, *Mishneh Torah Hilchot Teshubah* (Return to God), V,
1-3.

6: We, on the contrary, are convinced that our
Law agrees with Greek philosophy, which establishes
with convincing proofs the contention that man's
conduct is entirely in his own hands, that no compulsion is exerted, and that no external influence is
brought to bear upon him that constrains him to be
either virtuous or vicious. The only exceptions, as
has been said above, are the instances where he may
by nature prove to be so constituted as to find it easy
or hard, as the case may be, to do a certain thing;

but that he must necessarily do, or refrain from doing, a thing is absolutely untrue.—Maimonides, *Shemonah Perakim* (The Eight Chapters on Ethics), VIII (*The Eight Chapters of Maimonides on Ethics*, edited, annotated, and translated by Joseph I. Gorfinkle, New York, 1912).   (Revised by Tr.)

7: It is an essential characteristic of man's nature that he should of his own free will act morally or immorally, doing just as he prefers. That makes it obligatory, therefore, to teach him the ways of righteousness, to command and exhort him to walk therein, to punish and reward him according to his deserts. The object of it all is that man shall accustom himself to the practice of good deeds, and acquire the virtues corresponding to those good deeds; and furthermore, that by learning to abstain from evil deeds he may eradicate the vices that may have taken root in him. Let no man suppose that his characteristics have reached such a state where they are no longer subject to change, for any one of them may be altered from the good to the bad, and vice versa; and, moreover, all these changes are a matter of his own free will.—Maimonides, *Shemonah Perakim*, VIII (Gorfinkle, *l. c.*).   (Revised by Tr.)

8: The actions of a man are completely in the keeping of his free will, he can do them or leave any of them undone.—R. Moses b. Nachman, *Commentary to* Genesis xxii. 1.

9: Thus free will abides with man. Although God's anticipatory knowledge remains entirely without limitation, yet it does not deprive man of his free will.—Isaak b. Shishat, *Legal Opinions*, Nr. 119.

10: Moral conduct, however, is not decreed for man, since he is free; that is wholly in our own control, and as regards it we may boast that we possess the knowledge of God.—From the *Pentateuchal Tosafot to* Numbers xxxii. 1.

11: There are men who deny the freedom of the will. Such men, however, repudiate not only religion, but all moral action. If Judaism turns against this erroneous belief, it does so not merely from its own standpoint, but also because it is in itself false and immoral.—Joseph Albo, *Ikkarim* (Book of Principles), I, 9.

MODERN JEWISH LITERATURE

VII,   1: The freedom with which Judaism endows man consequently means *purity of heart*. This constitutes a contradiction, a denial of original sin. It is therefore instructive to observe that the Psalmist conceives a pure heart as something not yet in his possession but still to be created of God, and that it is this for which he supplicates. "Create in me a pure heart, O God; and renew a stedfast spirit within me" (Ps. li. 12). The gift of a pure heart at birth is not to be longed for, because its creation is left to be the object and the task of one's whole life. This is likewise the ultimate meaning of ethical freedom. It should not be looked upon as originally present as fact, as datum, but be conceived as task, and always remain so regarded.

If freedom and purity are thus wedded, that will make it impossible to regard purity as an innate possession or as the gift of God: on the contrary it will constitute the ideal of man.—Hermann Cohen, "The Significance of Judaism for the Progress of Religion" (in *Proceedings of the Fifth International Congress of Free Christianity and Religious Progress*, Berlin—Schöneberg, 1911, pp. 385-400), p. 394.   (Revised by Tr.)

2: But the Jew knows this also, that as man separated from God through his own guilt, he must again approach Him through his own moral deed. And however much the soul is saddled with sin, full freedom and ability still remain for doing better. Moral regeneration must be an outgrowth of one's own power, *the sanctifying of man is his own work; by great struggles must he obtain peace with himself, the spiritual equilibrium* which is the guarantee of peace with God, atonement.   Inspired by this incentive, the Jew celebrates his Day of Atonement, unfailingly sustained by the thought that the all-merciful God inclines towards every repentant sinner, but that within himself alone lie the sources of moral regeneration.—Max Dienemann, *Judentum und Christentum*, pp. 34-35.

3: Judaism has kept alive nevertheless, has saved its external treasures, and has not allowed itself to be dimmed.   It has not permitted its belief in God to be disfigured or alloyed with foreign elements.   It has not allowed the doctrine of original sin to be grafted on to it, though great pains have been spent in the attempt to deduce that idea from the Scriptures.   It has not permitted the annihilation of mankind's title to nobility, but has clung to the conviction that man has been invested by God with the power of free self-determination and self-improvement; that despite the sensual propensity innate in man's nature, he is vested with the power of conquering it and of reaching by his own exertions the goal of elevation and ennoblement.—Abraham Geiger, *Das Judentum u. s. Geschichte,* I, p. 145 (Newburgh, *l. c.,* p. 159). (Revised by Tr.)

4: This capacity which man possesses of full freedom to choose for himself, and therefore to elevate himself, to strive toward perfection by his own efforts, and to attain it by honest endeavor, this capacity Akiba has presented with pregnant brevity, as the base and center of Judaism, in his dictum: "All is foreseen, freedom is given," and Judaism has steadily held fast to it.—Abraham Geiger, (*l. c.*) II, p. 19 (Newburgh, *ibid.,* p. 228). (Revised by Tr.)

5: Judaism knows no constraint of the will such as follows from the doctrine of hereditary sin as an inevitable consequence. The antinomy between human freedom of the will and divine foreknowledge, to be sure, cannot be solved any more than the antinomy in the domain of philosophy between man's freedom of will and the law of causality. Here we must, with Maimonides, acquiesce in the thought that we can form no idea of God's knowledge, which possesses in common with man's knowledge only the similarity of name. The *consciousness* of freedom which we possess, however, is a fact that cannot be disputed, and is at the same time the absolute presupposition for all moral action by man. We believe in no hereditary sin which serves to propagate evil in mankind, and we believe in no predestination which vetoes all moral self-determination of the human being and will not consent to allow the good to be considered as man's moral deed, but holds it to be entirely but an effect of divine grace. We are free, and can by the exercise of our own faculties battle our way through to moral perfection, because we are made in the likeness of God and created in His image. Even after when we have sinned, we have not incurred thereby the loss of our moral freedom. We are still able to extricate ourselves from the power of sin and to repattern our lives to correspond with the image of God which we bear.—Guttmann, *Die Idee der Versöhnung in Judentum*, pp. 8-9.

6: You yourself create the future for yourself by making good or bad use of the past and the present, for precisely according to this freely chosen program of yours does God shape your future, whether as recompense or as education; and thus it is the human being himself who in a measure prepares his own future.—S. R. Hirsch, *Choreb*, c. 6, §24.

7: Do not believe you are too weak! Do not believe because you have succumbed to sin so often that you cannot be victorious after all! *What God requires, for that He also gives power and strength.* Every man is endowed by Him at his entrance into this world with the power to be faithful to duty, and only for *Th'shuvah*, only for a *return* to inward purity need you strive, to become again what you once were.—S. R. Hirsch, *l. c.*, c. 79, §519.

8: He [man] can always assert his divine power of freedom by opposing the evil inclination (*yezer ha ra*) with the good inclination (*yezer ha tob*) to overcome it (Gen. vi. 5; viii. 21; B. Sira XV. 14; XVII. 31; XXI. 11; *Ber.* 5 a; *Kid.* 30 b; *Suk.* 52 a. b.; *Shab.* 152 b; *Eccl. R.* xii. 7; comp. F. Ch. Porter: "The Yezer ha Ra" in *Biblical and Semitic Studies,* 93-156; Bousset, *Wesen d. Rel.,* 462f.).— Kaufmann Kohler, *Jewish Theology,* p. 215 and note.

9: Judaism has always emphasized the freedom of the will as one of its chief doctrines. The dignity and greatness of man depend largely upon *his freedom, his power of self-determination.* He differs from the lower animals in his independence of instinct as the dictator of his actions. He acts from free choice and conscious design, and is able to change his mind at any moment, at any new evidence, or even through whim. He is therefore responsible for his every act or omission, even for his every *intention.* This alone renders him a *moral* being, a child of God; thus the moral sense rests upon freedom of the will. (See Dilmann, *H. B. d. alttestamentl. Theol.,* 301f., 375; *J. E.,* art. Freedom of Will.)—Kaufmann Kohler, *ibid.,* p. 231 and note.

10: The insistence of Judaism on unrestricted freedom of will for each individual entirely excludes hereditary sin. This is shown in the traditional explanation of the verse of the Decalogue: "Visiting the iniquity of the fathers upon the children unto the third and fourth generation of them that hate Me" (Ex. xx. 5). According to the Rabbis the words "of them that hate Me" do not refer to the fathers, as would appear to be the meaning of the passage, but to the children and the children's children. These are to be punished only when they hate God and follow the evil example of their fathers (*Sanh.* 27 b).— Kaufmann Kohler, *Theol. d. Judentums,* p. 179 (*Jewish Theology,* p. 236). (Revised by Tr.)

11: Man endowed with freedom of action, illumined by the Divine commandments laid down for him, finds in his own will the center of gravity of his existence. As his fate—his life and his death— is assumed to be in the strictest sense morally conditioned, the very idea of fate loses all the incompatibility that it must otherwise have for his moral consciousness.—Max Wiener, *Die Anschauungen der Propheten von der Sittlichkeit,* p. 108.

12: By having made Ezekiel's teaching of freedom its own, Judaism acknowledges that the center of gravity of life lies within ourselves; that man is not subject to fate but rather can choose a fate of his own.—Max Wiener, *Die Religion der Propheten,* p. 63.

See also:

HERMANN COHEN, *Innere Bezhg. d. Kant. Philos. z. Judentum,* 1910, pp. 54ff.
——— *Religion u. Sittlichkeit,* 1907, p. 134.
——— *Streiflichter über jüdische Rel. u. Wissenschaft, in "Neue jüdische Monatshefte,"* 1917, Nr. 10, p. 701.
MAX DIENEMANN, *Judentum u. Christentum,* 1914, pp. 8, 13f., 16ff., 27.
ABRAHAM GEIGER, *Das Judentum u. s. Gesch.,* 1865, I, p. 24; 1865, II, p. 19.
GUTTMANN, *Die Idee der Versöhnung im Judentum, Hefte "Vom Judentum,"* Nr. 2, pp. 6ff.
S. R. HIRSCH, *Choreb,* 1837, c. 6 §30; c. 79 §519.

———— *Ges. Schr.*, I, 1902, p. 300; II, 1904, p. 393; III, 1906, p. 284; IV, 1908, pp. 416, 424.

BENZION KELLERMANN, *Der ethische Monotheismus d. Propheten*, 1917, pp. 44ff.

KAUFMANN KOHLER, *Grundr. e. syst. Theol. d. Judentums*, 1910, pp. 21; 126f., 161, 170, 175, 177f., 179f., 181f., 183, 185f., 124.

M. LAZARUS, *Die Ethik d. Judentums*, I, 1899, p. 94; II, 1911, pp. xxxif., 70.

H. STEINTHAL, *Über Juden u. Judentum*, 1906, p. 129.

LUDWIG VENETIANER, *Jüdisches im Christentum*, 1913, pp. 40-41.

MAX WIENER, *Die Anschauungen d. Propheten v. d. Sittlichkeit*, 1907, pp. 97, 103, 109.

CHRISTIAN AUTHORS

VIII,   1: In the second place, in this same connection the fact that, in spite of all recognition, however strong, of a radically perverse tendency in human nature and will, *the thought of human freedom and responsibility is never given up.* The very core of Jewish pious consciousness protests against the annulment of freedom. Annulment of freedom would signify annulment, as its corollary, of the law. That is why the fact is so emphasized that God's law stands in opposition to the evil impulse in man. Man has to choose between the two. Josephus expressly calls attention to the way that the Pharisees oppose the thought of freedom to the fatalism of the Essenes.— Wilhelm Bousset, *Die Religion des Judentums*, pp. 465-6.

2: The second distinguishing mark to indicate that man's being is made in the image of God is his freedom of will. God left man after He had created him, to the sway of his own powers of self-determination (Ben-Sira xv. 14). He showed him good and evil (Ben-Sira xvii. 7) and admonished him to beware of all wrong. He also gave him commandments to explain how he should conduct himself towards his fellowmen (Ben-Sira xvii. 14; compare The Fourth Book of Ezra VII. 21, 72).—Ludwig Couard, *Die Religiösen u. sittlichen Anschauungen d. alttest. Apokr. u. Pseudepigr.*, p. 106.

3: Nevertheless, the false converse of the postulate that recompense is certain for virtue, requital for wickedness, is alien to Deuteronomy. It does not assert, as popular opinion did later, that all human sorrow is evidence of grave prior guilt. No less does Jeremiah (xxxi. 29f.) dispute the proverb that is quoted also by Ezekiel (xviii. 2), by the use of which at that time they were wont to sneer at the misunderstood doctrine of requital found in Exodus xx. 5b: "The fathers have eaten sour grapes, and the children's teeth are set on edge." On the contrary, it is taught that everyone must suffer for his own guilt (compare also Deuteronomy xxiv. 16); accordingly, no one is able to remove the moral responsibility that rests heavily on his shoulders, and that precisely is the proof that the requirements of *Yahveh* are conceived as not impossible of human accomplishment.—Emil Kautzsch, *Biblische Theol. d. A. T.*, pp. 245-246.

4: For the present time, however, it is precisely he [Isaiah] who turns with special vigor to, and makes definite moral demands upon, the national and individual will; and he everywhere assumes that man is able to fulfil the conditions which God attaches to the grant of His mercy, that human nature is capable of turning towards God, of putting its trust in Him and of complying with His will, compare i. 16f., 19; vii. 9; viii. 11ff.; x. 20ff.; xxii. 12ff.; xxviii. 16ff.; xxx. 15; xxxi. 6, etc., etc.—Justus Köberle, *Sünde u. Gnade,* pp. 168-169.

5: The basic presupposition of the contrast between the pious and the wicked is the persuasion that it lies within the choice of man to be a pious or a wicked person. In point of fact, this has been at all times the dominant conviction in Judaism which has never been altered essentially, or even so much as materially influenced by the companion conviction of the universality of sin.—Justus Köberle, *l. c.,* p. 345.

6: That, in truth, Judaism refuses to recognize the doctrine of predestination, is correctly stressed by Volz (*l. c.,* p. 117). A religion that calls attention to the freedom of the will with such emphasis as the Jewish religion, could not find any room for a real doctrine of predestination.—Justus Köberle, *ibid.,* p. 662.

7: The individual in ancient Israel was already independent even in regard to his attitude toward moral duty. The doctrine of paralyzing determinism suited the old Israelitish consciousness as little as the doctrine of *nationalism* in moral matters. The older Hebrew literature resounds, indeed, regularly and unmistakably with imperatives and interdictions, therefore with appeals to moral decision.—Eduard König, *Geschichte d. alttest. Religion,* pp. 385-386.

8: But on that account [notwithstanding Hosea v. 7, Isaiah i. 4] there is in human nature, according to them, no compulsion to sin. It would never occur to them to assume, as dogmatics had done for a long time, that at the time of Adam's fall such a change took place in human nature, originally created good, that ever since a propensity to sin adheres to it.   The narrative itself in Genesis iii. does not carry this meaning.—Karl Marti, *Geschichte d. israelitischen Religion*, p. 198.

9: According to Israel's ethical-religious view of life, the dominion of evil over man is not absolutely fixed; on the contrary, it rests with the *free self-decision* of man to say whether he prefers to listen to *Yahveh's* commandment and in obedience to His will cast away the evil and choose the good.   The Israelite has, for that reason, a vivid consciousness of *personal responsibility for his course of action,* and every sinful act reports itself to his consciousness as personal guilt which is threatened with Divine judgment.—Eduard Riehm, *Alttest. Theol.,* p. 178.

10: Finally, any man in whom the freedom of ethical self-determination is paralyzed, so that he is not able to *begin* an *action* himself, that man is not able to achieve a heroic deed, to attain sanctification, —for him the holiness of God will always remain something external and strange—he will never become "God's friend."   Hence, it follows that the true religion, as we find is the case with the Israelitish people, not only does not preclude the development of free human personality, but on the contrary, furthers the expansion of man's self-esteem, self-consciousness, self-confidence, and his desire to achieve great things.—Wladimir Solowjoff, *Judentum u. Christentum*, p. 23.

11: And quite definitely for later Judaism, man's moral independence is a fundamental principle, a basic assumption in support of his zeal for the Law and his hopes of the future.—Emil Schürer, *Geschichte d. jüd. Volkes im Zeitalter Jesu*, II, p. 461.

12: However strongly the *social connection of men* and the duties arising from them are stressed by the prophet, just as strongly does he go on to lay the emphasis upon *the moral responsibility resting upon the individual:* Everyone suffers for *his own guilt* (Ezekiel xviii. 10-20). The ethical error, widely spread nowadays, which declares that *a man's morality is the product also of the social milieu that is shaping him,* that the time and place and the position in life to which a man is born necessarily determine also what his whole character development shall be, is unconditionally rejected by Ezekiel (Ez. xviii. 20). —Franz Walter, *Die Propheten in ihrem soz. Beruf u. d. Wirtschaftsleben ihrer Zeit*, pp. 205-206.

See also:

WILHELM BOUSSET, *Die Religion d. Judentums*, 1906, pp. 465f., 468, 474, 586f.

LUDWIG COUARD, *Die relig. u. sittl. Anschauungen d. alttest. Apok. u. Pseudepigr.*, 1907, pp. 136f.

MAX HALLER, *Religion, Recht u. Sitte*, 1905, p. 109.

——— *Der Ausgang der Prophetie*, 1912, p. 9.

EMIL KAUTZSCH, *Biblische Theol. d. A. T.*, 1911, pp. 201f., 358.

AUGUST KLOSTERMANN, *Gesch. d. Volkes Israel*, 1896, pp. 11f.

JUSTUS KÖBERLE, *Sünde u. Gnade*, 1905, pp. 64, 168f., 345ff., 456, 473, 495f., 514, 552, 570, 652, 662f., 670f.

EDUARD KÖNIG, *Gesch. d. alttest. Religion*, 1912, p. 386.

KARL MARTI, *Gesch. d. alttest. Religion*, 1907, pp. 197f.

EDUARD RIEHM, *Alttest. Theol.*, 1899, pp. 71, 183f., 185, 217f., 278f.

RUDOLF SMEND, *Lehrb. d. aittest. Religionsgesch.*, 1899, p. 310.

BERNHARD STADE, *Gesch. d. Volkes Israel*, 1888, II, pp. 12, 303.

PAUL VOLZ, *Mose*, 1907, pp. 80ff.

FRANZ WALTER, *Die Propheten*, 1900, p. 85.

FERDINAND WEBER, *Jüd. Theol. auf Grund d. Talmud*, 1897, pp. 215ff., 218, 224ff., 231ff., 239f., 311.

[R. TRAVERS HERFORD. *The Pharisees*, 1924, Chap. V, D, pp. 138-146 ('The Torah and the Moral Law).—Tr.]

[For a valuable list of English books on Jewish subjects, see also "Books of Reference" in *The Jewish Year Book*, London, 1928, pp. 273-344.—Tr.]

V

REWARD AND PUNISHMENT

Introduction by Dr. Simon Bernfeld

The ethics of Judaism is built upon its teaching concerning the freedom of the will, which endows man with the moral power to determine what he will do or leave undone, with a capacity to vanquish his sinful impulses, and to sanctify himself in disposition, intent, and open action. But by that, in addition, it also lays upon him a great responsibility. The teaching of Judaism regarding reward and punishment is founded upon this responsibility.

Its conception of the consequences of good and evil developed in Judaism from naïve hope for reward and fear of punishment in the beginning to the very highest ethical consciousness in the end: "The reward of a good deed is a good deed, and the punishment of sin is a sin." The Jewish philosophers of religion all agree (there is only one opinion on the subject) that in the Biblical writings promise of reward and threat of punishment have for their aim the education of the people, according to their powers of apprehension, in the observance of the Divine commandments and the living of an immaculate life (compare also pp. 138-139, VI, 1). Therefore, as a reward for

125

doing what is pleasing in the sight of God, earthly welfare at first is promised, and earthly trials are threatened as punishment for the transgression of the Divine commandments (Leviticus xxvi. 3ff.; Deuteronomy vii. 9f.; xi. 13ff.; xxviii. 1ff.). But even this teaching does not confine reward and punishment merely to the personal destiny of the individual; on the contrary, it declares that the righteousness practiced by the individual and the community carries an entail of happiness and welfare for the community, just as for evil practices the individual and the community are punished. The happiness promised in the Torah and in the prophetic writings is not merely material and personal, but ideal conditions for the community are included: undisturbed peace, public welfare and social harmony, in which all participate and through which alone man's spiritual ascent is made possible.

Jeremiah and Ezekiel, the prophets who lived at the time of the dissolution of the Jewish state, in their religious teaching about good and evil placed in the foreground man's individual responsibility for his actions and accordingly interpreted reward and punishment also in an individual sense. They opposed the distributive view, so widespread among their contemporaries, that found expression in a popular proverb: "The fathers have eaten sour grapes, and the children's teeth are set on edge" (Jeremiah xxxi. 29-30 and Ezekiel xviii. 2). Since their time the doctrine of reward and punishment developed in Judaism branched out in these two directions: the imposition of high moral duties on the community to the fulfillment of which is attached communal happiness, material and spiritual, and the non-fulfillment of which disastrously affects the commonweal. This does not abrogate the responsibility of the individual within his personal sphere; indeed, it is more vigorously emphasized. In that personal sphere what a man is morally is made to be dependent upon himself, and he himself has to bear the consequences also of his own deeds.

With the rise of the conception that reward and punishment could be individual as well as communal, however, the problem raised by the suffering of the righteous and the happiness of the wicked obtruded itself. That problem forms the main theme of the didactic poem Job; with it the prophet Jeremiah also struggles (xii. 1), and *Koheleth* voices it in the words, "There is a righteous man that perisheth in his righteousness, and there is a wicked man that prolongeth his life in his evil-doing" (Ecclesiastes vii. 15). This state of affairs, so often encountered in life, was to find explanation in eschatology, with its doctrine of a just settlement awaiting both a pious or a sinful life in this world, in an *eternal* life *in a future world*. The beginnings of eschatology meet us in the later writings of the Bible (Daniel xii. 2-3). Its development took place in apocryphal literature and in the Talmud. "Not in this life is the pious deed rewarded" (*Kiddushin* 39 a). "The pious deed that a human being performs in this life receives him and precedes him in the future world, and the sin that a human being commits in this life holds him fast and precedes him on the Day of Judgment" (*Sotah*

3 b). Reward and punishment in the next life, according to most apothegms in the Talmud and the unanimous interpretation of Jewish religious philosophy, are of a purely spiritual nature. To be sure, in isolated Talmudical utterances and in some popular ethical writings the notion of reward and punishment in the next world is more akin to the popularly naïve interpretation.

Nevertheless, independently of the notion of reward and punishment there developed in the Talmud and in Jewish religious philosophy in agreement with it, as well as in most popular ethical writings, the doctrine that the good must be done without hope of reward and the evil must be avoided on other grounds than fear of punishment. The reward of the good lies in the good itself, and the punishment of evil in the evil itself. Evil pollutes the soul that God gave to man pure.

BIBLE

I,   1: I the LORD thy God am a jealous God, visiting the iniquity of the fathers upon the children unto the third and fourth generation of them that hate Me; and showing mercy unto the thousandth generation of them that love Me and keep My commandments.—Exodus xx. 5-6; Deuteronomy v. 9-10.

2: The LORD, the LORD, God, merciful and gracious, long-suffering, and abundant in goodness and truth; keeping mercy unto the thousandth generation, forgiving iniquity and transgression and sin;

and that will by no means clear the guilty; visiting the iniquity of the fathers upon the children, and upon the children's children, unto the third and unto the fourth generation.—Exodus xxxiv. 6-7.

3: If ye walk in My statutes, and keep My commandments, and do them; then I will give your rains in their season, and the land shall yield her produce, and the trees of the field shall yield their fruit. And your threshing shall reach unto the vintage, and the vintage shall reach unto the sowing time; and ye shall eat your bread until ye have enough, and dwell in your land safely. And I will give peace in the land, and ye shall lie down, and none shall make you afraid; and I will cause evil beasts to cease out of the land, neither shall the sword go through your land. And ye shall chase your enemies, and they shall fall before you by the sword. And five of you shall chase a hundred, and a hundred of you shall chase ten thousand; and your enemies shall fall before you by the sword. And I will have respect unto you, and make you fruitful, and multiply you; and will establish My covenant with you. . . . But if ye will not hearken unto Me, and will not do all these commandments; and if ye shall reject My statutes, and if your soul abhor Mine ordinances, so that ye will not do all My commandments, but break My covenant; I also will do this unto you: I will appoint terror over you, even consumption and fever, that shall make the eyes to fail, and the soul to languish.—Leviticus xxvi. 3-9, 14-16.

4: Know therefore that the LORD thy God, He is God; the faithful God, who keepeth covenant and mercy with them that love Him and keep His commandments to a thousand generations.—Deuteronomy vii. 9.

5: And it shall come to pass, because ye hearken to these ordinances, and keep, and do them, that the LORD thy God shall keep with thee the covenant and the mercy which He swore unto thy fathers.— Deuteronomy vii. 12.

6: And it shall come to pass, if ye shall hearken diligently unto My commandments which I command you this day, to love the LORD your God, and to serve Him with all your heart and with all your soul, that I will give the rain of your land in its season, the former rain and the latter rain, that thou mayest gather in thy corn, and thy wine, and thine oil. And I will give grass in thy fields for thy cattle, and thou shalt eat and be satisfied. Take heed to yourselves, lest your heart be deceived, and ye turn aside, and serve other gods, and worship them; and the anger of the LORD be kindled against you, and He shut up the heaven, so that there shall be no rain, and the ground shall not yield her fruit; and ye perish quickly from off the good land which the LORD giveth you. —Deuteronomy xi. 13-17.

7: Behold, I set before you this day a blessing and a curse: the blessing, if ye shall hearken unto the commandments of the LORD your God, which I command you this day; and the curse, if ye shall not hearken unto the commandments of the LORD your God, but turn aside out of the way which I command you this day, to go after other gods, which ye have not known.—Deuteronomy xi. 26-28.

8: Say ye of the righteous, that it shall be well with him; for they shall eat the fruit of their doings. Woe unto the wicked! it shall be ill with him; for the work of his hands shall be done to him.—Isaiah iii. 10-11.

9: For, behold, the LORD cometh forth out of His place to visit upon the inhabitants of the earth their iniquity; the earth also shall disclose her blood, and shall no more cover her slain.—Isaiah xxvi. 21.

10: In those days they shall say no more: 'The fathers have eaten sour grapes, and the children's teeth are set on edge.' But every one shall die for his own iniquity; every man that eateth the sour grapes, his teeth shall be set on edge.—Jeremiah xxxi. 29-30.

11: And the word of the LORD came unto me, saying: 'What mean ye, that ye use this proverb in the land of Israel, saying: The fathers have eaten sour grapes, and the children's teeth are set on edge? As I live, saith the Lord GOD, ye shall not have occasion any more to use this proverb in Israel. Behold, all souls are Mine; as the soul of the father, so also the soul of the son is Mine; the soul that sinneth, it shall die.

But if a man be just, and do that which is lawful and right, and hath not eaten upon the mountains, neither hath lifted up his eyes to the idols of the house of Israel, neither hath defiled his neighbour's wife, neither hath come near to a woman in her impurity; and hath not wronged any, but hath restored his pledge for a debt, hath taken nought by robbery, hath given his bread to the hungry, and hath covered the naked with a garment; he that hath not given forth upon interest, neither hath taken any increase, that hath withdrawn his hand from iniquity, hath executed true justice between man and man, hath walked in My statutes, and hath kept Mine ordinances to deal truly; he is just, he shall surely live, saith the Lord GOD.

If he beget a son that is a robber, a shedder of blood, and that doeth to a brother any of these things, whereas he himself had not done any of these things, for he hath even eaten upon the mountains, and defiled his neighbour's wife, hath wronged the poor and needy, hath taken by robbery, hath not restored the pledge, and hath lifted up his eyes to the idols, hath committed abomination, hath given forth upon interest, and hath taken increase; shall he then live? he shall not live—he hath done all these abominations; he shall surely be put to death, his blood shall be upon him.

Now, lo, if he beget a son, that seeth all his father's sins, which he hath done, and considereth, and doeth not such like, that hath not eaten upon the mountains, neither hath lifted up his eyes to the idols of the house of Israel, hath not defiled his neighbour's wife, neither hath wronged any, hath not taken aught to pledge, neither hath taken by robbery, but hath given his bread to the hungry, and hath covered the naked with a garment, that hath withdrawn his hand from the poor, that hath not received interest nor increase, hath executed Mine ordinances, hath walked in My statutes; he shall not die for the iniquity of his father, he shall surely live. As for his father, because he cruelly oppressed, committed robbery on his

brother, and did that which is not good among his
people, behold, he dieth for his iniquity. Yet say ye:
Why doth not the son bear the iniquity of the father
with him?   When the son hath done that which is
lawful and right, and hath kept all My statutes, and
hath done them, he shall surely live. The soul that
sinneth, it shall die; the son shall not bear the iniquity
of the father with him, neither shall the father bear
the iniquity of the son with him; the righteousness
of the righteous shall be upon him, and the wickedness of the wicked shall be upon him.

But if the wicked turn from all his sins that he
hath committed, and keep all My statutes, and do that
which is lawful and right, he shall surely live, he shall
not die.   None of his transgressions that he hath committed shall be remembered against him; for his
righteousness that he hath done he shall live. Have I
any pleasure at all that the wicked should die? saith
the Lord GOD; and not rather that he should return
from his ways, and live?

But when the righteous turneth away from his
righteousness, and committeth iniquity, and doeth according to all the abominations that the wicked man
doeth, shall he live?   None of his righteous deeds that
he hath done shall be remembered; for his trespass
that he trespassed, and for his sin that he hath sinned,
for them shall he die. Yet ye say: The way of the
Lord is not equal. Hear now, O house of Israel: Is
it My way that is not equal? is it not your ways that
are unequal?   When the righteous man turneth away
from his righteousness, and committeth iniquity, he
shall die therefor; for his iniquity that he hath done

shall he die.   Again, when the wicked man turneth away from his wickedness that he hath committed, and doeth that which is lawful and right, he shall save his soul alive.   Because he considereth, and turneth away from all his transgressions that he hath committed, he shall surely live, he shall not die.   Yet saith the house of Israel: The way of the Lord is not equal.   O house of Israel, is it My ways that are not equal? is it not your ways that are unequal?   Therefore I will judge you, O house of Israel, every one according to his ways, saith the Lord GOD.   Return ye, and turn yourselves from all your transgressions; so shall they not be a stumblingblock of iniquity unto you.   Cast away from you all your transgressions, wherein ye have transgressed; and make you a new heart and a new spirit; for why will ye die, O house of Israel?   For I have no pleasure in the death of him that dieth, saith the Lord GOD; wherefore turn yourselves and live.—Ezekiel xviii. 1-32.

12: The LORD preserveth the faithful, and plentifully repayeth him that acteth haughtily.—Psalms xxxi. 24.

13: Also unto Thee, O Lord, belongeth mercy; for Thou renderest to every man according to his work.—Psalms lxii. 13.

14: The LORD preserveth all them that love Him; but all the wicked will He destroy.—Psalms cxlv. 20.

15: His own iniquities shall ensnare the wicked, and he shall be holden with the cords of his sin.—Proverbs v. 22.

16: The way of the LORD is a stronghold to

the upright, but ruin to the workers of iniquity.—
Proverbs x. 29.

17: Behold, the righteous shall be requited in the
earth; how much more the wicked and the sinner!—
Proverbs xi. 31.

18: Evil pursueth sinners; but to the righteous
good shall be repaid.—Proverbs xiii. 21.

19: A just balance and scales are the LORD'S;
all the weights of the bag are his [1] [man's] work.—
Proverbs xvi. 11.

20: The violence of the wicked shall drag them
away; because they refuse to do justly.—Proverbs
xxi. 7.

21: He that soweth iniquity shall reap vanity.—
Proverbs xxii. 8.

22: The end of the matter, all having been
heard: fear God, and keep His commandments; for
this is the whole man. For God shall bring every
work into the judgment concerning every hidden
thing, whether it be good or whether it be evil.—
Ecclesiastes xii. 13-14.

PALESTINIAN APOCRYPHA

II a,   1: Know, therefore, my children that two
spirits wait upon man—the spirit of truth and the
spirit of deceit. And in the midst is the spirit of
understanding of the mind, to which it belongeth to
turn whithersoever it will.

And the works of truth and the works of deceit
are written upon the hearts of men, and each one of
them the Lord knoweth.

[1] The English version follows a different interpretation.—Tr.

And there is no time at which the works of men can be hid; for on the heart itself have they been written down before the Lord. And the spirit of truth testifieth all things, and accuseth all; and the sinner is burnt up by his own heart, and can not raise his face to the judge.—*The Testaments of the Twelve Patriarchs,* IV. 20 (Charles, in Charles, *l. c.,* II).

2: Recompense shall follow, and the reward be made manifest; deeds of righteousness shall awake, and deeds of iniquity shall not sleep.—*The Fourth Book of Ezra,* VII. 35 (Box, in Charles, *l. c.,* II).

3: So shall none then pray for another on that Day, neither shall one lay a burden on another; for then every one shall bear his own unrighteousness or righteousness [all alone].—*Ibid.,* VII. 105 (Box, *ibid.*).

JEWISH-HELLENISTIC LITERATURE

III,   1: For wisdom itself is the reward of wisdom; and justice, and each of the other virtues, is its own reward.—Philo, *On Special Laws,* II; *On the Honor Due to Parents* (C.-W. 259).

2: However, the reward of such as live exactly according to the laws, is not silver or gold; it is not a garland of olive-branches or of smallage, nor any such public sign of commendation; but every good man is content with the witness that his own conscience bears him.—Josephus, *Against Apion* (*The Works of Josephus,* tr. by W. Whiston; from the last London ed., Philadelphia, 1856), II, 31. (Revised by Tr.)

Talmudical Literature

V,   1: Antigonos of Socho . . . used to say, Be not like servants who minister to their master upon the condition of receiving a reward; but be like servants who minister to their master without the condition of receiving a reward; and let the fear of Heaven be upon you.—*Ethics of the Fathers*, I, 3 (Singer's *Prayerbook*, p. 271).

2: Do the things for the sake of the Creator and occupy yourself with them for their own sake, do not make a crown of them in order to boast with it, nor likewise a spade in order to dig with it.—*Nedarim* 62 a.

3: The recompense of a good deed is a good deed, and the reward of a sin is a sin.—*Ethics of the Fathers*, IV, 2 (see above, p. 73, V. 3).

4: The pious deed that a human being performs in this life, receives him and precedes him in the future world, and the sin that a human being commits in this life, holds him fast and precedes him on the Day of Judgment.—*Sotah* 3 b.

5: Moses taught (Exodus xx. 5; xxxiv. 7; Deuteronomy v. 9): "Visiting the iniquity of the fathers upon the children and upon the children's children." Ezekiel annulled it by teaching (xviii. 4): "The soul that sinneth, *it* shall die."—*Makkot* 24 a.

6: The holy One, blessed be He, punishes man only when his measure is full [does not punish man until his cup of offense is full to the brim].—*Sotah* 9 a.

7: The human being is judged only by the actions he has already performed.—*Rosh ha-Shanah* 16 b; *Bereshit Rabbah* c. 53.

8: A good intention is reckoned by God as a deed, an evil intention is not reckoned by God as a deed.—*Tosefta Peah*, c. 1.

9: If a man contemplated fulfilling a commandment, and was compelled to desist from it, the verse ascribes it to him as though he had done it.—*Berachot* 6 a (Cohen *l. c.,* p. 28). (Revised by Tr.)

10: The measure with which one measures will be measured out to him—i. e. as man deals, he will be dealt with.—*Sanhedrin* 100 a [Rodkinson, *B. T.,* vol. viii (16), p. 318], and *Mishnah Sotah,* I, 7.

11: "Happy is the man that feareth the Lord, that delighteth greatly in His commandments" (Psalms cxii. 1). In His commandments, not in any recompense for their observance.—*Abodah Zarah* 19 a.

MIDDLE AGES

VI,   1: How are we to understand what is said everywhere in the Torah: If you obey you will fare thus, and if you do not obey, you will fare thus, and all the earthly promises as satiation and hunger, war and peace, etc.? All those pronouncements have come true and will come to pass endlessly. If we act in accordance with all the commandments of the Torah, those temporal goods will all be granted us; and if we transgress them, the evils mentioned will befall us. And notwithstanding that this is so, those goods are none of them the real recompense for the keeping of the commandments, nor those evils the real punishment for the transgression of the commandments. Rather, is this matter to be understood thus: God has revealed unto us His Torah, which is a tree of life, and he who executes everything that is written in the Torah and apprehends it (the Torah) rightly, attains therewith eternal life, i. e. does so according to the measure of his deeds and of his knowledge. Besides we are promised that if we execute God's commandments in joy and to gratify our soul's desire and are always absorbed in their wisdom, as recompense God will ward off from us everything that would prevent our continued observance of the Torah, such as illness, the calamity of war, famine, and the like, and He will also grant us temporal happiness that will aid in furthering the observance and the knowledge of the Torah, such as contentment, peace, enough possessions, and the like, so that we would not need to struggle every day for the bare necessaries of life, but could at full leisure and exempt from care be occupied with the study of God's Torah, in order thus to become participants of eternal life.—Maimonides, *Mishneh Torah Hilchot Teshubah* (Return to God), IX, 1.

2: A man must not say: I desire to keep the commandments of our Torah and be intently occupied with its wisdom so that I may obtain all the blessings that it promises or so that I may procure eternal life. Nor should he say: I wish to keep clear of sins in order to escape the disaster that is threatened in the Torah in punishment, or so that I shall not incur the loss of eternal life. One must not serve God in this manner, for he who serves God thus, does it only *out of fear* of God. That is not the way the prophets served God, nor it is the way approved of wisdom. He who serves God out of love for Him, occupies himself with the Torah and the commandments and walks in the way of wisdom, not for the sake of worldly advantage, nor from fear of misery, nor because he desires to obtain happiness, but he serves the truth because it is the truth. . . . That is what our father Abraham did, whom God declared to be His friend because he served Him from pure love. That is what God commanded us through Moses, "And thou shalt love the Eternal, thy God . . ." And if man loves God with true love, he will, out of love to Him, soon be doing everything that is commanded of him. What is the true love of God? It is a love of God that is great and strong, so very much so that the soul is tied fast to and constantly wrapt in it, as if it were love-sick. . . . Indeed, still more, the love of God takes up its abode in the heart of those that love Him, and are wrapt in that love, as it is commanded of us, ". . . with all thy heart and with all thy soul." Our old sages have said: If any one should perchance say: I am going to study the Torah so that I become rich, or in order that I be called 'Rabbi,' or in order that I obtain recompense in the future life,— then the word is pointed out to him, "That thou shouldest love the Eternal." And that means: Everything that you do, you shall do out of love only.— Maimonides, *l. c.*, X, 1-4.

3: The perfect man is forbidden to say: If I perform these good deeds and refrain from evil deeds, what is then the recompense that I am to receive therefor? . . . Our sages likewise have already issued a warning against the view that anything external whatever is the final aim and end of the service of God and of the keeping of the commandments.   As Antigonos of Socho says. . . . And that is what they call a servant of God out of love. . . . It is clear that this is the intent of the Torah and the true intent of our sages. . . . Such a degree of disinterestedness was attained by Abraham who served God out of love, and it is towards this goal that all human beings must strive.   Now, since the sages knew that this was difficult in practice and not every man could attain it, . . . for that reason they made concessions to men taken as they run, but exhorted them nevertheless and sought to strengthen their disposition and heart to the point where they might reach the truth. —Maimonides, *Commentary to the Mishnah*, Introduction to *Sanhedrin* I.

MODERN JEWISH LITERATURE

VII,   1: The Bible speaks often and impressively of the punishment of sin, as well as of the reward of piety, of *tangible, earthly* reward.   That teaching had its uses and a place of importance in the history of the education of the people of Israel, as he who knows the history of man will understand without being told.   The goal and the result of this course of development in Judaism is, however, a definite conclusion that purity, freedom, and disinterestedness are unconditional requirements of the good deed, and that its reward is found in the constant need of its repetition.   How this thought had become the possession of the community, the entire religious literature of the middle ages gives proof, declaring unanimously that only that deed may be reckoned a good deed that is willed and done for its own sake.—Leo Baeck, *Das Wesen des Judentums* (2d. ed.), pp. 192-193.

2: The conception of "joy in the pious action" precludes its being performed for the sake of reward, be it for reward in this world or the next.—M. Güdemann, *Das Judentum i. s. Grundzügen,* p. 86.

3: In Judaism divine grace is not offered as a bait to make men believe, but as an incentive to moral improvement. The God of holiness, who inflicts wounds upon the guilty soul by bitter remorse, offers also healing through His compassion.—Kaufmann Kohler, *Jewish Theology,* p. 117.

4: Only superior minds could ascend to that higher ethical conception where compensation is no longer expected, but man seeks the good and happiness of others and finds therein his highest satisfaction. As Ben Azzai expresses it, "The reward of virtue is virtue, and the punishment of sin is sin" (Aboth IV, 2). At this point justice merges into divine holiness. —Kaufmann Kohler, *l. c.,* 124.

5: The evil strokes of destiny come upon the righteous, not because he deserves them, but because his divine Friend is raising him to still higher tests of virtue. This standpoint, never reached even by the pious sufferer Job, is attained by Rabbinic Judaism when it calls the visitations of the righteous "trials of the divine love" (*Ber.* 5 a, after Deut. viii. 5; Prov. iii. 12). Thus evil, both physical and spiritual, receives its true valuation in the divine economy. Evil exists only to be overcome by the good.   In His *paternal goodness* God uses it to educate His children for a place in His kingdom.—Kaufmann Kohler, *ibid.*, pp. 177-178.

6: When the Rabbis speak of paradise and hell, describing vividly the delights of the one and the torments of the other, these are to them only metaphors of the agony of sin and the happiness of virtue. True piety serves God neither from fear of punishment nor as servants obey a master from desire for reward, but from pure love of God and truth.—Kaufmann Kohler, *Theol. d. Judentum*, p. 231 (citation from the *Mishneh Torah* by Maimonides) (Kohler, *Jewish Theology*, p. 308).   (Revised by Tr.)

7: But side by side with references to reward and punishment in Rabbinical literature stand numerous sayings which repudiate alike the idea that reward is the reason for obedience of the law or that it is the proper motive of its fulfillment, and these sayings were well-known and universally endorsed. The oldest representative of the specifically Rabbinical mode of thought, if not its originator, was Antigonos of Socho, the immediate successor to Simon the Just, and he was the author of the sentence: "Be not like unto servants who serve their master with a view to recompense, but be like unto servants who serve their master without the expectation of reward, and let the fear of Heaven be upon you" (Aboth 1:3).—M. Lazarus, *Die Ethik des Judentums*, I, p. 133 (Szold, *l. c.*, I, pp. 174-175).   (Revised by Tr.)

See also:

HERMANN COHEN, *Religion u. Sittlichkeit*, 1907, pp. 145f.
FELIX PERLES, *Boussets "Religion d. Judentums,"* 1903, pp. 125f.
MAX WIENER, *Die Religion d. Propheten*, 1912, pp. 39f.

CHRISTIAN AUTHORS

VIII.   1: An important point of view against which the book of Job is one long contention is the conception of ethics as a sort of commercial transaction between God and man. "Can a man be profitable unto God, as he that is wise may be profitable unto himself?" says Eliphaz (Job xxii. 2). In other words, it is impossible to acquire any merit in relation to God, upon which one can afterward presume.— Hugo Dingler, *Die Kultur der Juden*, p. 103.

2: Another equally plain thesis of the Old Testament, recurring therein with innumerable modifications, treats of Divine *requital* with relation to good and evil; that is the great thought that is contained also in the ten commandments, "Who visits iniquity, but shows mercy unto those that love Him and keep His commandments." This belief may have been externalized often enough in ancient Israel, and requital may have been too much looked for in the outward destinies of men; yet the belief remains one of the most important principles of all moral religion, indeed of every higher view of life, that the natural and the moral world-order are not mutually exclusive ultimately, however often they may seem to be at odds with each other. Instead, the course of the world in its final aim serves the good and not the evil, and is conducive to building up and not to destroying, and there in the end is a requital.—Hermann Gunkel, *Was bleibt v. A. T.?* pp. 19-20.

3: It would be no slight error, of course, were one to assume that the idea of requital originated with these prophets (Jeremiah and Ezekiel) and accordingly that Ezekiel was the creator of "individualism." Rather have they only formulated these ideas. For as in every highly cultivated people, so in ancient Israel, religion and morality had for a long time past formed an alliance.—Hermann Gunkel, *l. c.*, pp. 81-82.

4: Ezekiel desires at any cost to establish three lines of thought on a sure footing: (a) Every sinner is punished visibly by means of external penalty, and every righteous person so rewarded.   (b) No other individual is ever punished for the sin or rewarded for the righteousness of another.   (c) At all times, only the ethical-religious complexion of the last decisive moment counts in the appraisal of the ensuing deed. Ezekiel's theory marks a culmination, and at the same time a turning-point, in the history of thought in regard to requital.   Only by him is the dogma of requital expressed so clearly, without any limitation, made so strictly individual in application, and related so wholly to this world.   In considering it, one must take into account, above all, the fact that it constitutes the bluntest application of a *lofty moral conviction.*   This theory of requital is indeed nothing else than the application to individuals of the belief, held by the prophets, in a moral order in the universe.

Ezekiel is by no means to be credited with implanting this belief once for all in Judaism. . . . Nowhere, however, is the postulate of this account of righteousness adhered to with such energy as in Judaism. In the face of all seemingly contradictory experiences, Ezekiel's theory succeeds absolutely in holding its own.—Justus Köberle, *Sünde und Gnade,* pp. 218-219.

5: It became the general custom always to regard the relationship between one's behavior and one's lot only *from this ethical viewpoint* of just Divine requital. The basic conception on which the whole view of life rested thus was ethical. Thereby it acquired an otherwise missing stability and definiteness, in which respects Judaism soared high above the moral indifference and the life at random which prevailed in most nations possessing a similar outward civilization. In the same way, moreover, this moral principle was a safeguard against the stark resignation and the impotent pessimism, into which the confidence in a moral world-order watched over by the gods finally sunk among other peoples of high standing.—Justus Köberle, *l. c.,* p. 278.

6: On the other hand, it deserves to be stressed that the thought of a reward other than the fulfillment of the Divine will is absolutely unknown to the prophets. The right motive for action is never the thought of external reward but an inner impulsion. The impetus does not emanate from the outer world but, in the last analysis, from God.—Karl Marti, *Religion d. A. T.,* p. 54.

7: Hand in hand with the ever progressive in-

tensification of religion [with making religion ever
more and more inward] the individual comes to cease
to feel that his relation of *Yahveh* is mediated through
membership in his people, that religion now is not
so much a matter between "Yahveh and the people"
as between "*Yahveh* and the soul."   And all that
previously applied to his people is now simply trans-
ferred and made to apply to the relation between
Yahveh and the individual Jew.   They shall say no
more, "Our fathers have eaten sour grapes, from that
were our teeth set on edge" (Jeremiah xxxi. 29); nor
will *Yahveh* any more "visit the iniquity of the
fathers upon the children."   Rather, everyone will
bear his own guilt, that is, he will receive in this life
the reward of his own deeds.—Joh. Meinhold,
Geschichte d. jüd. Volkes, p. 24.

8: That the pre-exilic prophets do not exclude
its application to individuals from their thought of
requital, but wittingly admit it, is proved by their
repeated entreaties to return to *Yahveh* which are
addressed to the people for *individual acceptance;*
each of them shall return from his evil way, and
amend his ways and doings (Jer. xviii. 11), every
individual shall take away the foreskin of his heart
(iv. 4).   The prophets, it is true, wish that all of
them may return to *Yahveh*, yet they regard the decision as the *personal* affair of every individual and
promise redemption to the *returning* fragment.—
Friedrich Nötscher, *Die Gerechtigkeit Gottes b. d.
vorexilischen Propheten*, p. 69.

9: This postulate [of just Divine requital] finds
support (a) in the confident expectation that the

dream of a "State of God" and of a "People of God" will some day be perfectly and completely realized; (b) in the consciousness that in the privilege of communion with his God the pious man possesses an inner happiness of life that far surpasses all mundane prosperity and abundantly compensates for every outward misfortune; (c) in the presentiment that this communion with God is an eternal good, outlasting death. —Ed. Riehm, *Alttest. Theol.*, p. 359.

See also:

W. COSZMANN, *Die Entwicklung d. Gerichtsgedankens b. d. alttestamentlichen Propheten*, 1915, pp. 95ff., 155f., 199.

BERNHARD DUHM, *Die Theol. d. Propheten*, 1875, p. 184.

HEINRICH EWALD, *Gesch. d. Volkes Israel*, 1864, IV, pp. 357f.

HERMANN GUNKEL, *Was bleibt v. Alten Testament?* 1916, pp. 19f.

———— *Die Propheten*, 1917, pp. 81, 90.

JULIUS HAPPEL, *Weltgericht, Weltbegnadigung u. Neuordnung d. Welt nach dem 1. Buch Moses* (an essay in *Die Zeitschrift für Missionskunde und Religionswissenschaft*, 25. Jahrg., Heft 11).

PAUL KLEINERT, *Die Propheten Israels in sozialer Beziehung*, 1905, pp. 51f.

JUSTUS KÖBERLE, *Sünde u. Gnade*, 1905, pp. 54, 141f., 187, 218ff., 277f., 383, 625f.

EDUARD KÖNIG, *Geschichte der alttestamentlichen Religion*, 1912, p. 387.

HANS MEINHOLD, *Geschichte d. jüd. Volkes*, 1916, p. 23.

FRIEDRICH NÖTSCHER, *Die Gerechtigkeit Gottes b. d. vorexilischen Propheten*, 1915, pp. 50, 54ff., 60f., 64, 66f., 74f., 86f.

ERNEST RENAN, *Histoire du peuple d'Israel*, 1891, III, p. 78.

EDUARD RIEHM, *Alttestamentliche Theologie*, 1889, pp. 359f.

ERNST SELLIN, *Die alttestamentliche Religion*, 1908, pp. 55, 57f.

RUDOLF SMEND, *Lehrbuch d. alttestamentlichen Religionsge-schichte*, 1899, p. 432.

BERNHARD STADE, *Geschichte d. Volkes Israel*, II, 1888, pp. 303, 516ff.

[R. TRAVERS HERFORD, *The Pharisees*, 1924, Chap. V, B, pp. 123-135 (Merit and Reward).—Tr.]

VI

EQUALITY OF ALL HUMAN BEINGS

Introduction by Dr. Samson Hochfeld

The ethics of Judaism is dominated by the principle of universalism, that is, it knows no difference in its requirements and regulations between Jew and non-Jew. What it commands applies universally. Any separation of men according to descent and belief into classes or nationalities or races or religions is meaningless for it. It would be not only to defame, but completely to misconstrue Jewish ethics, were one to assume that it attributes a greater binding force to the commandments of righteousness, truth, and love, where some question among Jews themselves is at issue than where the claims of those of other faiths have to be taken into consideration.

Just as in this case of moral obligation, Judaism likewise makes no distinction of any kind whatever between man and man in respect to his eligibility for morality. The human being as such is both the object and the subject of morality. All children of this world are at the same time children of God, qualified and able to realize the good and to extend its dominion in the world more and more. The moral inclination is innate in every man, and it is incumbent

150

on him to develop it to ever greater power in the
struggle with his proclivities and appetites.

The Messianic teaching of Judaism grew to be
the grand expression of this view concerning the
moral vocation of all human beings, that outlook on
the future which, upon its highest summit, contem-
plates a kingdom of God upon earth, a moralization
of all peoples and nations as the ultimate goal aimed
at in the development of humanity.

The idea of the election of Israel which, at first
glance, seems to contradict the teaching that all human
beings are on an equal footing in respect of morality,
upon closer inspection will be seen rather to be conso-
nant with it. The deepest meaning of God's bestowal
of grace upon Israel is a mission to influence the rest
of mankind by leading the way in morals: it must
not keep its ethical gifts to itself, but is to communi-
cate them to all peoples so that they too may ascend
to ever higher levels of humanization.

Judaism is so far from making moral worth dependent upon the practice of its ceremonial precepts
that it promises to the pious, that is, to the morally
good, regardless of race or religion, a share in the
everlasting bliss. For this reason it has eschewed
missionary propaganda on a large scale, although it
does not refuse admission to the convert who comes
of his own free will and from disinterested motives.
The absence of all missionary activity in the Judaism
of the last two thousand years does not signify a want
of confidence in the power of its own faith to win
recruits, but is in keeping with its conviction that the

fulfillment of ethical requirements is possible of achievement also outside of its own circle.

BIBLE

I,   1 : And it shall come to pass in the end of days, that the mountain of the LORD'S house shall be established as the top of the mountains, and shall be exalted above the hills; and all nations shall flow unto it.   And many peoples shall go and say: 'Come ye, and let us go up to the mountain of the LORD, to the house of the God of Jacob; and He will teach us of His ways, and we will walk in His paths.'   For out of Zion shall go forth the law, and the word of the LORD from Jerusalem.—Isaiah ii. 2-3, and Micah iv. 1-2.

2 : Neither let the alien, that hath joined himself to the LORD, speak, saying: 'The LORD will surely separate me from His people.' . . . —Isaiah lvi. 3.

3 : Also the aliens, that join themselves to the LORD, to minister unto Him, and to love the name of the LORD, to be His servants, every one that keepeth the sabbath from profaning it, and holdeth fast by My covenant: even them will I bring to My holy mountain, and make them joyful in My house of prayer; their burnt-offerings and their sacrifices shall be acceptable upon Mine altar; for My house shall be called a house of prayer for all peoples.—Isaiah lvi. 6-7.

4 : And they [the heathen nations] shall bring all your brethren out of all the nations for an offering unto the LORD, upon horses, and in chariots, and in

litters, and upon mules, and upon swift beasts, to My holy mountain Jerusalem, saith the LORD, as the children of Israel bring their offering in a clean vessel into the house of the LORD. And of them also will I take for the priests and for the Levites, saith the LORD.—Isaiah lxvi. 20-21.

5: At that time they shall call Jerusalem the throne of the LORD; and all the nations shall be gathered unto it, to the name of the LORD, to Jerusalem; neither shall they walk any more after the stubbornness of their evil hearts.—Jeremiah iii. 17.

6: For then will I turn to the peoples a pure language, that they may all call upon the name of the LORD, to serve Him with one consent.—Zephaniah iii. 9.

PALESTINIAN APOCRYPHA

IIa, 1: Which race is honorable? The race of man. Which race is honorable? They that fear the LORD. Which race is dishonorable? The race of man. Which race is dishonorable? They that transgress the commandments.—Ben-Sira x. 19.

JEWISH-HELLENISTIC LITERATURE

III, 1: And then indeed He will raise up His kingdom for all ages over [all] men. He who once gave a holy law to godly men, to all of whom He promised to open out the earth and the world, and the portals of the blessed, and all joys, and everlasting sense and eternal gladness. And from every land they shall bring frankincense and gifts to the house of the great

God; and there shall be no other house for men even in future generations to know but only that which He has given to faithful men to honor.   For mortals call that alone the house of the great God.—*The Sibylline Books*, Book III, 767-776 (Lanchester, in Charles, *l. c.*, II).

2: God welcomes virtue, even if it sprouts from the lowly born.—Philo: *On Rewards and Punishments, On Curses* (M. II, 433; C.-W. 152).

3: [If, then, any one proves himself a man of such a character—namely, of virtue, goodness, wisdom—in the city he will appear superior to the whole city;] and if a nation do so it will be the lord of all the other nations, as the head holds the place of preëminence among the members of the body, not more for the fame to be had thereby than for advancing the interests of those that see.   (For continual observation of good models usually stamps impressions closely resembling them on all souls which are not utterly obdurate and intractable.)—Philo, *On Rewards and Punishments* (M. II, 426; C.-W. 114; Yonge, *l. c.*)   (Revised by Tr.)

4: This is the mind in which the prophet says that God walks as in his palace; for the mind of the wise man is in truth the palace and the house of God. And he who is the God of all things is peculiarly the God of this mind; and again this mind is by a peculiar form called his people, not the people of any particular rulers but of the one only and true ruler, the Holy One of holies.—Philo, *On Rewards and Punishments* (M. II, 428; C.-W. 123; Yonge, *ibid.*)

5: Every man's intellect is connected with the

Divine reason, being an impression of, or a fragment, or a ray of that blessed nature.—Philo, *On the Creation of the World* (M. I, 25; C.-W. 146; Yonge, *ibid.*) (Revised by Tr.)

6: We must not, therefore, give in to those persons who seek to creep stealthily into the possession of a property belonging to others, namely, nobility of birth, as though it were of right their own, and who, with the exception of those whom I have mentioned, might justly be looked upon as enemies, not only of the race of the Jews but of all the human race in every quarter: of the one because they give a truce to those of the same nation, allowing them to despise sound and stable virtue, through trusting implicitly in the virtue of their ancestors; and of the others because, even if they could attain to the highest and most absolute perfection of all excellence, they would still derive no advantage themselves, because of their not having irreproachable fathers and grandfathers, than which I do not know that there can be a more mischievous doctrine.—Philo, *On Virtues, On Nobility* (M. II, 444; C.-W. 226; Yonge, *ibid.*)

TALMUDICAL LITERATURE

V, 1: Despise not any man.—*Ethics of the Fathers*, IV. 3 (Singer's *Prayerbook*, p. 283).

2: "*One* law shall be to him that is home-born, and unto the stranger" (Exodus xii. 49). In respect of all commandments of the Torah, Scripture places the stranger on a footing of equality with the home-born.—*Mechilta, ad loc.*

3: The righteous of all nations will have a share in the world of eternal bliss.—*Tosefta Sanhedrin* 13, 2.

4: Rabbi Meir taught: Whence do we conclude that even a heathen who is occupied with the Torah is to be deemed equal to the high-priest? It is said, "Ye shall therefore keep My statutes, and Mine ordinances, which if a man do, he shall live by them" (Leviticus xviii. 5). It is not said there, priests, Levites, or Israelites, but a *man*. Thence you may learn that even a heathen who occupies himself with the Torah is equal to the high-priest.—*Abodah Zarah* 3a.

5: [The heathen Antoninus] once asked [Rabbi Yehudah, the patriarch], "Will I have a share in the world to come?" To which the latter answered "Yes."—"But is it not written, 'And there shall not be any remaining of the house of Esau' (Obadiah 18)?"—"Only if he commits Esau's acts [of violence]."—*Abodah Zarah* 10b.

6: He who teaches wisdom, even if he is of the nations of the world, is calle da sage.—*Pesikta Chadata* to *Purim* (*Bet ha-Midrash*, ed. Jellinek, VI, p. 57).

7: It has been taught: If a heathen employs the Divine Name in prayer, at its conclusion one may pronounce "Amen."—Rabbi Tanchuma says, "When a heathen greets thee, thou canst say 'Amen' thereto.'—*Yer. Berachot* VIII, 6 (ed. Shitomir, 55a).

8: The Holy One, blessed be He, rejects no creature. The portals are opened and he who desires to enter may come and enter. For thus it is written,

"Open ye the gates, that the righteous nation that keepeth faithfulness may enter in" (Isaiah xxvi. 2). It is not said there, priests, Levites, or Israelites, but "that the righteous nation may enter in."—*Sifra*, section *Achare Mot; Shemot Rabbah*, c. 17.

9: Heaven and earth I call to be witnesses, be it non-Jew or Jew, man or woman, man-servant or maid-servant, according to the work of every human being does the holy spirit rest upon him.—*Yalkut*, §42.

10: "Ye shall therefore keep My statutes, and Mine ordinances, which if a man do, he shall live by them" (Leviticus xviii. 5).—R. Jeremiah used to say: You might ask whence do we conclude that even a heathen if he follows the Torah is equal to the high-priest? It is said, "which if a man do, he shall live by them." It is likewise written "And this is the law of man" [1] (Second Samuel vii. 19) — it is not written there: the law of the priests, Levites, and Israelites, but the law of man. Likewise it is not written, Open the gates that priests, Levites, and Israelites may enter, but, "Open ye the gates, that the righteous nation that keepeth faithfulness may enter in" (Isaiah xxvi. 2). Likewise it is not written, This is the gate of the LORD, through which priests, Levites, and Israelites shall enter, but, "This is the gate of the LORD; the righteous shall enter into it" (Psalms cxviii. 20). Likewise it is not written, Rejoice, ye priests, Levites, and Israelites, in the LORD, but, "Rejoice in the LORD, O ye righteous" (Psalms xxxiii. 1). Likewise it is not written, Do good, O

---

[1] The English version follows a different interpretation.—Tr.

LORD, unto the priests, Levites, and Israelites, but, "Do good, O LORD, unto the good" (Psalms cxxv. 4)—from all of which you can conclude that even a heathen if he follows the Torah is equal to the priest.—*Sifra, ad loc.*

11: "They encamped in the wilderness," the Torah was given in an open land, publicly, at a place that belongs to no one. For, had it been given in the land of Israel, the latter might have said to the heathen nations that they had no share in it; therefore it was given in an open land, in all publicity, at a place that belonged to no one race or nation, and whoever desires to accept it, let him come and take it. . . R. Jose says, indeed, it is written, "I have not spoken in secret, in a place of the land of darkness" (Isaiah xlv. 19), etc.; when I gave it the first time, I did not give it in secret, not in a place of the land of darkness, not in a place of secrecy, nor did I speak to the descendants of Jacob, "I give it to you alone."—*Mechilta* to Exodus xix. 2.

12: The Torah has been revealed in the wilderness between fire and water, and just as these belong equally to all inhabitants of the earth, the Torah, too, is given to all inhabitants of the earth.—*Mechilta* to Exodus xx. 2.

13: It is written, "And another shall call himself by the name of Jacob" (Isaiah xliv. 5)—those are the righteous proselytes; "and another shall subscribe with his hand unto the LORD" (*ibid.*)—those are the repentant sinners; "and surname himself by the name of Israel" (*ibid.*), and by that are meant all the

"God-fearing" [heathens who join themselves to the One God].—*Gerim* iv, 2.

14: "The LORD loveth the righteous" [Psalms cxlvi. 8]—why does He love the righteous? Because their virtue is not a possession that has been inherited. . . . If a man desired to be a Levite or a Cohen [a priest], he could not be one, if his father was not a Levite or a Cohen [priest]. But if any one desires to become a righteous person, he can become a righteous person even if he is a heathen; for the righteous are not descended from a given race, but they have acquired this merit through themselves; for that reason it is written, the LORD loveth the righteous.—*Midrash Tehillim* to Psalm cxlvi; *Bamidbar Rabbah*, c. 8.

15: Whether Israelite or heathen—he who executes a righteous deed, God will recompense him for it.—*Tanna Debe Elijahu*, c. 13 (compare *Yer. Peah* I, 1: "God does not leave unrequited even the heathen who do good works.")

16: "Let Thy priests be clothed with righteousness" (Psalms cxxxii. 9)—by that are meant also the righteous heathen who lead a priestly life.—*Yalkut* to Isaiah §429 (compare also *Otiyyot de R. Akiba*, second recension, letter *Zayin*—*Bet ha-Midrash*, ed. Jellinek, III, p. 28).

17: Rabbi Simeon b. Lakish teaches: The stranger who accepts the Torah from inner conviction is to be rated higher than those hosts of Israelites who stood at Mount Sinai and accepted the Torah when they heard the thunders and saw the lightnings.—*Tanchuma*, section *Lech Lecha*.

18: The proselytes are loved [by God], for everywhere [in the Torah] they are placed on an equal footing with the Israelites. It is written "I have loved you [children of Israel], saith the LORD" [Malachi i. 2]. . . and likewise it is written of the strangers, "He [God] loveth the stranger, in giving him food and raiment" (Deuteronomy x. 18). The Israelites are called [God's] servants, and likewise the strangers, for it is written, "Also the aliens, that join themselves to the LORD, to be His servants" (Isaiah lvi. 6). Of Israel's offerings it is said that they are acceptable to the LORD, for it is written, "That they [the holy gifts of the children of Israel] may be acceptable before the LORD" (Exodus xxviii. 38), and also of the sacrifices of the strangers it is written, "Their [those of the aliens that join themselves to the LORD] burnt-offerings and their sacrifices shall be acceptable upon Mine altar" (Isaiah lvi. 7). Of Israel it is written, "The LORD is thy keeper" (Psalms cxxi. 5) and likewise it is written of the strangers, "The LORD preserveth the strangers" (Psalms cxlvi. 9)! Of the Israelites it is written that they minister [unto the LORD], "But ye shall be named the priests of the LORD, men shall call you the ministers of our God" (Isaiah lxi. 6) and likewise it is written of the strangers, "Also the aliens, that join themselves to the LORD, to minister unto Him" (Isaiah lvi. 6).—*Gerim* IV, 2.

19: The *righteous heathen* who serve God are equal to the priests.—*Otiyyot de Rabbi Akiba*, §7.

20: The non-Jews outside of the land [Palestine] are not to be looked upon as idolaters, since they merely kept up the usages of their forefathers.—*Chul-lin* 13 b.

MIDDLE AGES

VI,   1: All Israelites will have a share in eternal life and likewise the righteous of the other nations.—Maimonides, *Mishneh Torah Hilchot Teshubah*, III, 5.

2: Not only is the Jewish tribe sanctified by the highest degree of human holiness, but every human being, regardless of differences of birth, in whom is the spirit of love and the knowledge empowering him to devote his life exclusively to the service of God and to the dissemination of His knowledge, who walks uprightly before Him and has cast off the yoke of the many earthly desires pursued by the rest of men, of him also it may be said that God is his portion and his eternal inheritance, and that God will provide for his needs, as He did for the priest and the Levite of yore.—Maimonides, *Mishneh Torah Hilchot Shemit-tah* (Concerning the Sabbatical Year), XIII, 13 (Kohler, *Jewish Theology*, p. 404). (Revised by Tr.)

3: As to your question regarding the nations: Know that God requires the heart, and that all depends upon the allegiance of the heart, the intent. Therefore our ancient sages said: The righteous of the nations of the world will have a share in the world to come, if they have acquired what they were capable of acquiring of the knowledge of the Creator and have ennobled their souls by means of good qualities. And there is no doubt that everyone who ennobles his soul through the integrity of his personal qualities and through a sound apprehension of the Creator, assuredly has a share in the world to come.   Therefore our sages have said, a heathen who is engaged in the study of the Torah is to be deemed equal to the high-priest. —Maimonides, *Letters* (ed. Lichtenberg) II, 23d ff.

4: Such as become converts to Judaism are called Israelites or Jews, even if they are descended from other nations.—Joseph Albo, *Ikkarim* (Book of Principles) IV, 42.

Modern Jewish Literature

VII,   1: However great the difference between man and man, to have been made in the image of God is the character all of them bear, the likeness common to them all.   This is what makes the human being a human being, that denotes he is a human being.   God's covenant is with all men, as it is with all worlds.   Not merely this one or that one bears the image of God, but simply man as man; for this constitutes the basis and the meaning of all human life.   By whatever phrasing the Holy Writ expresses it, that man is made in the image of God, every human being is "the child of God."   He is that by his very humanity and for his humanity.   The highest is in everyone.   In the essential and decisive elements, they are all alike.   His place and task are assigned to each, but human nobility is in all.   To deny that even *to one,* would mean to deprive all of it.   Beneath every line of demarcation between races and nations, castes and classes, between those that rule and those that serve, those that give and those that receive, beneath all differences even of talents and powers stands the more basic term, "human being." Whoever bears a human countenance is created and called to be a revelation of human dignity.—Leo Baeck, *Das Wesen des Judentums* (2d ed.), p. 161.

2: The recognition that we owe to the other man is accordingly unconditional and unlimited; for it rests exclusively upon the fact that since he is a human being, he is a fellow human being, being of my being, dignity of my dignity. The saying from Leviticus that Akiba called the determinant sentence of the Bible, that is usually rendered "thou shalt love thy neighbor as thyself," signifies more precisely: "Thou shalt love thy neighbor, he is like thee." In this *"like thee"* lies the whole content of the monition. The conception of his standing as a fellow human being is contained therein: he is like you, he is essentially your equal, you and he are one as the possessors of a common humanity. And this counsel is not mere philosophy and visionary sentimentality, but an unconditional commandment, the affirmation of a clear and distinct requirement that we shall honor any and every other who is like ourselves. Not because he does this perhaps or that, or is looked upon as this or that, are we to esteem him, but simply because he is a human being.—Leo Baeck, *l. c.,* p. 205.

3: As the One and Only God signifies the God of morality, He is not here in the first place for the *individual,* nor even for the family, tribe, and nation, but for all mankind.—Hermann Cohen, *Religiöse Postulate, a Lecture,* p. 14.

4: All nations, therefore, without any exception, from the remotest islands, must go up with the Jews towards Jerusalem. And there must not remain any difference between the children of Israel and the sons of the foreign lands. For they too will become priests and Levites. We are approaching the time when the "new covenant" will be made; for "the Torah will be written into the heart." We are approaching the time when they will say, "Thou art our Father; Abraham hath not known us."—Hermann Cohen, *l. c.,* pp. 14-15.

5: Accordingly, the purport of the sentence "God has chosen Israel" is that he who formulated it and he who takes it up and repeats it as his profession, believes in a God Who desires to perpare the way to Himself for all mankind, Who since He gave the property of being His children to all men therefore selected someone to be the bearer of His message to mankind. —M. Dienemann, *Israels Erwählung,* p. 4.

6: But all men are created in the divine image, not the forefather of one nation or another only, but the progenitor of all, from whom the whole human race has descended, *endowed with equal rights.*— Abraham Geiger, *Das Judentum u. s. Geschichte,* I, p. 42 (Newburgh, *l. c.,* p. 54).

7: Judaism broke down the barriers of narrow nationality; it is not birth that makes the Jew, but conviction, the profession of faith. So he also who is not born of Jewish parents but accepts the true faith becomes a Jew, fully entitled to equal rights and privileges. Proselytism in the more exalted meaning of the term, signifying the adoption of the conviction

by those hitherto outsiders because they willingly declare themselves to be in full agreement therewith—
that kind of proselytism is a product of Judaism.—
Abraham Geiger, *l. c.*, pp. 88-89 (Newburgh, *ibid.*,
pp. 101-102). (Revised by Tr.)

8: But God is the Father of all men, to Whom
everyone stands in the relation of a child and unto
Whom everyone may find the way at any time whatever if he seek it sincerely.   These are the contempla-
tions, to the manifestation of which the New-Year's
Day presents the natural occasion through its univer-
salistic character, and which also constitute the substance of the Messiah-hope of Judaism.—M. Güdemann, *Das Judentum i. s. Grundzügen*, pp. 103-104.

9: Judaism allows, as has already been demonstrated, that there are equally righteous persons also
outside of its circle, and it concedes eternal bliss as well
to them.   Even upon its followers it has no higher reward to bestow.   Judaism does not know of a kingdom of heaven into which only Jews find admittance,
or into which entrance is granted only on the strength
of a Jewish symbol.—M. Güdemann, *l. c.*, p. 105.

10: But Judaism concedes the merit of everyone
who is instrumental in the exaltation of God upon
earth.   That this shall be realized, at length, and "the
world be perfected under the kingdom of the Almighty," as it is expressed in the concluding prayer
of the daily service, is the hope of Judaism for the future of mankind.—M. Güdemann, *ibid.*, p. 105.

11: We Jews have another conception of the God
of love.   Because we believe in a God of love Who
created *all* men in His image, we believe that progress

upward takes place in the history of mankind irre-
sistibly, and therefore we believe in the triumph of
the idea of atonement in the life of the nations. Every
civilized people that is the bearer of an idea is in the
service of *all* mankind.   Molding its ideal, fulfilling
the mission assigned to it, it enriches and extends the
possessions of the whole body of mankind, it contributes to the saving work of directing mankind towards
its ultimate destiny.   The day is coming when the
existence of this situation will become common
knowledge and the covenant of brotherhood embracing all mankind be consciously adopted.   Then will
Judaism's conception of atonement, the true idea of
atonement, have won the victory.   It does not hold
that the Messiah redeems mankind from sin, but declares that when mankind shall have set itself free
from the sway of sin through *its own powers of
amendment,* and shall have matured to true moral
perfection, *then, for it, the Messiah will have come.*—
Jakob Guttmann, *Die Idee der Versöhnung im Judentum* (Heft Nr. 2, *"Vom Judentum"*) pp. 14-15.

12: On the other hand, we dispute that there is
a man in the world who by reason of his colour, of
his appearance, or of his descent has lost the power of
valuing himself morally and of remaining true to his
moral dignity.   Consequently, we oppose racial hatred with all our might.—Emil G. Hirsch, *The Contributions of Judaism to Free Religion*— (in *Proceedings of the Fifth International Congress of Free Christianity and Religious Progress,* Berlin-Schöneberg
1911), p. 381.

13: Of all religions in the world it is indeed Ju-

daism that does *not* say: outside of me there is no salvation!   Indeed it is precisely the Judaism that is de-
famed because of its alleged particularism which
teaches that the good and honest persons of all nations
walk towards the most blissful goal!   It is precisely
the *Rabbins,* decried because of their alleged particularism, who more than any others point to the procla-
mation by the mouth of the prophets and singers of a
superb morning-tide of humanity, telling how it is
not priests, Levites, and Israel who are named there,
and how the righteous, the honest, and the good persons of all nations would be encompassed also in this
most magnificent blessing.—S. R. Hirsch, *Ges. Schr.*
I, p. 155.

14: Our song (Psalms viii) means that only as
the *Tzorere ha-Shem* [adversaries of God] disappear
will *Ojeb* [enemies] and *Mitnakem* [avengers] also
disappear from human society; that only as right consciousness of God is attained, will right consciousness
of man also obtain dominion in every human heart
and every human soul; that consciousness of the One
and Only God and Father of mankind which teaches
us both to discern, esteem, and love the divinity even
in the last man who has sunk to the lowest depths,
that cannot be lost, and to own in him the child of
God, the brother.   It is this consciousness which does
away with human enmity. . . .—S. R. Hirsch,
l. c., p. 394.

15: He [R. Akiba] used to say: Beloved [of
God] is man, for he was created in the image of God;
but it was by a special love that it was made known
to him that he was created in the image of God, as it

is written, "For in the image of God made He man" (Genesis ix. 6) (*Ethics of the Fathers*, III, 18; see above, p. 95, V, 1). R. Akiba speaks here of all human beings, which reading the Biblical verse here cited, permits, for it is addressed to all descendants of Noah and not only to Israel.—R. Yom-Tob Lipman Heller, in *Tosafot-Yom-Tob* (Commentary to the *Mishnah*), *ad loc.*

16: First and foremost, however, it was in Israel that ethics broke down national barriers for the first time, counted all human beings as children of God, and cherished the mental vision of a distant future in which all human beings would serve God unanimously and harmoniously in purity and holiness, in righteousness and love.—Max Joseph, *Zur Sittenlehre d. Judentums*, p. 18.

17: The first covenant of God was made with Noah, as the representative of mankind, after the flood. It was intended to assure him and all coming generations of the perpetual maintenance of the natural order without a second interruption by flood, and at the same time it demanded of all mankind in return the observance of certain laws, such as never to shed, or eat, blood. Here, at the very beginning of history, religion is presented as the *universal* basis of human morality, so developing at the outset the fundamental principle of Judaism that it rests upon a *religion of humanity*, which it desires to establish in all purity. As the idea of a common humanity thus forms its beginning, so Judaism will attain its final goal only in a divine covenant comprising all humanity.—Kaufmann Kohler, *Theol. d. Judentums*, pp.

37-38.   (*Jewish Theology*, p. 48). (Revised by Tr.)

18: That Israel, and with Israel all mankind, was redeemed, not at the Red Sea, but at Sinai, is a thought reiterated (in Rabbinic teaching) in a number of passages; in the allegory, for instance, that God bade Moses write the Torah in seventy languages in order that *all* nations might have a share in it. Again, it is said that "the Torah was revealed publicly, in the unclaimed desert. Since the Israelites might have maintained that the other nations had no part in it if it had been given in the land of Israel, it was published in the open desert. It is the property of the whole world; every one is at liberty to assume the responsibilities it imposes" (*Mekhilta Yithro Parshath Bachodesh*).—M. Lazarus, *Die Ethik des Judentums*, I, p. 25 (Szold, *l. c.*, pp. 29-30). (Revised by Tr.)

19: Though its first appeal was to the nation whose language it spoke, yet the ethics of Judaism, even in its oldest form, was preëminently inter-human. In its essentials, its fundamental thought concerning the reason and aim of morality, it was not a national but an universal ethics. In other words, moral knowledge was not held to have been effectuated for Israel alone; it was for the world at large. The ideals of correct conduct were proclaimed, not only for the members of that race in the midst of which they were conceived, but for the whole of mankind. That all mankind may join in the effort to grasp and realize these ideals is the burden of the most earnest prayers, the object of the unstilled longing, and the ever-renewed hope of all noble souls.—M.

Lazarus, *l. c.,* p. 144 (Szold, *ibid.,* p. 189). (Revised by Tr.)

20: The whole of mankind is called to coöperate in the establishment of the moral order, in the work of moulding the world of ideas, and their realization in actual life.—M. Lazarus, *ibid.,* p. 149 (Szold, *ibid.,* p. 196).

21: From the standpoint of true Judaism, all the inhabitants of the earth are created for happiness.— Moses Mendelssohn, *Jerusalem,* p. 170.

22: But what is "revealed" to us through the prophets is simply and plainly our task: to love God and to walk in His ways, and this task is set for all peoples.—H. Steinthal, *Über Juden u. Judentum,* p. 14.

23: Judaism, as a religious community or a religious system, never harbored any pretensions to the sole disposal of the means of grace; it does not claim that membership in it is a guarantee of salvation of the soul, nor does it deny salvation of the soul to anyone who was not born a Jew. Everyone—thus runs the Talmudic doctrine (*Megillah* 13 a)—who rejects idolatry is a Jew, and only the perfecting of himself morally procures eternal salvation for any man.— Ludwig Venetianer, *Jüdisches im Christentum,* pp. 27-28.

24: The fundamental presupposition of the Mosaic doctrine, the belief in the One and Only God, the Creator of heaven and earth, necessarily suggested the companion thought that all men were the children of God and accordingly led to the recognition of an obligation to a brotherly attitude towards all children

EQUALITY OF ALL HUMAN BEINGS   171

of men. For in Mosaism the moral law flows from the belief in the One and Only, the Holy God Who called men to emulate Him. As did God Himself, therefore so also His moral commandment had in like manner to encompass all those created in His image.— *Begründung der öffentlichen Erklärung über die interkonfessionelle Stellung des Judentums* (in *Verhandlungen u. Beschlüsse der Rabbiner-Versammlung in Berlin*, am 4. u. 5. Juni, 1884), p. 87.

See also:

MARTIN BUBER, *Vom Geist des Judentums*, 1916, p. 32f.
HERMANN COHEN, *Religiöse Postulate* (a lecture delivered at the second general meeting of the Verband der Deutschen Juden, the 13th of October, 1907, in Frankfurt a. M.).
——— *Religion u. Sittlichkeit*, 1907, p. 154.
——— *Nächstenliebe im Talmud*, 1888, p. 23.
I. ELBOGEN, *Die Religionsanschauungen d. Pharisäer*, 1904, pp. 55ff.
ABRAHAM GEIGER, *Das Judentum u. seine Geschichte*, 1865, I, pp. 25, 42, 88f.; II, 1865, pp. 10, 21f., 177f.
E. GRÜNEBAUM, *Die Fremden (Gerim) nach rabbinischen Gesetzen* (*Jüdische Zeitschrift für Wissenschaft und Leben*, 1870, Jahrgang VIII), pp. 49ff.
M. GÜDEMANN, *Das Judentum in seinen Grundzügen*, 1902, pp. 43f., 104f.
EMIL G. HIRSCH, *The Contributions of Judaism to Free Religion*, 1911, p. 381.
S. R. HIRSCH, *Gesammelte Schriften*, I, 1902, pp. 158, 394; II, 1904, p. 455; IV, 1908, p. 421.
BENZION KELLERMANN, *Der ethische Monotheismus der Propheten*, 1917, pp. 54ff.
KAUFMANN KOHLER, *Grundrisz einer syst. Theologie d. Judentums*, 1900, pp. 94, 165, 190, 228f., 296, 298ff., 301, 305f., 312.
L. LAZARUS, *Zur Charakteristik d. talmudischen Ethik*, 1877, p. 43.

M. LAZARUS, *Die Ethik d. Judentums*, I, 1899, pp. 28f., 92,
123f., 144f., 147ff., 153ff., 161, 163f., 166f.; II, 1911,
pp. 356f.

H. STEINTHAL, *Über Juden u. Judentum*, 1906, p. 106.

———— *Zu Bibel u. Religionsphilosophie*, II, 1895, p. 222.

MAX WIENER, *Die Anschauungen d. Propheten v. d. Sittlichkeit*, 1909, pp. 33, 64f., 70, 133.

———— *Die Religion d. Propheten*, 1912, pp. 20, 48.

CHRISTIAN AUTHORS

VIII,   1: The whole thinking human world strives
after a perfecting of mankind, that is, after the highest
in the way of entire outer and inner unfoldment of
life that it is possible for the whole of the species to
reach, which while it rules over the earth, is also
bound down to the earth. That consummation is
nothing else than the kingdom of God, for the coming
of which Jesus asks. The prayer, while it is in its
origin Israelitish, is in its meaning comprehensibly
human.—Wolf Wilhelm Graf Baudissin, *Zur Gesch.
d. alttest Religion*, p. 48.

2: In so far as Amos, and later Micah, emphasize
first and foremost the moral factor in the *Yahveh-
religion*, this religion of itself lays *claim to universal
validity*. "*Yahvism* must present itself for acceptance
to all in whose bosom a human heart beats."—A.
Bertholet, *Stellg. d. Israeliten u. d. Juden z. d.
Fremden*, p. 95.

3: Consequently, a more accurate consideration
of the Psalms helps to throw light on just that side
of the faith of the Jewish community to which no
other pre-Christian community makes even a remote
approach, "the hope for a kingdom of God, to which

all human beings are called and in which everything in heaven and upon earth is in harmony with God's will."—A. Bertholet, *l. c.,* p. 194.

4: *Ben-Sira* is a loyal son of his people. Yet even to him the thought of the unity of the human race is very active.—Wilhelm Bousset, *Die Religion d. Judentums,* p. 95.

5: The religion of the Jew ascribes to all men and peoples without exception a noble descent and a spiritual-moral value. It alone speaks distinctly and clearly of the descent of all men from a single common progenitor. This idea of the uniform descent of all men and peoples, which was either unknown to the ancient world or of which it did not become impressively conscious, at least which is not clearly expressed in the traditions of the other peoples, has a great social and moral significance for human life. It peremptorily introduces the thought of the community of tasks and aims in life for the whole human race and spreads light over the whole history of mankind.—(Bishop) Chrysanth, *Die Religionen d. alten Welt in ihrer Beziehg. z. Christentum,* III, p. 168.

6: In a religion, which alone among all religions had a clear conception of the descent of all men from one single father and which set the value of the human being so exceedingly high, there could be no room for a generic differentiation between nation and nation, for a division into higher and lower races, into peoples fundamentally barbarian and non-barbarian. The Jews were the only people of the ancient world who possessed a correct, all-embracing historical view of the life of man and of human society, an outlook in which even the Greeks, foremost among the peoples of heathendom, were wanting. They [the Jews] never could lose the consciousness of the unity of all peoples, and of the higher general purposes of existence applicable to the whole body of mankind. Their exclusiveness had only a temporary significance and led in quite the opposite direction.— (Bishop) Chrysanth, *l. c.,* p. 326.

7: And now, what is the attitude of the Torah of Israel towards this true humanity? On its very first page this beacon word shines out to greet us, "And God created man in His own image, in the image of God created He him." This one sentence would suffice to prove the Divine origin of the Holy Writ of Israel.—Heinrich Cornill, *Das A. T. u. d. Humanität,* p. 9.

8: And what sort of spirit does our Israelitish table of the genealogy of nations breathe? (Genesis x.) No self-seeking interest, no base motive can be perceived there. On the contrary, it is a view of life that comprehends the whole world, that sees in mankind a large family composed of God's children, who as the children of One Heavenly Father are brothers one of another. Its spirit, therefore, is that of the most genuine and lofty humanity, as it has grown upon religious soil into a true daughter of heaven—the practical application and a necessary consequence of the doctrine that God created man in His own image.— Heinrich Cornill, *l. c., p.* 10.

9: The ideality and universality of religion— these are the two new grand apprehensions which Jeremiah has given to the world. Every man as human is born a child of God. He is not made a child of God through the forms of any particular religion or outward organization, but he becomes such in his heart, through circumcision of the heart and of the ears. A pure heart and a pure mind are all that God requires of man [anteceding moral action].—C. H. Cornill, *Der israel. Prophetismus*, p. 98 [The *Prophets of Israel* (tr. by S. F. Cockran, 2d ed. Chicago, Open Court Pub. Co., 1897), p. 98]. (Revised by Tr.)

10: According to Jeremiah, all men and all nations are destined and called upon to turn to God and become His children. Deutero-Isaiah sees in this program the final aim of the history of the world, towards which its entire course and development are striving.—C. H. Cornill, *l. c.*, p. 130 (Cockran, *l. c.*, p. 140). (Revised by Tr.)

11: There was thus no longer any stringent reason for confining this religion to a single country, such as Canaan or Judah, or even to a single people, such as Israel. Nay, more, since this was the true religion, and was therefore called from the first by its deepest aspirations and final destiny to enlighten and guide all men and all peoples alike (see Vol. II, pp. 106sqq.), it must of necessity, as soon as its national limitations ceased to be required, go forth all the more boldly and mightily to every nation without distinction; and now that this tendency, originally implanted in it, could move with freedom and was endeavoring to realise its object, every member, in proportion to the liveliness of his communion, necessarily felt the strength of the impulse to labor in this direction. *No stranger who desired to submit himself to its loftiest claims ought any longer to be denied all its blessings;* but, on the other hand, every member of that people which had hitherto been its support, and which had been the first to experience its glory, must have felt a burning zeal kindling within him to discharge to its ultimate author his debt of gratitude for its beneficent power, by spreading it far and wide, and proclaiming the 'God of Israel' amongst all the heathen.—Heinrich Ewald, *The History of Israel* (tr. by J. E. Carpenter, 2d ed. London, Longmans, Green & Co., 1880), Vol. V., pp. 26-27.

12: He who like Moses understands, in the first place, that there exists only one true God and that all human beings without distinction are equal before Him; and in the second place also that the sovereignty of this God and His will are alone indestructibly eternal for all human beings, just as they are immutably uniform amidst all the fluctuations of circumstance; and in the third place that this One true God is He Who encompasses all human beings in equal measure, in His might punishing their departures from His will and still more advancing in His infinite love to meet them:—such an one, if he is at the same time inspired by such pure and ever constant but also such an intense love for his people as well as *for all human beings* as Moses, and if like the latter he is qualified to act as the leader and molder of his people, will also be able to draw the correct outlines of that community of the true God which is the only genuine one. . . . —Heinrich Ewald, *Die Lehre d. Bibel v. Gott oder Theol. d. alten u. neuen Bundes,* I, p. 204.

13: Equality of rights for all peoples and therefore peace on earth, that is the ultimate thought of the religion of the Old Testament.—Hermann Gunkel, *Kriegsfrömmigk. i. A. T.* (*"Internat. Monatsschrift,"* Jahrg. 9, Heft 8, column 758).

14: Hence, to the prophet it was a matter of course that fundamental moral laws exist which are binding upon all peoples, and over the observance of which *Yahveh,* as a Being of absolute morality and at the same time as the Master and Judge of all, has strict supervision.—Emil Kautzsch, *Biblische Theol. d. A. T.,* p. 226.

15: The thought that the heathen also are called to salvation, that some day they would worship *Yahveh* and belong to the kingdom of God, never ceased to be a subject of the prophetic sermon.—Johannes Nikel, *Das A. T. u. d. Nächstenliebe,* p. 36.

16: The *third* chief difference between the Old Testament religion and the other religions of antiquity lies in this fact that in the former alone is the holy and righteous God, infinitely exalted above the world, simultaneously apprehended as the God Who in condescending, sin-forgiving mercy becomes a Redeemer and Savior to all who seek Him, and becomes so latterly not arbitrarily but in a moral-religious sense. As such, He founds a kingdom of God upon earth, by means of a series of special revelations and deeds of salvation, in the first instance for Israel and then for all mankind.—Eduard Riehm, *Alttest. Theologie,* p. 26.

17: We feel it, with a still greater degree of clearness and certainty than in the latter [Isaiah], that the kingdom God desires cannot be bound to the confines of Israel, but as the kingdom of the good, is intended to be for mankind, for every individual human being directly.—Ernst Sellin, *Der alttestamentl. Prophetismus*, p. 57.

18: What particularly attracts notice here [in the wisdom of Ben-Sira] is the complete withdrawal of the thought that God's mercy rests especially upon Israel. Even the law is here given to man, God's eternal covenant is made with him; nay, more, it is expressly emphasized that God's compassion applies *to all human beings*, and that the shortcoming which calls forth this compassion has its roots in the natural disposition of man.—Bernhard Stade, *Geschichte d. Volkes Israel*, II, p. 303.

19: The principle of the equality of human beings does not in the least suffer thereunder [under the election of Israel]; the Israelites have, as far as their worthiness comes into consideration, no advantage at all over other peoples. For that reason, the prophets regard the relationship of Israel to God as one that is morally conditioned, which can just as well be acquired by any other people through the fulfillment of the moral conditions.—Franz Walter, *Die Propheten*, p. 250.

20: The Torah as God's revelation of salvation that is complete and perfect in itself was *originally* intended *for the whole body of mankind*. We find this already expressed in the *Pesikta*. Here it is said (fol. 107a), the Torah was given in the third month (*Sivan*), the planets of which are the Gemini, in order to indicate that the Torah is given to both, to Jacob and also to Esau (the nations of the world) as far as he repents. For that very reason, its revelation occurred in a manner perceptible to all human beings.— Ferdinand Weber, *Jüd. Theologie auf Grund d. Talmud,* p. 19.

21: Such proselytes have all the predicates that are attributed to Israel. Their descendants can even attain to the priesthood (*Bamidbar Rabbah,* c. 8). Nay, more, the Lord prefers, in a certain sense, the proselyte to the son of Israel; for while he stood at Mount Sinai and received there the great impressions that stimulated him to believe, the proselyte has come to believe without these incentives (*Tanchuma* to *Bereshith Lech Lecha,* 6). Moreover, God accepts and honors also those proselytes as members of God's people who join themselves to Israel not for the sake of God but from other motives, as the Gibeonites (*Bamidbar Rabbah,* c. 8). And He desires that the proselyte be treated gently and that for ten generations nothing bad be said of heathens in his presence, in order not to remind him of his heathen origin and thus to offend him (according to *Sanhedrin* 94 a); likewise, because of Exodus xxii. 20a ("And a stranger shalt thou not wrong"), one shall not remind the descendant of a proselyte of the doings of his ancestors (according to *Baba Metzia* 4, 10).—Ferdinand Weber, *l. c.,* p. 77.

22: Nevertheless, the homogeneity of the human race as well as of the world is unquestionable. He Who created Israel called also the nations into being (*Sifra* to Leviticus xviii. 1; cf. Romans ii. 29).— Ferdinand Weber, *ibid.,* pp. 199-200.

23: Not an unfriendly word against the non-Jew can be found in it [in the Halachah]. Only the greatest and most universal love of mankind is again and again expressed and required. That is the overwhelming impression the reader receives. And this love that does not make any distinction, to which conceptions like "savage" or "barbarian" are absolutely foreign, extends to the departed as well as the living. It reaches out beyond death and the grave to the gates of celestial bliss, as we read in the Talmud (Tractate *Sanhedrin* 105 a), "The righteous *of all* nations will have a share in the eternal bliss!"—J. Weigl, *Das Judentum*, p. 92.

24: According to *Yore Deah* 148 and 178, the Israelite shall, to be sure, abstain from participation in the religious festivals and usages of other persuasions; but he must not do anything that would disturb the latter or mar the festal joy of those of another faith. Judaism commands its people to respect the religious convictions of other human beings, for all human beings are eligible to come to God. As an offshoot of this tolerance, the Israelitish love of one's fellow-man extends in all its plenitude beyond death and the grave. Thus we read Mar Samuel's words, "Before the Creator's throne no difference prevails between Jew and non-Jew, since there are noble and virtuous men among the latter also."—J. Weigl, *l. c.*, p. 112.

25: But the chief claim of the Hebrew world to our regard lies in the fact that the ideals of democracy which today are winning acceptance among all civilized races first developed within this area. Though the great military despotisms of Egypt, Babylonia, Assyria, and Persia that flourished in these lands have caused people to think of autocracy and the East together, it is nevertheless true that under the iron heel of these very despotisms there grew and blossomed a tiny flower, precious as any poppy that now blows in Flanders fields. It is the flower of human freedom, of the rights of man, of the possibility of self-determination, of the duty of brotherhood.   Certain ancient kings of Babylon and Egypt were the first to express these ideals, but their teachings were vague and fell upon poor soil, and so they died and left no trace in human institutions. It was in the soil of the barren steppe lands that encircle Palestine and among the nomadic tribes of the wilderness that the seeds of democracy first took root. Among the Aramean tribes that under the leadership of Abraham and Jacob found a home in southern Palestine . . . each man had equal rights and responsibilities and the chieftain was the servant of all. Whenever the independence of this liberty loving group was endangered, each man rose to put down the despot.   In time their ideals regarding the fundamental rights of man and his duties to his fellows were expressed in definite laws, and all later democratic legislation is largely an unfolding of what is there set forth in principle.—Bailey and Kent, *History of the Hebrew Commonwealth* (New York, Scribner, 1922), pp. 13-14.   (Added by Tr.)

26: Amos, though not a priest or a prophet but only a herdsman, felt a divine call to go to Bethel at the time of a great national festival and cry out against all this wickedness. He denounced the rich and ruling classes, the grafters who used public office for private gain. He fearlessly proclaimed that the first duty of rulers is to protect the rights of the poor and defence-less; that riches gained by exploiting the poor are a disgrace and a menace; and that God cannot be bribed to wink at evil, even by the richest sacrifices. Democ-racy, brotherhood, and the religion of kindness are his great teachings. These are all the greater because in Amos they are clearly heard for the first time in Hebrew, if not in world history.

It seems as if the genius of the Hebrew people, balked in its attempt to realize a true democracy in the forms of government, had now burst out in the moral realm. All its pent-up passion for justice and brotherhood, finding at last a mouthpiece in Amos, leaped at once to revolutionary expression and de-manded in the name of *Jehovah*, the God of right-eousness, a full recognition of its claims. . . .

Besides marking the high-tide of literary art, this passage proclaims the revolutionary truth that God is on the side of the downtrodden and the poor, and that any religion which does not concern itself with the welfare of one's fellows is no religion at all. This is a great discovery, one that outranks any discovery or invention in the realm of science in its possible effect upon human civilization. In thirty centuries we have not yet lived up to it; it still stands as a protest against most of our civic and social institutions, and as a great ideal yet to be attained.—Bailey and Kent, *l. c.*, pp. 188-189.   (Added by Tr.)

27: But Hosea's positive teaching shows the greatness of his genius. He taught that the only corrective for such crimes is love—not a sentiment or an emotion but a principle of action; love that shows itself in righteousness, justice, kindness, fidelity. Finding in his own heart the presence of such love even toward his unfaithful wife, he reached the bold conclusion that God must love even while he punishes faithless Israel. God's justice and His love thus become the great arguments why men should love and be just. Hosea anticipated by eight centuries the teaching of Jesus that love to God and love to man are essential to the formation of a perfect society. His teaching is only another expression of the democratic spirit that all along had underlain Hebrew society; for we know now what havoc the principle of love always works with distinctions of caste, with aristocracies, oligarchies, plutocracies, and other manifestations of selfish individualism. Love is as dangerous to vested privilege as T N T powder.—Bailey and Kent, *ibid.*, p. 190. (Added by Tr.)

28: From Israel has come a moral code based on the Ten Commandments, which expresses, as well as mere laws can, the fundamental duties of man to God and to his fellow man. It sprang from an instinct for freedom and brotherhood, perhaps the earliest and certainly the most persistent manifestation of this instinct among the ancient peoples of the world. It is this code that is the basis not only of the constitutions but also of the everyday life of all the great democracies of the present day.—Bailey and Kent, *ibid.*, p. 355. (Added by Tr.)

See also:

WOLF WILHELM GRAF BAUDISSIN, *Zur Geschichte der alttesta-mentlichen Religion in ihrer universalen Bedeutung (Zwei akademische Reden. II, Nationalismus und Universalismus)*, 1914, pp. 41f., 47f.

ALFRED BERTHOLET, *Die Stellung der Israeliten und der Juden zu den Fremden*, 1896, pp. 176, 192, 194, 242f., 276f., . 281.

WILHELM BOUSSET, *Die Religion des Judentums*, 1906, pp. 94ff., 99, 157, 238ff., 334.

KARL BUDDE, *Die Religion des Volkes Israel*, 1905, pp. 31, 120, 199f.

T. K. CHEYNE, *Jewish Religious Life After the Exile*, 1901, pp. 216f.

HEINRICH CORNILL, *Das Buch Jeremia*, 1905, p. 168.
———— *Der israelitische Prophetismus*, 1912, pp. 36, 46f., 97f., 138f.

BERNH. DUHM, *Das Buch Jeremia* (in *Kurzer Handkommentar zum Alten Testament*, herausg. v. Karl Marti, 1901, Abtg. XI), p. 253.
———— *Die Theologie der Propheten*, 1875, p. 249.
———— *Israels Propheten*, 1916, pp. 128, 310, 317, 403.

HEINRICH EWALD, *Geschichte des Volkes Israel*, II, 1865, p. 170; IV, 1866, pp. 35ff., 50f.; V, 1867, pp. 125f., 175; VI, 1868, p. 406; VII, 1868, p. 4.
———— *Die Propheten des Alten Bundes*, 1867, I, p. 124.
———— *Die Lehre d. Bibel v. Gott oder Theologie d. Alten u. neuen Bundes*, II, 1873, p. 109.

FR. GIESEBRECHT, *Die Grundzüge der israelitischen Religions-geschichte*, 1919, p. 119f.

FERDINAND GREGOROVIUS, *J. Singer, Briefe berühmter christ-licher Zeitgenossen über die Judenfrage*, 1885, pp. 69f.

HERMANN GUNKEL, *Kriegsfrömmigkeit im Alten Testament* (*Internationale Monatsschrift*, Jahrg. 9, Heft 8, column 758).
———— *Die Propheten*, 1917, p. 100.

MAX HALLER, *Der Ausgang der Prophetie*, 1912, p. 19.

G. HEINZELMANN, *Die Bibel im Lichte des Krieges* (*Der Geisteskampf der Gegenwart*), 1915, Nr. 8.

J. HERRMANN, *Die soziale Predigt der Propheten*, 1911, pp. 26f.

EQUALITY OF ALL HUMAN BEINGS   185

EMIL KAUTZSCH, *Biblische Theologie des Alten Testaments*, 1911, pp. 226ff., 270ff., 298f.

RUD. KITTEL, *Judenfeindschaft oder Gotteslästerung?* 1914, p. 64.

PAUL KLEINERT, *Die Propheten Israels in sozialer Beziehung*, 1905, p. 57.

AUGUST KLOSTERMANN, *Geschichte des Volkes Israel*, 1896, pp. 68f., 89f., 106f.

JUSTUS KÖBERLE, *Sünde und Gnade*, 1905, pp. 121f., 252f., 304.

EDUARD KÖNIG, *Geschichte des Reiches Gottes*, 1908, pp. 68, 72, 141.

———— *Geschichte der alttestamentlichen Religion*, 1912, p. 340.

———— *Prophentenideal, Judentum und Christentum*, 1906, pp. 10f.

A. KUENEN, *Volksreligion und Weltreligion*, 1883, pp. 141, 143, 172.

KÜPER, *Das Prophetentum d. Alten Bundes*, 1870, pp. 38f., 70, 164, 235, 271, 273f.

KARL MARTI, *Die Religion des Alten Testaments*, 1906, pp. 59f.

———— *Geschichte der israelitischen Religion*, 1900, p. 176.

HANS MEINHOLD, *Geschichte des jüdischen Volkes*, 1916, p. 41.

———— *Jesaja und seine Zeit*, 1898, p. 46.

GEORGE F. MOORE, *Die Eigenart der hebr. Geschichtsschreibung im alttestamentlichen Zeitalter* (28. *Bericht der Lehranstalt für die Wissenschaft des Judentums*, 1910) pp. 73f.

JOHANNES NIKEL, *Das Alte Testament u. d. Nächstenliebe*, 1913, pp. 36f.

EDUARD RIEHM, *Alttestamentliche Theologie*, 1889, pp. 268, 270, 409f.

L. SEINICKE, *Geschichte des Volkes Israel*, I, 1876, p. 39.

ERNST SELLIN, *Der alttestamentliche Prophetismus*, 1912, pp. 17, 25, 56f., 59f., 73, 187ff., 192, 229f., 232f.

———— *Die alttestamentliche Religion in Rahmen der anderen altorientalischen*, 1908, pp. 9f., 43f.

RUDOLF SMEND, *Lehrbuch der alttestamentlichen Religionsgeschichte*, 1899, pp. 310f., 439f.

BERNARD STADE, *Geschichte des Volkes Israel*, I, 1887, pp. 5f., 551; II, 1888, pp. 69f., 294, 303.

W. STAERK, *Neutestamentliche Zeitgeschichte,* II, 1907, pp. 5, 24, 49f.

GEORG STERNBERG, *Die Ethik des Deuteronomiums,* 1908, p. 27.

B. STOSCH, *Die Prophetie Israels in religionsgeschichtlicher Würdigung,* 1907, pp. 502, 546ff.

———— *Die Universalität des absoluten Gottes bei Jesaja* ("*Evangelische Kirchenzeitung,*" 89. Jahrg., Nr. 25), 1915, p. 304.

PAUL TORGE, *Aus Israels Propheten,* 1914, p. 13.

FRANZ WALTER, *Die Propheten in ihrem sozialen Beruf und das Wirtschaftsleben ihrer Zeit,* 1900, p. 250.

FERDINAND WEBER, *Jüdische Theologie auf Grund des Talmud und verwandter Schriften,* 1897, pp. 9, 19, 200, 263.

J. WEIGEL, *Das Judentum,* 1911, pp. 157f.

JULIUS WELLHAUSEN, *Israelitische und jüdische Geschichte,* 1907, pp. 221ff.

[HARTLEY BURR ALEXANDER, *Nature and Human Nature,* Chicago, 1923, Chap. XIV, pp. 460-492 (Hebraism as a Mode of Philosophy).

EDWARD CHAUNCEY BALDWIN, *Our Modern Debt to Israel,* Boston, 1913, Chap. II, pp. 18-88 (The Prophets); Chap. V, pp. 134-151 (The Debt of Israel and the World to Hebrew Law); Chap VIII, pp. 200-209 (The Message of Israel to the Modern World).—Tr.]

VII

THE WILL TO LIVE

Introduction by Dr. Leo Baeck

The sense of reality is characteristic of Judaism. Yet it knows nothing of the realism which recognizes only that which can be touched and handled. All reality capable of manifestation in the forms of might, mass, and dominion, on the contrary, it declares to be transitory and fleeting. It is the reality which is disclosed in the good, the meaning of life which reveals itself in the moral deed, the power to create this true reality displayed by man which wins its recognition. This sense of reality is closely intertwined with the will to the good, the desire to fashion and shape, to labor and be active. Religion here not only lends dignity to the will to live, but it also requires it. God has given man life, "life and good." Life is thus for man a possession that he is to guard, a problem that he is to solve. "Thou shalt live," upon this commandment as a base all the others are built; "that thou mayest live," upon this promise are all the others founded.

Such an attitude toward life insures a definite, affirmative relation to the world in which it is carried on. The world is not semblance and not delusion; it is not the abode of misery and of pain; rather is it the scene of life's task, the field of duty. The life of man is a part of the world, so much so that the world, as the wondrous allegory of the Bible is intended to show in ever new metaphors, participates in his joy and in his sorrow, in his godliness and in his iniquity, exults with him and laments with him. From the ground which he tills, to the kingdom of God for which he is to work so that it shall be established upon earth, in everything the world is given also to man to shape, that he may give proof in it of the will to the good, the will to live. It is in this activity and labor that he shall experience the blessing that is vouchsafed him in the world. "Thou shalt rejoice in all the good that the Eternal, thy God, giveth thee."

Of course, Judaism also knows that asceticism has its place; it realizes the necessity of abstaining from many things that life contains. Every religion takes cognizance of what is merely material in life, of what is ordinary and base in it. Judaism is especially aware that he only has the true will to live who also has the will to endure and to renounce. In particular, the conception of law as the way that God marks out, and the conception of divine commandment, in the fulfillment of which alone man finds his road to freedom, have taught Judaism self-discipline, have insisted that the moral will which sets the bounds and indicates the direction shall be stronger than mere desire. A great "thou shalt not" resounded in Judaism as in no other religion.

Hence arose here, too, the resolution to demonstrate possession of power of foregoing things for the sake of God; to deny oneself many a permissible thing, thereby to establish the power of the mind over the body. Judaism had its Nazarites, its circle of Essenes and of those that followed them, and even such extremists as the followers of Isaac Luria, the mystic; it has kept fastdays and known vows; it has extended the bounds of what was forbidden. To cope with the fact that the body is encompassed by the exigencies of everyday life, it has set up the dietary laws. Whatever their purpose in the beginning, Judaism has been carried by them along the road to asceticism, not the one leading to self-denial and chastisement and the mortification of the flesh as an end in itself, but to the one leading out of bondage to the merely earthy. Through them it has cultivated a conscious will to self-discipline. By means of these and the other "thou shalt not" laws, the Jew has learned moderation, how to rise above mere desire and prove stronger than things material.

Here, too, the will to live sought and found expression; the will to that life which man not only takes as he receives it but which he also fashions and forms himself. This is the decisive factor in Judaism. The commandment of God gave life its meaning for Judaism and thus obedience to it could be required here: "Thou shalt choose life, that thou mayest live, thou and thy seed."

1. MORALITY AND JOY OF LIFE

BIBLE

I,   1: And thou shalt rejoice before the LORD thy God, thou, and thy son, and thy daughter, and thy

man-servant, and thy maid-servant, and the Levite
that is within thy gates, and the stranger, and the
fatherless, and the widow, that are in the midst of
thee.—Deuteronomy xvi. 11; see also Deuteronomy
xvi. 14.

2: And thou shalt rejoice in all the good which
the LORD thy God hath given unto thee, and unto
thy house, thou, and the Levite, and the stranger that
is in the midst of thee.—Deuteronomy xxvi. 11.

3: He is God; that formed the earth and made it,
He established it, He created it not a waste, He formed
it to be inhabited.—Isaiah xlv. 18.

4: Serve the LORD with gladness; come before
His presence with singing.—Psalms c. 2.

5: Lo, children are a heritage of the LORD; the
fruit of the womb is a reward.—Psalms cxxvii. 3.

6: Happy is every one that feareth the LORD,
that walketh in His ways. When thou eatest the labor
of thy hands, happy shalt thou be, and it shall be
well with thee. Thy wife shall be as a fruitful vine,
in the innermost parts of thy house; thy children
like olive plants, round about thy table. Behold,
surely thus shall the man be blessed that feareth the
LORD.—Psalms cxxviii. 1-4.

7: I know that there is nothing better for them
[the sons of men], than to rejoice, and to do good[1]
so long as they live. But also that every man should
eat and drink, and enjoy pleasure for all his labor,
is the gift of God.—Ecclesiastes iii. 12-13.

8: Behold that which I have seen: it is good, yea,

[1] This rendering is faithful to the Hebrew text. The English version seems to
follow a forced interpretation.—Tr.

it is comely for one to eat and to drink, and to enjoy pleasure for all his labor, wherein he laboreth under the sun, all the days of his life which God hath given him; for this is his portion. Every man also to whom God hath given riches and wealth, and hath given him power to eat thereof, and to take his portion, and to rejoice in his labor—this is the gift of God.—Ecclesiastes v. 17-18.

9: So I commended mirth, that a man hath no better thing under the sun, than to eat, and to drink, and to be merry, and that this should accompany him in his labor all the days of his life which God hath given him under the sun.—Ecclesiastes viii. 15.

10: Go thy way, eat thy bread with joy, and drink thy wine with a merry heart; for God hath already accepted thy works. Let thy garments be always white; and let thy head lack no oil. Enjoy life with the wife whom thou lovest all the days of the life of thy vanity, which He hath given thee under the sun, all the days of thy vanity; for that is thy portion in life, and in thy labor wherein thou laborest under the sun.—Ecclesiastes ix. 7-9.

11: Rejoice, O young man, in thy youth; and let thy heart cheer thee in the days of thy youth, and walk in the ways of thy heart, and in the sight of thine eyes; but know thou, that for all these things God will bring thee into judgment.—Ecclesiastes xi. 9.

12: 'Go your way, eat the fat, and drink the sweet, and send portions unto him for whom nothing is prepared; for this day is holy unto our Lord; neither be ye grieved; for the joy of the LORD is your strength.'—Nehemiah viii. 10.

PALESTINIAN APOCRYPHA

IIa,   1: Deny not thyself the good that the day bringeth thee, and let not the part in joy overpass thee.—*Ben-Sira* xiv. 14.

2: Give not thy soul to sorrow, and let not thyself become unsteadied with care. Heart-joy is life for a man, and human gladness prolongeth days.—*Ben-Sira* xxx. 21-22 (Box and Oesterley, in Charles, *l.c.*).

3: Wine is as good as life to a man, if it be drunk moderately; what life has a man that is without wine? for it was created from the beginning to make men glad.—*Ben-Sira* xxxiv. (=xxxi) 27.

4: Speak, thou that art the elder, for it becometh thee, but be humble minded; and hinder not music. Pour not out words where there is wine. . . . A concert of music in a banquet of wine is as a signet of carbuncle set in gold. As a signet of an emerald set in a work of gold, so is the melody of music with pleasant wine.—*Ben-Sira* xxxv. (=xxxii) 3-6.

JEWISH-HELLENISTIC LITERATURE

III,   1: It is purification for the mind if thou preservest the body clean.—Pseudo-Phokylides, *Nuthetikon*, 215.

2: [And Moses is above all other men skillful in training and disciplining persons of good natural disposition in the practice of virtue by frugality and abstinence, endeavoring to remove costly excess from their characters,] but at the same time not approving unnecessary rigor, like the lawgiver of Lacedaemon, nor undue indulgence, like him who taught the Ionians and the Sybarites luxury and license, but keeping a middle path between the two, so that he relaxed what was overstrict and tightened what was too loose, merging the excesses which are found at each extremity into moderation, so as to produce a harmony and consistency of life void of reproach.—Philo: *On Special Laws*, IV; *On Coveting* (M. II, 352; C.-W. 102) (Yonge, *l.c.*). (Revised by Tr.)

TALMUDICAL LITERATURE

V, 1: "I praise mirth" [Ecclesiastes viii. 15]. This means that the righteous man rejoices when he performs a meritorious act. . . . This teaches that the Divine Presence [*Shechinah*] comes not by sadness, by indolence, by hilarity, by levity, by gossip, or by senseless talk, but through rejoicing in a meritorious deed.—*Shabbat* 30 b (Rodkinson, *l. c.*, Vol. I, pp. 47-48; compare *Yer. Sukkah* V, 1: The holy spirit rests only upon a cheerful disposition).

2: Rabbi Yehudah taught in the name of Samuel: It is said, "Ye shall therefore keep My statutes, and Mine ordinances, which if a man do, he shall live by them" (Leviticus xviii. 5), by them he shall *live*, but not die because of them.—*Yoma* 85 b.

3: All commandments of the Torah have been given that one may *live* by them, and where it is a question of preserving human life [*pikkuach nefesh*], none remains valid except the prohibitions of idolatry, of incest, and of the shedding of blood.—*Tosefta Shabbat*, c. 15.

4: Man must not torment himself with fasting.

. . . It is written, "And man became a living soul" (Genesis ii. 7)—the soul that I have given thee, maintain it living.—*Taanit* 22 b.

5: It is written, "[And the priest shall] make atonement for him [for the Nazarite], for that he sinned by reason of the dead" (Numbers vi. 11). How did he sin by reason of the dead? By abstaining from wine. Here you may make the transition from the lighter to the weightier conclusion: if he is a sinner who only denies himself the enjoyment of wine, how much more is he who foregoes all enjoyments. Thence you may learn that he who imposes fasting upon himself is a sinner.—*Nedarim* 10 a and *Nazir* 19 a.

6: It is written, "The merciful man doeth good to his own soul" (Proverbs xi. 17). Once upon a time, Hillel the older acted in compliance with this principle. One day he bade farewell to his disciples; these asked him, 'Whither goest thou?' He replied, 'To execute a pious work—I am going to bathe myself.' 'Is that a pious work?' 'Yes, indeed! You see, do you not, how the statue of the ruler that is exhibited in public must be kept clean? Should I, created in the image of God, not keep myself clean?'—*Vayyikra Rabbah*, c. 34.

7: No festal joy without wine.—*Pesachim* 109 a.

8: In the future, man will be called to account for abstaining from permitted enjoyments that he might have allowed himself.—*Yerushalmi Kiddushin* IV, 12.

9: He who sees beautiful things or beautiful trees shall say, "Blessed be He Who created them as part of His world."—*Bereshit Rabbah*, c. 58.

MIDDLE AGES

VI,   1: What we said of life and death, we also
say with respect to man's obligation to make use of
all means that subserve his health, his food, his raiment, his habitation, and the refinement of his habits,
and to abstain from everything that is contrary
thereto.—Bachya ibn Pakuda, *Chobot ha-Lebabot*
(Duties of the Heart), IV, p. 217.

2: You must never deprive your body of the
necessaries of life, nor procure too much for the soul
and thus weaken the body; in doing that you would
weaken both.   Offer your body the food that will
sustain it, and offer your soul doctrines of wisdom
and morality, even beyond its power of comprehension.—Bachya, *l. c.,* VIII, p. 391.

3: By no means would it be for the welfare of
the world for all men to withdraw from it, for that
would lead to the breaking up of civilization and to
the cessation of propagation, whereas it is written
in Isaiah (xlv. 18), "He created it not a waste, He
formed it to be inhabited."—Bachya, *ibid.,* IX, p.
409.

4: The divine law imposes no asceticism on us.
It rather desires that we should keep all in equipoise,
granting every mental and physical faculty its due,
i. e., as much as it can bear, without overburdening
another faculty at its expense. . . . Our law, as a
whole, is divided between *fear, love, and joy,* each
of which provides a way of approach to God.   Thy
contrition on a fast day does no more [to bring thee]
nearer to God than thy joy, if it is the outcome of a

devout heart on the Sabbath and holy days. . . .
Thou thankest Him in mind and word, and if thy
joy lead thee so far as to sing and dance, it becomes
worship and a bond of union between thee and the
Divine Influence.—Yehudah ha-Levi, *Kuzari*, II, 50
(Hirschfeld, *l. c.*). (With addition by Tr.)

5: According to our view a servant of God is
not a person who detaches himself from the world,
lest he be a burden to it, and it to him; or who hates
life, which is one of the bounties which God grants
to him. . . . On the contrary, he loves the world
and a long life, because it affords him opportunities
of better deserving the world to come. The more
good he does the larger will his claim be to the next
world. Yehudah ha-Levi, *l. c.*, III, 1 (Hirschfeld,
l. c.). (Revised by Tr.)

6: Someone might say: Since after all envy,
covetousness, ambition, and the like, are bad qualities, I am going to turn away from them more and
more and direct my steps towards the other extreme:
I will eat no meat, drink no wine, remain unmarried,
and not dwell in a good house, or wear good clothes.
That also is a method of bad conduct, which is forbidden. Scripture calls him who treads this path a
sinner. It is for that reason that our sages teach that
only those enjoyments shall a man deny himself
which our Torah forbids, but that he shall not
through vows and oaths forbid himself what is permitted. Thus our sages have also said: Is it not
enough discipline for you to give up what the Torah
forbids, that you deny yourself yet other things?
Accordingly, they who are always chastising them-

selves are not on the right way.   Maimonides, *Mish-neh Torah Hilchot Deot,* III, 1.

7: When the ignorant observed saintly men act-ing thus, not knowing their motives, they consid-ered their deeds of themselves virtuous, and so, blindly imitating their actions, thought thereby to become like them.   They chastised their bodies with all kinds of afflictions, imagining thus to acquire perfection and moral worth, and by this means to approach nearer to God, as if He hated the human body, and desired its destruction.   It never dawned upon them that these actions instead were bad, and resulted in moral imperfection of soul.—Maimonides, *Shemonah Pera-kim* (The Eight Chapters on Ethics), IV (Gor-finkle, *l. c.*).   (Revised by Tr.)

8: The real duty of man is, that in the adoption of whatever measures he may for his well-being and the preservation of his body in good health, his ob-ject should be to maintain in perfect condition these instruments of the soul, which the limbs of the body really are, so that his soul may not be hampered in its own work of acquiring the moral and mental virtues.—Maimonides, *l. c.,* V (Gorfinkle, *ibid.*). (Revised by Tr.)

9: Thus, just as the body becomes exhausted by hard labor, and then recovers by rest and refresh-ment, so it is necessary for the mind to have the relaxation which it gains by gazing upon pictures and other beautiful objects, that its weariness may be dispelled.—Maimonides, *ibid.,* V (Gorfinkle, *ibid.*).   (Revised by Tr.)

10: Bodily cleanliness leads to the sanctifying of

the soul and protects it from reprehensible opinions and evil designs. The sanctifying of the soul again is productive of an earnest striving to become god-like, according to the word of Scripture, "Sanctify yourselves therefore, and be ye holy; for I am holy, the LORD who sanctify you" (Leviticus xi. 44 and xx. 7-8).—Maimonides, *Mishneh Torah Hilchot Tumat Ochlin* (On Defilement of Food), XVI, 12.

11: Be mindful of cleanliness of body, it is a means of acquiring purity of soul.—Salomo Alami, *Iggeret Musar*.

12: The Divine Law contains certain precepts and directions that are not submitted to the subjective judgment of the individual; thus, for example, philosophical ethics wavers between asceticism and epicureanism, while Judaism takes the middle course. It rejects love of pleasure, but it does not require asceticism. Asceticism is even deemed by it to be unwarrantable.—Joseph Albo, *Ikkarim* (Book of Principles), I, 8.

MODERN JEWISH LITERATURE

VII,   1: Certainly Judaism does not require that the life of its followers be an ascetic one; we rather wish to rejoice in God's glorious nature, and in our own existence, and to gladden others; to enjoy life ourselves and to have others share in our enjoyment; for it is written in the Talmud, "*Atid adam liten din ve-cheshbon al kol ma she-rau ejnav velo achal.*" "One day man will be called to account for abstaining from those enjoyments which he saw were allowed and obtainable" (Talmud *Yerushalmi Kiddu-shin,* end of fourth section). Consequently, we are to make use of the gifts of the merciful Creator; how-ever, our enjoyment must be a moderate one, inter-mixed with abstemiousness and self-denial, it must never be regarded as an end, but merely as a means of life. *"Perishut mebia lijde tohorah, tohorah me-bia lijde kedushah."* "Abstinence leads to purity, purity leads to holiness" (Talmud *Abodah Zarah* 20 b).—M. Bloch, *Die Ethik i. d. Halacha,* p. 42.

2: The sentient soul, so Judaism enjoins, must enlist itself in the service of the moral task. There-fore, the attitude of Judaism toward life and the world, and toward civilization is one of joyous af-firmation. It sees in them not something that di-verts us from God, but something that, rightly un-derstood, leads us to God; all labor in the progress of civilization becomes for the Jew not a matter of indifference religiously, but the discharge of a task set by religion, an enterprise of value also for molding the moral character of the individual and of future generations.—M. Dienemann, *Judentum u. Christen-tum,* p. 22.

3: It [Judaism] has not thought of this earth as a vale of tears, nor pictured the reward to come be-yond the grave in brilliant colors. It has never com-manded us to despise this earth as something vain and sinful. It has never demanded that all joy in life on earth should be crushed, because our stay here is but a time of probation. Judaism does not know such morbid sentimentality.—Abraham Geiger, *Das*

Judentum u. s. Geschichte, I, p. 96 (Newburgh, *l. c.*, p. 110).   (Revised by Tr.)

4: Fleeing off by itself out of the world would really have been the natural step for Judaism to take in view of its suffering and heavy trials; hermit-like brooding ought to have made its appearance, and yet such courses of conduct were never recognized as worthy action.   On the contrary, isolation from society was reproved, labor for humanity, recognition of the goodness of God in nature and in the human world were at all times recognized and praised as the innermost kernel, the foundation of all moral will and endeavor.—Abraham Geiger, *l. c.*, II, p. 20 (Newburgh, *ibid.*, p. 229).   (Revised by Tr.)

5: The joy, however, which devotional preparations, performances, and practices give serves to prevent the broodings, scruples, and spirit of melancholy, which easily arise where the religious need cannot find discharge in regular devotional usages and abstinences.   Otherwise, that need will go like an unregulated river courses its own destructive ways and lose contact with wholesome life; fanaticism and mysticism will gain the upper hand and seen through their veil earthly existence will appear to the dimmed eye as a vale of tears from which flight alone can rescue one.   Everywhere sin and its advocate, the devil, stare such an one in the face, they spread their gloomy shadows even over the spell of married life, and in the constant struggle with them man resorts to self-tormenting practices which are intended to mortify the flesh and suppress in him every desire for indulgence.—M. Güdemann, *Das Judentum i. s. Grundzügen*, pp. 83-84.

6: But in what does holiness consist according to the teaching of Judaism? Must we, in order to approach this ideal, forcibly suppress every impulse of our physical nature? Must man, in order not to fail in his moral task, subdue all the earthly inclinations and instincts of his heart, and avoid as far as possible every contact with the outer world as imperiling the purity of his soul? That doctrine which originated with Paul is contrary to the idea of unity held by Judaism, for it places a chasm between nature and morality that cannot be spanned, and conceives of matter as the absolute opposite of mind. Perceiving in the flesh the starting point and occasion of sin, it demands as a postulate of religion the mortification of the flesh, a hostile and non-participating attitude toward the world, the renunciation of every pleasure of life. . . . For Judaism nature and morality are both included within an ideal unity, and this has always kept it safe from such exaggerations.— J. Guttmann, *Die Idee der Versöhnung im Judentum* (*"Vom Judentum,"* Heft Nr. 2), pp. 10-11.

7: Everywhere, *fasting in itself* is regarded as of no value, as in itself not meritorious at all. It has value only if a person really employs it as a means of improvement and emerges from its use the purer and the stronger for the victory over the animal [nature].—Otherwise, apart from what is prescribed, and unless suffering and struggle with sin call for it, fasting itself is a sin. For even the strength of your body is not yours to weaken arbitrarily: you are to use it for the good of your community and your-self.—S. R. Hirsch. *Choreb,* c. 33, §244.

8: And as for the Law, is it really a preventive of all the joys of life, a hindrance and an obstacle to the gratification of the natural human craving for pleasure? Examine the precepts and ordinances of the Law from beginning to end and tell me what legitimate desire it forbids man to gratify, what natural impulse it would destroy or extirpate?

On the contrary, it purifies and sanctifies even our lower impulses and desires by allowing us to apply them with wise limitation to the purposes designated by the Creator.

Righteousness is the Law's typical end and aim, the gratification of physical lust and passion is never its object. Therefore are the lower cravings to be subordinated to a higher law and limited as designed by the Creator's wisdom for His infinitely wise purposes; but as means to proper and necessary ends, the Law recognizes these desires to be perfectly moral, pure, and human, and that carrying them out is as just and as legitimate as the fulfillment of any other human task or mission.

What the Law, however, firmly and unyieldingly opposes is the deification of wealth and lust as the sole aim and controlling impulses of our lives. It not only permits their pursuit within the limits set by Divine wisdom, but declares the effort to gain the ends proper to these means a duty as sacred and binding as any other human obligation, and it condemns purposeless and unreasonable abstinence from permitted indulgences as sin (*Taanit* 11 and 22).—S.

R. Hirsch, *The Nineteen Letters of Ben Uziel*, XV,
p. 68 (Drachman, *l. c.*, pp. 138-139). (Revised
by Tr.)

9: But your God desires you to be not only
peaceful and secure, He called you to *Ssimchah*, to
joy, pure, human, and serene. He does not cause
the flowers to exhale fragrance and the fruits to ripen
in vain, *lo tohu beraah*—He did not create the earth
to be a waste, a vale of tears and of misery, but a
serene, joyful place of abode for happy and cheerful
beings, where everyone should enjoy his existence and
rejoice in his contacts and labors.—S. R. Hirsch, *Ges.
Schriften* I, p. 10-11.

10: Not pain and not sorrow, not chastisement
and not pining are the culmination of Judaism;
cheerfulness, gladsomeness, and joy are its holiest
ends. "Not in idleness and not in pain and dejec-
tion," nor in levity, does the Jewish spirit find its
abode; only where discreet joy dwells, it dwells also.
Levity flees before the earnestness of the Jewish Law,
but the Divine truth of the same Law dispels pain
and grief and teaches us to live a cheerful and happy
life upon earth.—S. R. Hirsch, *l. c.*, pp. 34-35.

11: But Judaism brings something still higher.
The unforbidden pleasures of the senses and of accomplishment by labor are not only admitted, allowed, approved, but even pleasure and work become
"Mitzvah"; even pleasure and labor become holy ac-
tivities, serving God, when stripped of all self-seeking.
The Jew is not only *permitted* to enjoy pleasure and
work, but it is his *duty* to do so.—S. R. Hirsch, *ibid.*,
p. 475.

12: But the same religion that restricts all its joys within the bounds of purity, morality, and human dignity, also teaches the positive value of every pure, moral joy. The apathetic, pining human being who is consumed with grief is not its ideal, but the cheerful, serene human being who works in God with gladness and also enjoys in God with gladness.—S. R. Hirsch, *ibid.*, p. 476.

13: Judaism makes man find God in the act of finding himself. Air and life, strength, freedom, and joy are God's heralds that escort man to Him. He builds his sanctuaries upon the luminous heights of life. Death and putrefaction find no place of lodgment in the rooms of His temple. Pain and sorrow must be cast off on arrival at its threshold. Its halls open at the knock of wakeful, active life. With the night that beckons the active man to rest, its portals likewise close.—S. R. Hirsch, *ibid.*, III, p. 294.

14: It was Judaism that first divined the truth that joy is a way to inner freedom and through this perception came the profound myth of the *Neshamah yetherah,* of the favored soul that descends to us on the Sabbath, fills our inner being with high spiritual joy and elevates us above all everyday miseries and above every earthly sorrow.—Wilhelm Jerusalem, *Der Kulturwert des Judentums* ("*Der Jude,*" 1917, Nr. 7), p. 483.

15: To be sure, passages in our Holy Scriptures not infrequently give touching expression to the fleeting nature of all things earthly and to man's weakness and misery; still the fundamental tendency of the Mosaic legislation, present also in the moral precepts in the Talmud and in the philosophy of religion, after all is directed toward preserving, lengthening, and perfecting life on earth. "Therefore choose life, that thou mayest live, thou and thy seed" (Deuteronomy xxx. 19).—Wilhelm Jerusalem, *l. c.,* p. 486.

16: In everything that anyone partakes of, he shall offer in prayer a suitable blessing. This will make eating more acceptable than fasting. Nevertheless, I do not desire to interdict fasting categorically, as I am not yet clear on that point. On the other hand, at certain times one should take what measures are requisite to reinvigorate all his limbs and senses and particularly the sense of sight, in order to be enabled to serve God in a whole and sound state. Even the penitent shall not inflict upon himself excessive chastisement. But it is good to control the appetites by means of small abstinences.—R. Jona (Land-Sofer), *Testament* [in *Derech Tobim* (The Way of the Good)].

17: *Jewish ethics was not bent upon extirpating the natural instincts of the human being: on the contrary, it aimed from the very beginning at guiding these instincts so that they should minister to the preservation of life and the promotion of civilization.*— Max Joseph, *Zur Sittenlehre des Judentums,* p. 16.

18: Never has the prevailing spirit in Judaism seen anything especially meritorious in resolving upon self-imposed poverty on principle.—Max Joseph, *l. c.,* p. 52.

19: Judaism does not consider the soul, the exclusive seat of the divine as opposed to the body. In fact, Judaism admits no complete dualism of spirit and matter, however striking some aspects of their contrast may be. The whole human personality is divine, just in so far as it asserts its freedom and molds its motives toward a divine end. In recognition of this fact Hillel claimed reverence for the human body as well as the mind, comparing it to the homage rendered to the statue of a king, for man is made in the image of God, the King of all the world (*Lev. R.* XXXIV, 3).—Kaufmann Kohler, *Jewish Theology,* pp. 208-209.

20: Because Judaism sees the attainment of human perfection only when the divine in man has reached complete development through the unimpeded activity of all his spiritual, moral, and social forces, it insists upon the full recognition of all branches of human society as instruments of man's elevation, either individually or collectively. It deprecates the idea that any force or faculty of human life be regarded as unholy and therefore be suppressed. It thus rejects on principle monastic renunciation and isolation, pointing to the Scriptural verse, "He who formed the earth created it not a waste; He formed it to be inhabited" (Isaiah xlv. 18).—Kaufmann Kohler, *l. c.,* p. 316.

21: Neither does Judaism begrudge man the joy of life which is the fruit of industry, nor rob it of its moral value. On the contrary, that ascetic spirit which encourages self-mortification and rigid renunciation of all pleasure is declared sinful (*Taan.* 11a). Instead, we are told that in the world to come man shall have to give account for every enjoyment of-

fered him in this life, whether he used it gratefully
or rejected it in ingratitude (*Yer. Kid.* IV, at the
close). Abstinence is declared to be praiseworthy
only in curbing wild desires and passions. For the
rest, true piety lies in the consecration of every gift
of God, every pleasure of life which He has offered,
and using it in His service, so that the seal of holiness
shall be imprinted even upon the satisfaction of the
most sensuous desires.—Kaufmann Kohler, *ibid.*,
p. 318.

22: In the Jewish view nature is by no manner
of means regarded as unholy. Every discussion, in
fact, pushes into the foreground the idea that nature is God's creation, "His handiwork." This in
itself is sufficient to indicate that as nature is not to
be deified, so also she is not to be considered godless,
god-forsaken, or arrayed against the divine.—M.
Lazarus, *Die Ethik des Judentums,* I, p. 245 (Szold,
l. c., Part Two, pp. 79-80).

23: That nature, the universe as a whole, or
matter in particular, is unconditionally opposed to
the ideal, that it is naught, worthy of annihilation
and contemptible in itself—of this Judaism has not
a word to say.—M. Lazarus, *l. c.*, pp. 245-246
(Szold, *ibid.*, II, pp. 80-81).

24: In a word, the fundamental view held by
the Jewish religion and by Jewish ethics as well is:
predominance of the spiritual, though without scorn
of the corporeal, coupled as well with effort to purge
the natural, the material, protect it from harm, and
to exalt and consecrate it by allying it with the spir-

itual.—M. Lazarus, *ibid.*, p. 274 (Szold, *ibid.*, II, pp. 121-122).   (Revised by Tr.)

25: Fun-making, diversions, dancing, and jollity of all sorts have room made for them in the economy of Jewish life, which is in no sense hostile to merriment.   The Rabbis, in fact, dignify the social pleasures with a moral sanction, preferably, however, when they are associated with the performance of some ideal task, as, for instance, the celebration of a marriage or a religious and patriotic festival.—M. Lazarus, *ibid.*, p. 284 (Szold, *ibid.*, II, pp. 136-137).   (Revised by Tr.)

26: The Jewish view of life, then, so far from despising or casting aside material possessions for moral or metaphysical or religious reasons, requisitions them for the service of morality.   Physical health and vigor, the ability to enjoy, and the capacity for work cheerfully exercised, constitute the elements of the natural organism in which the soul of morality acts and rules as the guiding force.—M. Lazarus, *ibid.*, p. 288 (Szold, *ibid.*, II, p. 143).

27: It is not enough for foolish men among non-Jews to avoid earthly pleasures that can be dispensed with.   They go on to deny themselves also the needful ones and to torture their bodies by flagellations and strange manipulations, which are not at all pleasing in the sight of God.   Precisely the contrary is taught us by our sages: A man must not torment himself at all (*Taanit* 22 b).—Moses Chayim Luzzatto, *Mesillat Yesharim,* c. 13.

28: The prophet always feels that he ought to be the advocate of the poor; not, however, because their poverty is the means of winning God's favor, but because they alone need a champion. The rich are up-braided, not for their wealth, but for the unfair manner in which many of them have acquired it. We hear harsh words spoken against the luxury and the squandering that occur among the well-to-do. But this censure is never born of the wrathfulness of the obscurantist living in seclusion, to whom riches and joy of life mean sin, but its source is the indignation felt over the dissipation of values, the thoughtful and just utilization of which would alleviate many and many a distress. Nowhere is a trace disclosed of that disdainful judgment of "temporal goods" loudly proclaimed where "this life" is looked upon more or less as a preparation for a future one, which alone has value.—Max Wiener, *Die Religion d. Propheten*, pp. 75-76.

See also:

MAX DIENEMANN, *Judentum u. Christentum*, 1914, p. 20.

ABRAHAM GEIGER, *Das Judentum u. s. Geschichte*, I, 1865 pp. 96, 155; II, 1865, pp. 20, 23.

GUTTMANN, *Die Idee der Versöhnung im Judentum*, 1909, pp. 10ff. (Heft: "Vom Judentum," Nr. 2, issued by the Verband der Deutschen Juden).

S. R. HIRSCH, *Choreb*, 1837, c. 9, §67; c. 62, §428, §429; c. 69, §466.

——— *Neunzehn Briefe*, 1836, XIV, p. 65; XV, p. 68.

——— *Gesammelte Schriften*, I, 1902, pp. 4, 32, 50, 54f., 106, 472f., 476f.; II, 1904, p. 36; III, 1906, pp. 33f., 38, 283, 358f., 453; IV, 1908, p. 410.

MAX JOSEPH, *Zur Sittenlehre des Judentums*, 1902, pp. 16, 19.

KAUFMANN KOHLER, *Grundrisz einer syst. Theologie d. Judentums*, 1910, pp. 14, 60, 99f., 239.

M. LAZARUS, *Die Ethik d. Judentums*, I, 1899, pp. 244, 249, 273, 281f.; II, 1911, pp. 135, 145.

RUDOLF LESZYNSKY, *Pharisäer und Sadduzäer*, 1912, p. 60.

M. SACKHEIM, *Sittlichkeits—und Mäszigkeitslehren im Judentum* (*Gemeindeblatt der Jüd. Gem. z. Berlin, Nr. 1, 1916*).

MAX WIENER, *Die Anschauungen d. Propheten v. d. Sittlichkeit*, 1909, p. 159.

———— *Die Religion d. Propheten*, 1912, p. 69.

CHRISTIAN AUTHORS

VIII,   1: Any leaning whatsoever toward asceticism is just as foreign to all the prophets as it is to the Law.   The aim of Old Testament piety is "life," to which concept belongs, according to the Hebrew view, not only long duration but also full unfoldment of all our human powers in the free handling of earthly goods.—Wolf Wilhelm Graf Baudissin, *Die alttest. Religion u. d. Armen*, p. 209.

2: However, we wish to lay stress upon the fact that in spite of all undervaluation of woman and in spite of the strong dread, intensified by the opposition to Hellenism, of sexual impurity and pollution, an *ascetic* frame of mind *properly speaking* had *never taken root* in Judaism.   Here and there, perhaps, isolated traces of such a tendency may be found, but on the whole Judaism kept its distance from this devious path and clung throughout to the divinely willed purpose of marriage.   Assuredly, Paul's leaning towards asceticism (I Corinthians vii.) cannot be explained by his rabbinical past.—Wilhelm Bousset, *Die Religion d. Judentums*, p. 493.

3: The Jewish religion was unacquainted even

with the false asceticism that characterized the majority of the old religions, consisting of doing violence to the individual life of the human being. In order to express their submission to God, the Jews fasted in times of misfortune and in case of death in the family, or on days of public misdeeds, as they entreated God for forgiveness. The Law prescribed only a single strict fast, on the Day of Atonement. . . .—(Bishop) Chrysanth, *Die Religionen d. alten Welt in ihrer Beziehung z. Christentum,* III, p. 279.

4: As at other points there appears also here [in the Proverbs of Solomon] in the Old Testament, a more friendly positive valuation of earthly goods— a conception which was restored in Christendom only by the sound sense of the reformers (see Augsburg Confession, article 16).—Karl Kautzsch, *Die Philosophie des Alten Testaments,* pp. 18-19.

5: On the other hand, the propensity to asceticism that is likely to be yoked with such conception of sin is foreign to Pharisaic Judaism. *Nowhere,* for example, in strictly Pharisaic writings is abstinence from marriage *recommended* as a manifestation of godliness. On the contrary, marriage is a duty to be performed for the sake of the Law and, may we add, for the sake of preserving the nation (compare *b. Yeb.* 63 b., *Ket.* 61 b). To be sure, there was much fasting among the Pharisees, and a boast was made of it (see Luke xviii. 12; Matthew vi. 16-18; ix. 14). It was not, however, done in the interest of an ascetic striving for perfection but as an expression of a penitential state of mind, or it was used for heightening zeal for prayer (see Chapter XXXII, 4). And even fasting on the Day of Atonement might be broken in certain extreme cases of necessity (compare *Mishnah Yom*. 8, 4ff.). It was forbidden to fast on the Sabbath; even he who uses the day to fast as a penitent obtains less benefit than he who spends the day joyfully (Yose ben Simra, Bacher, *Pal. Amor*. I, 111). Many utterances of the Rabbins show that the representatives of the official religion rejected every pronounced form of asceticism (see Bacher, *Tann*. I, 158—Yosua ben Chananja; *Tann*. II, 161—Yose ben Chalafta; *Bab. Amor*., p. 26; *Pal. Amor*. I, 364—Simeon ben Lakish, etc.; *Erub*. 54a; see also Geiger, *Das Judentum und seine Geschichte*, II, p. 20; M. Lazarus, *Die Ethik des Judentums*, §246f).—Justus Köberle, *Sünde und Gnade*, p. 518.

6: This repudiation of asceticism is by no manner of means to be explained as due to opposition to several ascetic secret sects, such as the Essenes, that arose at that time, nor, in later times, to opposition to Christianity. It is indeed most intimately connected with the whole Jewish idea concerning the relation of natural to moral life. The sound, sober, cool-headed tendency of the Jewish official religion, so averse to everything excessive, unbounded, extravagant, unnatural, mystically obscure, makes itself felt here also. The Pharisees and the Rabbins were not interested in speculating about evil as a cosmic force. Any and every confusion of moral evil and natural evil was uncongenial to them. Just as Satanology and demonology play but a slight rôle in the official

Rabbinical writings, so were the Rabbins likewise averse to all speculation about the ethical inferiority of what is material in man and in nature, and they rejected the corresponding ascetic consequences.—Justus Köberle, *l. c.*, pp. 518-519.

7: Above all, however, the formation of an ascetic mode of life as a custom was made impossible by the position taken with regard to the Law as the definitive ideal and the ultimate norm of religion. Whoever followed the trend of the time in this respect notwithstanding the ban thus put on it, strayed in so doing from genuine Judaism.—Justus Köberle, *ibid.*, p. 519.

8: In the fifth place, it must be remarked that at the Old Testament stage of the biblical religion, the fulfillment of *esthetic* duties also belongs to those classes of acts that are pleasing in the sight of God. This is shown for instance in the provision made for the cleansing of the person and the washing of the garments worn by the participants in a religious act, more especially in the act of the giving of the Law. —Eduard König, *Gesch. d. alttest. Religion*, p. 227.

9: The possession of *earthly goods* is expressly promised to the citizens of the kingdom of God (Genesis xii. b; xiii. 2, etc.), consequently their enjoyment is also permitted; the cultivation of the soil and the *subjugation of the gifts and forces of nature* are recommended (Genesis i. 28, "subdue the earth"); the virtue of diligence also is praised in industry and commerce (Proverbs xxxi. 15, 24f.) and slothfulness lashed with biting irony (xix. 24; xxii. 13; etc.), in an energetic protest against other phases of

Oriental sluggishness. Citizenship in the kingdom of God does not even require renunciation of the customary adornments of the person in social intercourse nor of ornament in general. This is plain, for example, from Abraham's bridal gift to Rebekah (Genesis xxiv. 22ff.), from Joseph's coat of many colors (xxxvii. 3b. as only in case of a princess: Second Samuel xiii. 18), and from Judah's signet-ring (Genesis xxxviii. 18). Such things also indicate a certain regard for the *arts;* indeed it may safely be assumed that the cultivation of the art of poetry and antiphonal song, of dancing and music was encouraged even in the oldest periods (Exodus xv. 1, 20f.). It follows, therefore, in spite of recent statements to the contrary that the negation of human civilization, the abstinence from rational, that is to say, moderate enjoyment of goods and pleasures was *not* included among the principles of the kingdom of God.— Eduard König, *Geschichte d. Reiches Gottes,* pp. 71-72.

10: And the problem is precisely the same in the case of the annual festivals. In the course of time, indeed, all of these assumed in Israel the character of historical memorial festivals of which the keynote, after Deuteronomy, was to be joy, a dignified, pure, chaste joy.—Ernst Sellin, *Die alttest. Religion,* pp. 14-15.

11: And still the prophets, notwithstanding their hard task as educators of a luxurious age debased by inebriety, are no pessimists, no gloomy reformers averse to all joy; on the contrary, the heart of the prophet also yearns for glad festive seasons (for instance, Isaiah, chapter xxxv) ; though, of course, these lay in the somewhat remote distance.—F. Walter, *Die Propheten in ihrem soz. Beruf u. d. Wirtschafts-leben ihrer Zeit,* p. 127.

12: The prophets are not opponents of a human existence that is embellished by art and cheerfulness. They do not begrudge their people glad enjoyment of life and they themselves frequently include mirth-ful features in their picture of the future: dance and joyous exultation, harvest festivals with merry round-elays. However, it is modest, rural joys to which they refer, even in their picture of the future.—F. Walter, *l. c.,* p. 228.

13: The prophets know no hostile dualism be-tween the temporal and the eternal, rather they aspire to a balance between the two, a reconciliation of the ethical-religious sphere with that devoted to the ac-quisition and enjoyment of the good things of life. Their attitude towards the latter, as our account has demonstrated, is anything but harsh and unfriendly. After all, it is one and the same human being that must take an active part in the two spheres of life.— F. Walter, *ibid.,* p. 72.

14: For that reason, temperance and moderation, the cleanliness of the body, of one's garments and dwelling, the development of the muscles by exer-cise, work, and also regulated recreation, are com-manded first and foremost. We may remark that it was precisely the Israelitish people of antiquity who excelled all others of their time in minute regulations concerning the care of personal and public health. Again, their observance was a matter of course, since they possessed the value of Divine ordinances because they were contained in the Law, particularly in Leviticus.—J. Weigl, *Das Judentum*, p. 85.

15: Joy in honestly acquired earthly goods, which are declared in Holy Writ to be a sign of God's blessing, is something that is permissible.   Judaism is a religion that affirms life joyously and gives its assent to every *regulated* enjoyment of the good things of this life.—J. Weigl, *l. c.*, p. 86.

16: Rational enjoyment of life is looked upon as freely permitted.   The conventional observances are not instances of asceticism in the sense of our common use of the word.   It is only fasting connected with vigil and prayer that may be looked upon as ascetic.—Julius Wellhausen, *Israelitische u. jüdische Geschichte*, p. 212.

17: For "the heinous conception that wedded life is less consecrated to God than the unmarried state is absolutely foreign to the Old Testament, and a product of a debased philosophy and asceticism."—Fritz Wilke, *Das Frauenideal u. d. Schätzung d. Weibes i. A. T.*, p. 54.

See also:

WOLF WILHELM GRAF BAUDISSIN, *Die altestamentliche Religion u. d. Armen* (Preussische Jahrbücher, Nr. 149, 1912), p. 209.

HEINRICH EWALD, *Geschichte des Volkes Israel*, I, 1864, p. 117f.; II, 1865, pp. 187, 357, 444.

FRANCKH, *Die Prophetie i. d. Zeit vor Amos* (Beiträge z. Förderung christl. Theologie, 1905, 9. Jahrg., Heft 1), p. 71.

JUSTUS KÖBERLE, *Sünde und Gnade*, 1905, pp. 450f., 518f., 563, 620.

EDUARD KÖNIG, *Geschichte der alttestamentlichen Religion,*
    1912, p. 104.
——— *Geschichte des Reiches Gottes,* 1908, pp. 68, 71, 138ff.,
    146, 215, 218f.
ERNST SELLIN, *Die alttestamentliche Religion,* 1908, p. 14f.
FRANZ WALTER, *Die Propheten in ihrem sozialen Beruf u. d.
    Wirtschaftsleben ihrer Zeit,* 1900, pp. 127, 239, 273.

2. TEMPERANCE

BIBLE

I,   1 : Woe unto them that rise up early in the
morning, that they may follow strong drink; that
tarry late into the night, till wine inflame them!   And
the harp and the psaltery, the tabret and the pipe,
and wine, are in their feasts; but they regard not
the work of the LORD, neither have they considered the operation of His hands.—Isaiah v. 11-12.

2 : Harlotry, wine, and new wine take away the
heart.—Hosea iv. 11.

3 : Wine is a mocker, strong drink is riotous; and
whosoever reeleth thereby is not wise.—Proverbs
xx. 1.

4 : He that loveth pleasure shall be a poor man;
he that loveth wine and oil shall not be rich.—
Proverbs xxi. 17.

5 : Be not among winebibbers; among glutton-
ous eaters of flesh; for the drunkard and the glutton
shall come to poverty; and drowsiness shall clothe
a man with rags.—Proverbs xxiii. 20-21.

6 : Who crieth; "Woe"? who "Alas"? who hath
contentions? who hath raving? who hath wounds
without cause? who hath redness of eyes?   They
that tarry long at the wine; they that go to try mixed

wine. Look not thou upon the wine when it is red, when it giveth its color in the cup, when it glideth down smoothly; at the last it biteth like a serpent, and stingeth like a basilisk. Thine eyes shall behold strange things, and thy heart shall utter confused things. Yea, thou shalt be as he that lieth down in the midst of the sea, or as he that lieth upon the top of a mast. "They have struck me, and I felt it not, they have beaten me, and I knew it not; when shall I awake? I will seek it yet again."—Proverbs xxiii. 29-35.

PALESTINIAN APOCRYPHA

IIa,   1: A workman that is given to drunkenness will never become rich; and he that contemneth small things will fall by little and little. Wine and women will make one wanton.—*Ben-Sira* xix. 1-2.

2: O LORD, Father and God of my life, give me not covetous eyes and keep concupiscence far away from me; let not the greediness of the belly nor lust of the flesh take hold of me; and give not over me Thy servant to an impudent mind.—*Ben-Sira* xxiii. 4-6.

3: Show not thy spiritedness in the use of much wine; for wine hath been the ruin of many.—*Ben-Sira* xxxiv. (=xxxi) 25.

4: And now, my children, I say unto you, be not drunk with wine; for wine turneth the mind away from the truth, and inspireth the passion of lust, and leadeth the eyes into error.—*The Testaments of the Twelve Patriarchs*, IV, 14, 1-2 (Charles, in Charles, *l. c.*, II).

5: For much discretion needeth the man who drinketh wine, my children; and herein is discretion in drinking wine, a man may drink so long as he preserveth modesty. But if he go beyond this limit the spirit of deceit attacketh his mind, and it maketh the drunkard to talk filthily, and to transgress and not to be ashamed, but even to glory in his shame, and to account himself honorable.—*Ibid.*, IV, 14, 7-8 (Charles, *ibid.*).

6: If ye drink wine in gladness, be ye modest in the fear of God. For if in [your] gladness the fear of God departeth, then drunkenness ariseth and shamelessness stealeth in.—*Ibid.*, IV, 16, 2 (Charles, *ibid.*).

JEWISH-HELLENISTIC LITERATURE

III,   1: What is it that is most beneficial to health? . . . Temperance . . .—*The Letter of Aristeas*, 237 (Andrews, in Charles, *l. c.*, III).

2: Sumptuous nourishment excites to wanton debauchery.—Pseudo-Phokylides, *Nuthetikon*, 55.

3: Keep within the right bounds in eating and drinking and speaking: Moderation in all things is the best, to overstep it—reprehensible.—Pseudo-Phokylides, *l. c.*, 63-64.

TALMUDICAL LITERATURE

V,   1: Ye shall be holy, temperate, and chaste, and approach God in this condition to consecrate yourselves to Him.—*Sifra* to Leviticus xix. 2.

2: The Torah teaches a mode of living wherein the human being shall not eat too much meat, but

only as much as he needs for the preservation of life.—
Chullin 84a.

3: Abstinence leads to purity, and purity . . .
to holiness.—*Abodah Zarah* 20 b.

4: Wine penetrates into every limb, the body becomes weak and the mind unsteady. . . . Where
the taking of wine gets the upper hand, reason
ceases.—*Bamidbar Rabbah*, c. 10.

5: Be not intoxicated, and thou wilt not sin.—
Berachot 29b (Cohen, *l. c.*, p. 196).

6: Where wine is, there is stumbling.—*Tanchuma*, section *Noah*.

7: A woman may drink one glass, with the second she already loses all dignity.—*Ketubot* 68 a.

8: Wine, taken moderately—is good, taken im-
moderately—bad.—*Tanna Debe Elijahu*, c. 7.

MIDDLE AGES

VI,   1: Our teachers say: If one has drunk a quarter (of a measure), he shall make no decisions; if
one has drunk a quarter (of a measure), he shall
not pray.—Bachya ibn Pakuda, *Chobot ha-Lebabot*
(Duties of the Heart), IX, p. 429.

2: The pious man is a ruler who exacts obedience from his senses, and from his mental as well as his
physical faculties, which he governs in accordance
with nature, as it is written: "He that ruleth his spirit
is better than he that taketh a city" (Proverbs xvi.
32) . . . He subdues his passions, keeping them in
bounds, but giving them sufficient latitude to satisfy

them as regards food, drink, cleanliness, etc.—Yehudah ha-Levi, *Kuzari*, III, 5 (Hirschfeld, *l. c.*). (Revised by Tr.)

3: The perfect Law which leads us to perfection recommends none of these things (such as self-torture, flight from society, etc.). On the contrary, it aims at the path of moderation for man in accordance with the dictates of nature, a life of eating, drinking, enjoying legitimate connubial joys, all in moderation, and living among people in honesty and uprightness, but not dwelling in the wilderness or in the mountains, or clothing oneself in garments of hair and wool, or afflicting the body.—Maimonides, *Shemonah Perakim* (The Eight Chapters on Ethics) IV (Gorfinkle, *l. c.*).

4: The words of our prophets and of the sages of our Law make it clear that they were bent upon moderation and the care of their souls and bodies, in accordance with what the Law prescribes.—Maimonides, *l. c.*, IV (Gorfinkle, *l. c.*). (Revised by Tr.)

5: Immoderate drinking of wine brings poverty, disgrace, discord; leads to slander, lewdness, murder; to loss of liberty, of honor, of sense.—From the *Pentateuchal Tosafot*, to Leviticus x. 9 (*Zunz, Zur Gesch. u. Lit.*, p. 145).

6: Accustom not thyself to banquets abroad; beware of inebriety, and thou wilt not have to regret base conduct and unseemly speech.—R. Asher b. Yechiel, from his *Testament* (Zunz, *l. c.*, pp. 148-149).

Modern Jewish Literature

VII,   1: The Jews have held their ground under the most difficult circumstances and the bodily and mental constitution which they preserved enabled them at the beginning of the modern period to participate at once in all cultural endeavors . . . Perhaps the most essential of the causes responsible for this survival is their standard of life, which put conduct in every particular under the control of religion. In this connection, account must be taken of the great significance that undeniably attaches to its numerous precepts for moderation and limitation of the material pleasures of life, in dietary and hygienic matters as well as in regard to education.—M. Güdemann, *Das Judentum in s. Grundzügen*, p. 82.

2: Young men, the call of the Torah is directed first of all to you: Do not play fast and loose with your health, your strength, your life! Avoid passion, avoid lust, avoid levity, avoid foolhardiness! Do not squander in the vestibule of life the powers that you will later miss in life's serious prime.—S. R. Hirsch, *Choreb*, c. 62, 429.

3: Yet, on the other hand, the great dangers connected with the boundless endeavor for increase of possession have never been misunderstood. In the Bible, wealth often appears as one of the principal sources of an enervating love of pleasure, and of senseless luxury, as a destroyer of public-mindedness and a dissolver of the strength of the people. The prophets very frequently lift up their voices in threats and woes against those of the rich whose

wealth serves them only for a life of luxury, so that
they lose power and heart for the common cause of
their people which is so grievously languishing, under the weakening and demoralizing influence of this
life of luxury.—Max Joseph, *Zur Sittenlehre d. Judentums*, p. 53.

See also:

M. BLOCH, *Die Ethik in d. Halacha*, 1886, p. 42.
S. R. HIRSCH, *Choreb*, 1837, c. 69, §466.
KAUFMANN KOHLER, *Grundrisz einer syst. Theologie d. Ju-
    dentums*, 1910, p. 239.
M. LAZARUS, *Die Ethik d. Judentums*, II, 1911, p. 79.
M. SACKHEIM, *Sittlichkeits—und Mäszigkeitslehren im Juden-
    tum* (*Gemeindeblatt d. jüdischen Gemeinde z. Berlin*, Nr.
    1, 1916).

CHRISTIAN AUTHORS

VIII, 1: In addition to all these various exhortations we come across many others that have in view
the right enjoyment of life.   Here the general rule
is: Enjoy what you possess in comfort, for death
after all will not be long in coming, and then you
will have to leave your wealth to others and a life
of pleasure may no longer be sought in the nether
world (*Ben-Sira* xiv. 11ff.)   As means of such
enjoyment Ben-Sira names wine and music that gladden the heart, beauty and charm that delight the eye
(xl. 20 ff.; xxxiv. [=xxxi] 27; xxxv. [=xxxii]
4f.).   In doing so, however, it is a settled postulate
that one shall sedulously endeavor to be moderate
(Tob. iv. 15; Ben-Sira xxxiv. [=xxxi] 27 f.).—
Ludwig Couard, *Die religiösen u. sittlichen Anschauungen d. alttest. Apokr. u. Pseudepigr.*, pp. 162-163.

2: The war of the prophets against alcoholism is all the more noteworthy, since Holy Writ otherwise does not by any means oppose drinking of wine in moderation. Thus Ecclesiasticus for example says, "Wine, if moderately partaken of, giveth man suitable strength; if thou drinkest it moderately, thou wilt remain sober. What manner of life hath he that shorteneth it through wine? In the beginning, wine was made to make men glad and not for drunkenness. Wine measurably drunk and in season produceth gladness of heart, and cheerfulness of mind. A moderate potion is wholesome for body and soul" (xxxi, xxxii ff.). But the havoc that had been wrought by the immoderate use of wine compelled the prophets to take a stand against alcoholism.— Franz Walter, *Die Propheten in ihrem sozialen Beruf u. d. Wirtschaftsleben ihrer Zeit,* p. 128.

VIII

KNOWLEDGE AND MORALITY

Introduction by Dr. Samson Hochfeld

Judaism teaches that even if knowledge be not the source of morality, it is still a mighty lever at its service. If the ethical impulses originate in the last analysis in feeling, yet are they purified, ennobled, and guided in right pathways through reflection and instruction. Only insight into the purpose and destiny of life protects a man against aberrations of moral feeling; only knowledge of what is possible and attainable prevents the moral energy from exhausting itself in useless acts due to ignorance of some kind of the real conditions of life. In cases of conflict, nothing else but the capacity to weigh and pass judgment on moral issues can ward off the danger of preferring the less important duty to the more urgent one.

The effort to attain to clearness in questions of morality through the use of rational reflection leads, furthermore, to this result: the individual moral actions of the human being arrange themselves into an organic series; the fulfillment of a duty is no longer left to the effervescence of feeling in each special case, but is taken up into a *conscious* striving to fashion one's *whole* life morally. Knowledge makes from the

225

brick of moral deeds a unified life-structure; it brings reconciliation into the discord and contrariness otherwise connected with the occurrence of conflicting dates and situations; it leads up to moral principles, to moral character. The moral character, or the ethical personality, that has become an inner unity is the highest stage of the moral development of the human being. In it, vividness of feeling and firmness of will unite with clearness of knowledge. Far from making the moral deed a cold intellectual product, or debasing it into an act of calculation, Judaism, on the contrary, shows it to be the way of ascent to the very highest peak of true humanity.

BIBLE

I, 1: And these words, which I command thee this day, shall be upon thy heart; thou shalt teach them diligently unto thy children, and shalt talk of them when thou sittest in thy house, and when thou walkest by the way, and when thou liest down, and when thou risest up.—Deuteronomy vi. 6-7.

2: My son, if thou wilt receive my words, and lay up my commandments with thee; so that thou make thine ear attend unto wisdom, and thy heart incline to discernment; yea, if thou call for understanding, and lift up thy voice for discernment; if thou seek her as silver, and search for her as for hid treasures; then shalt thou understand the fear of the LORD, and find the knowledge of God.—Proverbs ii. 1-5.

Palestinian Apocrypha

IIa,   1: Learn where is wisdom, where is strength, where is understanding; that thou mayest know also where is length of days, and happiness of life, where is the light of the eyes, and peace.—*Baruch* III. 14.

Greek Apocrypha

IIb,   1: For to think upon wisdom is perfection of insight, and he that keepeth vigil for her sake shall quickly be free from care. For she goeth about, seeking them that are worthy of her, and in their paths she appeareth unto them graciously, and meeteth them in every thought. For her true beginning is desire of instruction; and the care for instruction is love [of her]; and love [of her] is observance of her laws; and to give heed to [her] laws is the assurance of immortality and immortality bringeth near unto God. —*Wisdom of Solomon* VI. 15-19 (Holmes, in Charles, l.c., I).   (Revised by Tr.)

     2: Now wisdom is manifested under the forms of judgment [insight] and justice, and courage, and temperance. But judgment [insight] *or self-control* is the one that dominates them all, for through it, in truth, Reason asserts its authority over the passions.— *The Fourth Book of Maccabees* I. 18-19 (Townshend, in Charles, *ibid.*, II.   (With addition by Tr.)

Prayers

IV,   1: O put it into our hearts to understand and to discern, to mark, learn and teach, to heed, to do and to fulfil in love all the words of instruction in thy Torah.—Daily Introductory Prayer to the "Shema" (Singer's *Prayerbook*, p. 47).

2: Thou favorest man with knowledge, and teachest mortals understanding. O favor us with knowledge, understanding and discernment from Thee.—Eighteen Benedictions (*Ibid.*, p. 56).

TALMUDICAL LITERATURE

V, 1: An empty-headed man cannot be a sin-fearing man, nor can an ignorant person be pious.—*Ethics of the Fathers*, II. 6 (Singer's *Prayerbook*, p. 274).

2: Where there is no wisdom, there is no fear of God; where there is no fear of God, there is no wisdom.—*Ethics of the Fathers*, III, 21 (*ibid.*, p. 281).

3: Rabbi [the Patriarch, R. Yehudah the First] has said, "I marvel that they [the ancients] have not introduced the prayer for the granting of knowledge (see above, Prayers No. 2) for use on the Sabbath day, for how can a human being pray without knowledge?"—*Yerushalmi Berachot* IV, 3 and *Midrash Samuel* V, 9.

4: No man is free but he who is occupied with the study of Torah.—*Ethics of the Fathers*, VI, 2.

5: "For a day in thy courts is better than a thousand [days elsewhere]." Rabbi Yoshua ben Levi was of the opinion: One day in the study of the Torah is more acceptable to God than a thousand sacrifices.—*Yalkut* to Psalms lxxxiv. 11.

6: Who ranks higher, a prophet or a sage? It

follows from Psalms xc. 12 ["So teach us to number our days, that we may get us a heart of wisdom"] that the sage ranks higher than the prophet.—*Baba Batra* 12 a and *Yalkut, ad loc.*

7: Only poverty in knowledge is true poverty. In the West [in Palestine] they say: Hast thou acquired knowledge, thou hast all; hast thou acquired no knowledge, what hast thou?—*Bamidbar Rabbah,* c. 19.

8: If you employ yourselves with the study of the Torah, you will become master of the evil instincts.—*Kiddushin* 30 a.

9: The study of the Torah ranks higher than the building of the Temple, and the sacrifices.—*Erubin* 63 a and *Megillah* 16 b; cf. *Sanhedrin* 44 b.

10: The Torah only is meant by light.—*Megillah* 15 a.

MIDDLE AGES

VI,   1: He exhorted us to believe and do this, as well as made it known to us that by study and speculation we shall obtain that degree of conviction concerning each and everyone which the prophets have proclaimed to us as faith.—Saadyah, *Emunot ve-Deot* (Teachings of Revelation and Reason), Introd., p. 17.

2: All this confirms what we have asserted, that *tradition,* even though it is necessary, of course, for learners as a beginning, should never remain the sole prop for him who has it in his power to attain pure knowledge by the way of reason.—Bachya ibn Pakuda, *Chobot ha-Lebabot,* Introd., p. 15.

3: Men who are occupied with the study of the holy Torah, these are, so to speak, the men in the image of God. For without God's Torah, the human being is like an animal; he obtains the status of one bearing the image of God only through the knowledge and observance of the Divine Torah.—*Book of the Pious*, § 756.

4: [In the daily prayer] the first place—of the second group of blessings—is very appropriately given to the prayer for the intelligence and enlightenment requisite to obey God. Man prays to be brought near to his Master. He, therefore, says first: "Thou graciously givest reason to man," which is immediately followed by 'He who takes delight in repentance!' Thus 'wisdom,' 'knowledge' and 'intelligence' move in the path of the Law and worship. —Yehudah ha-Levi, *Kuzari*, III, 19 (Hirschfeld, *l.c.*).

5: One loves God only by dint of knowledge, and the degree of love corresponds to the degree of knowledge. On that account, man must be wholly devoted to the work of fathoming all branches of knowledge and obtaining the knowledge through the which he apprehends his Creator so far as in his power lies to conceive of Him.—Maimonides, *Mishneh Torah Hilchot Teshubah* (Return to God), X, 6.

6: If possible, my sons and daughters shall dwell in Jewish communities, so that their children acquaint themselves with Jewish life, and their sons as well as their daughters shall have the opportunity to receive instruction in the Divine Torah, even if they should be compelled to beg in order to be able to educate their children through religious instruction.—Eliezer Halevi, *Testament* (rendered into German by A. Berliner in *Jüdische Presse*, 1870), p. 90.

7: Love the teachers; run after them; strive for knowledge of your Creator; for the mind obtains its value only through knowledge.—R. Eliezer b. Isaac, *Orchot Chayyim* (Ways of Life), after M. Güdemann, *Geschichte d. Erziehungswesens u. d. Kultur d. abendländischen Juden*, I, p. 123.

8: As without fear of God there is no knowledge, so without knowledge there is no fear of God; on the contrary, it is only the fools who despise wisdom and discipline, that is, philosophy and natural sciences.— Immanuel b. Salomo Romi, *Commentary* to Proverbs i. 7.

9: Love of God and fear of God can be guided only by knowledge, and the prophet Isaiah already (xxix. 13) censures perfunctory divine worship given without the understanding heart. Besides, he who does not learn anything at all, cannot truly love God. —Lipman-Mühlhausen, *Nitztzachon* (Disputation), § 124.

10: Let God's commandments be your guides in choosing your ways in life and strive to acquire for yourself bliss in the life eternal. Take up your abode where Torah-study is being carried on; early in the morning hasten to prayer and to hours of occupation with the Torah. Attach yourself to wise men; associate with those who have in their heart reverence for God's commandments; keep aloof, not only from the dwellings of the wicked, but also from those who are only occupied with the study of the Torah and who only do God's commandments in order to boast and to give themselves airs.—Salomo Alami, *Iggeret Musar.*

MODERN JEWISH LITERATURE

VII,   1: And for the same reason it was impossible for the thought ever to arise, particularly with any semblance of religious sanction, that religion contained truths as its most precious treasure which men were forbidden to endeavour to know, which were to be taken only as matters of faith.—Hermann Cohen, "The Significance of Judaism for the Progress of Religion," *l.c.*, pp. 390-391.

2: And just because our houses of worship and our Divine services do not constitute our worship proper of God, but only form part of the paraphernalia of preparation for the worship of God throughout life, Israel's houses of worship are not Israel's holiest places, they are surpassed in holiness indeed by the *Bate Midrashot,* those places that are consecrated to the teaching and learning of the Torah, to the investigation and discernment of the Divine will, in order that life may *be lived* in worshiping God.— S. R. Hirsch, *Gesammelte Schriften,* I, p. 93.

3: Not the sinking into a state of ignorance, the brutalization, the besotting, stupefying, blunting and dulling of the mind and heart, but their illumination, enlightenment, and living development is the outcome awaited by the spirit of the teaching and of the Law which mankind is destined to receive from Israel's hands. Only the illumined mind is able and willing to receive the light of the Jewish teaching, only the

soul exalted to freedom is able and willing to receive
the blissful life of the Jewish Law.—S. R. Hirsch,
l.c., II, p. 42.

4: The center of gravity of Judaism does not lie,
however, in the sacred service; temple and priest, sacrifice and prayer are not the foremost bearers of
Jewish life; Israel's soul dwells in the Torah, in the
science and knowledge of the Divine teaching and of
the Divine Law.—S. R. Hirsch, *ibid.*, IV, p. 132.

5: In Judaism, once it was liberated from the
dominance of the priesthood, religion became *the in-
strument of universal instruction*, the *factor of general
spiritual and moral advancement*. In addition it endowed humanity with an *educational ideal*, destined
to regenerate its moral life far more deeply than Greek
culture could ever do. Its object was to *elevate all
classes of the people* by the living *word of God*, by the
reading and expounding of the *Scripture* for the dissemination of its truth among the masses.—Kaufmann
Kohler, *Jewish Theology*, pp. 354-355.

6: Or in other words: in the study of the Divine
teaching (Talmud-Torah), what matters is not
simply the knowledge but also the investigation, not
simply the *ideal content* alone, but also the *ideal occupation*.—L. Lazarus, *Zur Charakteristik d. talmudischen Ethik*, pp. 19-20.

7: The esteem in which the Rabbis held knowledge was based upon a threefold reason: Knowledge
is considered the highest and purest element of bliss,
an element, too, that can be enjoyed in this world;
moreover, it is the source of refined, unshakable convictions; and finally, it is therefore in itself an im-

portant feature of man's ethical task—the ethical pursuit pre-eminently worthy of man's spirit.—M. Lazarus, *Die Ethik d. Judentums*, I, p. 77 (Szold, *l.c.*, p. 99).

CHRISTIAN AUTHORS

VIII,   1: The Israelitish education offered this advantage over the education current among all heathen peoples, that it rests upon the knowledge of the One purely spiritual God and of His will as the highest law. Over the education current among the Greek people, in which the objective and universal at last sinks and disappears in the pretensions of the subjective caprice of the individual, it has in particular the advantage that the law of its God, in defiance of all variations in external life, remains unimpeachable in purity and holiness and serves as a beacon which sets before the human being, even in times of decadence, the inspiring task of seeing his true destiny in a higher life, one based on obedience to God's holy will.—G. Baur, *Geschichte d. Pädagogik*, p. 638.

2: An *influential new thought* enters into the religion of Israel. *Religion is culture*, religion and virtue are teachable. It is now a question of discipline and of education.—Wilhelm Bousset, *Die Religion d. Judentums*, p. 189.

3: As the Torah was the revelation which God had made to Israel, the study of it and the practical application of it were both associated with the "house of meeting." To study it was to ponder the meaning of the revelation. And to practice it was, among other things, to worship the God who had given it.

The Synagogue was intended to develop through religious fellowship the whole nature of those who met there, spiritual and moral, and by no means only intellectual.—Travers Herford, *Pharisaism, Its Aim and Its Method* (London, New York, 1912), pp. 82-83.

4: In fact, it was the ideal of nomistic Judaism that *every* Israelite should acquire an expert knowledge of the Law. Even though this was not attainable, still as many as possible were to be exalted to this ideal height.—Emil Schürer, *Geschichte d. jüd. Volkes im Zeitalter Jesu*, II, p. 384.

SOURCES

BIBLE
PALESTINIAN APOCRYPHA
> *Proverbs of Ben-Sira* (about 190 B.C.E.).
> *The Book of Enoch* (about 120 B.C.E.),
> *The Testaments of the Twelve Patriarchs* (about 100 B.C.E.).
> *The Psalms of Solomon* (about 45 B.C.E.).
> *Tobit* (about 40 B.C.E.).
> *The Syriac Apocalypse of Baruch* (about 70 C.E.).
> *The Fourth Book of Ezra* (about 85 C.E.).

GREEK APOCRYPHA
> *The Wisdom of Solomon* (about 50 C.E.)

JEWISH-HELLENISTIC LITERATURE
> *The Sibylline Books* (about 140 B.C.E.-80 C.E.).
> *Pseudo-Phokylides* (about 100 B.C.E.). *Nuthetikon.*
> *The Letter of Aristeas* (about 90 B.C.E.).
> PHILO (about 20 B.C.E.—54 C.E.):
>> *De opificio mundi.*
>> *De specialibus legibus,* II, *de septenario; de colendis parentibus.*
>> *De specialibus legibus,* IV, *de judice; de concupiscentia; de justitia.*
>> *De virtutibus, de caritate; de poenitentia; de nobilitate.*
>> *De praemiis et poenis, de execrationibus.*
>> *Fragments.*
> JOSEPHUS (37-about 100 C.E.), *Against Apion.*
>> *The Fourth Book of Maccabees* (falsely ascribed to Josephus).

PRAYERS
> Daily Prayer.
> Prayer for Sabbaths and Festivals.
> Prayer for the Day of Atonement.

TALMUDICAL LITERATURE
> (The dates indicate the time in which the works mentioned were collected and arranged. In most instances,

the origin of the passages cited goes back to a much older
period and occasionally dates back to the third century
B.C.E.).

Older Tannaitic Works (first and second centuries C.E.)
  Mishnah: Ethics of the Fathers, Sotah.
  Mechilta, Sifra, Sifre, Abot de Rabbi Nathan, Tosefta.

TALMUD (Palestinian=Yerushalmi: concluded about 375)
  *Berachot, Peah, Pesachim, Sukkah, Taanit, Kiddushin,
  Nedarim.*

TALMUD (Babylonian: concluded about 500)
  *Berachot, Shabbat, Erubin, Pesachim, Rosh ha-Shanah,
  Yoma, Sukkah, Megillah, Taanit, Ketubot, Kiddushin,
  Sotah, Nedarim, Nazir, Baba Metzia, Baba Batra, San-
  hedrin, Makkot, Abodah Zarah, Chullin, Niddah.*

MINOR TRACTATES:
  Derech Eretz Zuta, Gerim.

MIDRASH (sixth to twelfth centuries)
  *Tanna Debe Elijahu, Bereshit Rabbah, Shemot Rabbah,
  Vayyikra Rabbah, Bamidbar Rabbah, Debarim Rabbah,
  Echah Rabbati, Midrash to the Psalms, Midrash Samuel*
  (ed. Buber, Krakau, 1893), *Midrash Tanchuma, Yalkut Shimoni, Pesikta Chadata* (*Bet ha-Midrash*, ed. Jellinek, III, 1855), *Midrash Le-olam* (*Bet ha-Midrash*,
  ed. Jellinek, VI, 1877), *Otiyyot de Rabbi Akiba.*

MEDIEVAL LITERATURE
  Saadyah Gaon (892-942), *Emunot ve-Deot* (Teachings
  of Revelation and Reason).
  Bachya (about 1000), *Chobot ha-Lebabot* (Duties of the
  Heart) (cited after the edition by Stern, Vienna, 1853).
  Eliezer ben Isaac (about 1050), *Orchot Chayyim* (Ways
  of Life).
  Yehudah ha-Levi (1085-1140), *Kuzari.*
  The Book of the Pious (twelfth century).
  MAIMONIDES (Moses ben Maimon) (1135-1204):
    Commentary to the Mishnah (Introduction to *Sanhe-
    drin*, c. X).
    Shemonah Perakim (Eight Chapters on Ethics).
    MISHNEH TORAH: *Hilchot Deot* (On Ethics); *Hilchot
    Teshubah* (On the Return to God); *Hilchot Shemit-
    tah* (Concerning the Sabbatical Year); *Hilchot Tu-
    mat Ochlin* (On Defilement of Food).

Letters and Legal Opinions (ed. Lichtenberg, Leipzig, 1859).

ELEAZAR BEN YEHUDAH FROM WORMS (1160-1230), Rokeach.

MOSES BEN NACHMAN (1195-1270), Commentary to the Pentateuch.

Tosafot (Glosses) to the Pentateuch (twelfth to thirteenth century).

MOSES FROM EVREUX (about 1240), in Kol Bo (Compendium).

MOSES BEN JACOB FROM COUCY (about 1250), Sefer Mitzvot Gadol (The Great Law Book).

RABBI ASHER BEN YECHIEL (1250-1327), Testament.

IMMANUEL BEN SALOMO ROMI (1275-1340), Commentary to Proverbs.

ELIEZER HALEVI (died in 1357), Testament.

ISAAC BEN SHISHAT (1310-1407), Legal Opinions.

LIPMAN MÜHLHAUSEN (about 1400), Nitztzachon.

SALOMO ALAMI (about 1415), Iggeret Musar (Letter of Exhortation).

JOSEPH ALBO (1380-1444), Ikkarim (Book of Principles).

MOSES COHEN BEN ELEAZAR (second half of the fifteenth century), The smaller Book of the Pious.

The Book of Morality (fifteenth century).

MODERN JEWISH AUTHORS

BACH, Erlösung, Berlin, Zehlendorf, 1917.

BAECK, Das Wesen des Judentums, 2d ed., Frankfurt a.M., 1922.

BLOCH, Die Ethik in der Halacha, Budapest, 1886.

BUBER, Vom Geist des Judentums, Leipzig, 1916.

COHEN, HERMANN, Die Nächstenliebe im Talmud, Marburg, 1888.

———— Religion und Sittlichkeit (Jahrbuch für Jüdische Geschichte und Literatur), Berlin, 1907.

———— Religiöse Postulate (Bericht über die zweite Hauptversammlung des Verbandes der Deutschen Juden), Berlin, 1907.

———— Innere Beziehungen der Kantischen Philosophie zum Judentum (Jahresbericht der Lehranstalt für die Wissenschaft des Judentums), Berlin, 1910.

———— *Die Bedeutung des Judentums für den religiösen Fortschritt (Protokoll des 5. Weltkongresses für freies Christentum, 2.* Band), =[The Significance of Judaism for the Progress of Religion (Proceedings of the Fifth International Congress of Free Christianity and Religious Progress) Berlin-Schőneberg, 1911, pp. 385-400].

———— *Gesinnung (Vom Judentum,* Heft 5-6), Berlin, 1916.

———— *Streiflichter über jüdische Religion und Wissenschaft (Neue Jüdische Monatshefte,* Nr. 10), Berlin, 1917.

DIENEMANN, *Judentum und Christentum,* Frankfurt a.M., 1914.

———— *Die jüdische Wertung des Gesetzes und der Gerechtigkeit (Korrespondenzblatt des Verbandes der Deutschen Juden,* Nr. 14), Berlin, 1914.

———— *Israels Erwählung (Vom Judentum,* Heft 3-4), Berlin, 1914.

DUBNOW, *Shto Takoje Jewreskaja Istorija,* tr. into German by Isr. Friedländer, under the title of *Die jüdische Geschichte,* Berlin, 1898.

ELBOGEN, *Die Religionsanschauungen der Pharisäer (Jahresbericht der Lehranstalt für die Wissenschaft des Judentums),* Berlin, 1904.

ELLGUTHER, *Die soziale Gesetzgebung der Bibel (31. wissenschaftl. Bericht der "Philomathie"),* Neisze, 1902.

FRANKEL, *Der gerichtliche Beweis nach mosaisch-talmudischem Rechte,* Berlin, 1846.

FREUDENTHAL, *Spinoza, sein Leben und seine Lehre,* Band I, Stuttgart, 1904.

GEIGER, *Das Judentum und seine Geschichte,* Bd. I, II, Breslau, 1865.

GRÜNEBAUM, *Die Fremden (Gerim) nach rabbinischen Gesetzen (Geigers "Jüdische Zeitschrift für Wissenschaft und Leben,"* Jahrg. VIII), Breslau, 1870.

GÜDEMANN, *Geschichte des Erziehungswesens und der Kultur der abendländischen Juden,* 3 Bde., Vienna, 1880-88.

———— *Das Judentum in seinen Grundzügen und nach seinen geschichtlichen Grundlagen,* Vienna, 1902.

GUTTMANN, *Die Idee der Versöhnung im Judentum* (*Bericht über die vierte Hauptversammlung d. Verb. d. Deutschen Juden*), Berlin, 1909.

HELLER-WALLERSTEIN, Yom-Tob Lipman (1579-1654), *Tosafot-Yom-Tob, Commentary to the Mishnah.*

HERZFELD, *Geschichte des Volkes Jisrael*, Braunschweig, 1847-57.

HIRSCH, E. G., *The Contributions of Judaism to Free Religion* (Proceedings of the Fifth International Congress of Free Christianity and Religious Progress), Berlin-Schöneberg, 1911.

HIRSCH, S. R., *Neunzehn Briefe über Judentum*, Altona, 1836.

——— *Choreb*, Altona, 1837.

——— *Gesammelte Schriften*, Frankfurt a.M., 1902-1908.

JERUSALEM, *Der Kulturwert des Judentums* ("*Der Jude,*" Nr. 7), Berlin, 1917.

——— "*Du sollst zum Segen werden*" (*Gemeindeblatt*, XI, 2), Berlin, 1921.

JOEL, *Religiös-philosophische Zeitfragen*, Breslau, 1876.

JONA (Land-Sofer), *Testament in Derech Tobim* (The Way of the Good), Frankfurt a.M., 1717.

JOSEPH, *Zur Sittenlehre des Judentums*, Berlin, 1902.

KELLERMANN, *Der ethische Monotheismus der Propheten und seine soziologische Würdigung*, Berlin, 1917.

KOHLER, *Grundrisz einer systematischen Theologie des Judentums auf geschichtlicher Grundlage*, Leipzig, 1910.

LAZARUS, L., *Zur Charakteristik der talmudischen Ethik*, Breslau, 1877.

LAZARUS, M., *Die Ethik des Judentums*, I, II, Frankfurt a.M., 1899, 1911.

LESZYNSKY, *Pharisäer und Sadduzäer*, Frankfurt a.M., 1912.

LUZZATTO, *Mesillat Yesharim* (The Way of the Pious), tr. into German by Wohlgemuth, Berlin, 1906.

MAIMON, *Lebensgeschichte*, I, Berlin, 1792.

MARX, *Ethik und Religion* (*Straszburger Israelitische Wochenschrift*, Nr. 18), Gebweiler i. E., 1910.

MENDELSSOHN, *Jerusalem*, Berlin, 1783.

PERLES, *Boussets "Religion des Judentums,"* Berlin, 1903.

RABBINERVERSAMMLUNG zu Berlin am 4./5. Juni 1884, Bericht über d. Verhandlungen und Beschlüsse.

SELIGMANN, *Vom Wesen der jüdischen Moral (Gemeinde-blatt,* Nr. 12), Berlin, 1916.

STEINTHAL, *Zu Bibel und Religionsphilosophie,* I, II, Berlin, 1890, 1895.

———— *Über Juden und Judentum,* Berlin, 1906.

VENETIANER, *Jüdisches im Christentum,* Frankfurt a.M., 1913.

WIENER, *Die Anschauungen der Propheten von der Sittlichkeit,* Berlin, 1909.

———— *Die Religion der Propheten,* Frankfurt a.M., 1912.

ZUNZ, *Zur Geschichte und Literatur,* Berlin, 1845.

CHRISTIAN AUTHORS

BÄHR, *Symbolik des mosaischen Kultus,* I, Heidelberg, 1837.

BAUDISSIN, *Die alttestamentliche Religion und die Armen,* Berlin, 1912.

———— *Zur Geschichte der alttestamentlichen Religion in ihrer universalen Bedeutung,* Berlin, 1914.

BAUR, *Geschichte der Pädagogik (Encykl. des gesamten Erziehungs- und Unterrichtswesens,* hrsg. v. K. A. Schmid, Bd. V), Leipzig, 1883.

BERTHOLET, *Die Stellung der Israeliten und der Juden zu den Fremden,* Freiburg i. B., 1896.

BOUSSET, *Die Religion des Judentums im neutestamentlichen Zeitalter,* Berlin, 1906.

BUDDE, *Die Religion des Volkes Israel,* Gieszen, 1905.

CASPARI, *Die israelitischen Propheten,* Leipzig, 1914.

CHEYNE, *Jewish Religious Life After the Exile,* Putnam, New York and London, 1898-1901, tr. into German by Stocks under the title of *Das religiöse Leben der Juden nach dem Exil,* Gieszen, 1905.

CHRYSANTH (Bishop), *Religij Drewnjago Mira we ich otnoshenij ke christjanstwu* (The Religions of the Ancient World in their Relation to Christianity), St. Petersburg, 1878.

CORNILL, *Das Buch Jeremia,* Leipzig, 1905.

———— *Das Alte Testament und die Humanität,* Leipzig, 1895.

———— *Der israelitische Prophetismus*, Straszburg, 1900.

COSSMANN, *Die Entwicklung des Gerichtsgedankens bei den alttestamentlichen Propheten*, Gieszen, 1915.

COUARD, *Die religiösen und sittlichen Anschauungen der alttestamentlichen Apokryphen und Pseudepigraphen*, Gütersloh, 1907.

DINGLER, *Die Kultur der Juden*, Leipzig, 1919.

DUHM, *Die Theologie der Propheten*, Bonn, 1875.

———— *Das Buch Jeremia*, Tübingen, 1901.

———— *Israels Propheten*, Tübingen, 1916.

EWALD, *Geschichte des Volkes Israel*, Göttingen, 1864ff.

———— *Die Propheten des Alten Bundes*, I, Göttingen, 1867.

———— *Die Lehre der Bibel von Gott*, Leipzig, 1871.

FELDMANN, *Israels Religion, Sitte und Kultur in der vormosaischen Zeit*, Münster, 1917,

FRANCKH, *Die Propheten in der Zeit vor Amos*, Gütersloh, 1905.

GIESEBRECHT, *Die Geschichtlichkeit des Sinaibundes*, Königsberg, 1900.

———— *Die Grundzüge der israelitischen Religionsgeschichte*, Leipzig, 1908.

GREGOROVIUS, in J. Singer, *Briefe berühmter christlicher Zeitgenossen über die Judenfrage*, Vienna, 1885.

GRESZMANN, *Mose und seine Zeit*, Göttingen, 1913.

GUNKEL, *Kriegsfrömmigkeit im Alten Testament (Internationale Monatsschrift*, Heft 8), Leipzig, 1915.

———— *Was bleibt vom Alten Testament?* Göttingen, 1916.

———— *Die Propheten*, Göttingen, 1917.

HALLER, *Religion, Recht und Sitte in den Genesis-Sagen*, Bern, 1905.

———— *Der Ausgang der Prophetie*, Tübingen, 1912.

HAPPEL, *Weltgericht, Weltbegnadigung und Neuordnung der Welt nach dem 1. Buch Moses (Zeitschrift für Missionskunde und Religionswissenschaft*, Nr. 25, Heft 11).

HEGEL, *Vorlesungen über die Philosophie der Geschichte*, Leipzig, 1907.

HEINZELMANN, *Die Bibel im Lichte des Krieges (Geisteskampf der Gegenwart*, Nr. 8), Gütersloh, 1915.

HERFORD, *Pharisaism, Its Aim and Its Method*, New York and London, 1912 (tr. into German by R. Perles under the title of *Das Pharisäische Judentum*, Leipzig, 1913).

HERRMANN, *Die soziale Predigt der Propheten*, Berlin, 1911.

HÖLSCHER, *Die Propheten*, Leipzig, 1914.

JEREMIAS, *Moses und Hammurabi*, Leipzig, 1903.

KAUTZSCH, EMIL, *Biblische Theologie des Alten Testaments*, Tübingen, 1911.

—————— *Die bleibende Bedeutung des Alten Testaments*, Tübingen, 1912.

KAUTZSCH, KARL, *Die Philosophie des Alten Testaments* (*Religionsgeschichtliche Volksbücher*, VI. Reihe, 6. Heft), Tübingen, 1914.

KITTEL, *Judenfeindschaft oder Gotteslästerung?* Leipzig, 1914.

—————— *Das Alte Testament und das deutsche Christentum* (in *Allgem. Evangelisch-lutherische Kirchenzeitung*, 55. Jahrg., Nr. 17) Leipzig, 1922.

KLEINERT, *Die Propheten Israels in sozialer Beziehung*, Leipzig, 1905.

KLOSTERMANN, *Geschichte des Volkes Israels bis zur Restauration unter Esra und Nehemia*, München, 1896.

KÖBERLE, *Sünde und Gnade im religiösen Leben des Volkes Israel bis auf Christum*, München, 1905.

KÖNIG, *Prophetenideal, Judentum und Christentum*, Leipzig, 1906.

—————— *Geschichte des Reiches Gottes bis auf Jesus Christus*, Berlin, 1908.

—————— *Geschichte der alttestamentlichen Religion*, Gütersloh, 1912.

KUENEN, *Volksreligion und Weltreligion* (German ed.), Berlin, 1883.

KÜPER, *Das Prophetentum des Alten Bundes*, Leipzig, 1870.

LÖHR, *Geschichte des Volkes Israel*, Straszburg, 1900.

MARTI, *Geschichte der israelitischen Religion*, Königsberg, 1900.

—————— *Die Religion des Alten Testaments unter den Religionen des vorderen Orients*, Tübingen, 1906.

MEINHOLD, *Jesaja und seine Zeit*, Leipzig, 1898.

———— *Die Propheten in Israel von Moses bis auf Jesus*, Langensalza, 1909.

———— *Geschichte des jüdischen Volkes von seinen Anfängen bis gegen 600 n. Chr.*, Leipzig, 1916.

MEYER, *Ursprung und Anfänge des Christentums*, II, Stuttgart u. Berlin, 1921.

MOORE, *Die Eigenart der hebräischen Geschichtsschreibung im alttestamentlichen Zeitalter (Bericht der Lehranstalt für die Wissenschaft des Judentums)*, Berlin, 1910.

NIKEL, *Das Alte Testament und die Nächstenliebe*, Münster, 1913.

NÖTSCHER, *Die Gerechtigkeit Gottes bei den vorexilischen Propheten*, Münster, 1915.

NOWACK, *Die Entstehung der israelitischen Religion*, Straszburg, 1895.

PERKINS, *The Attitude of the Liberal Christian toward the Jew* (Proceedings of the Fifth International Congress of Free Christianity, pp. 371-378), Berlin-Schöneberg, 1911.

PFLÜGER, *Der Sozialismus der israelitischen Propheten*, Berlin, 1914.

RENAN, *Histoire des origines du Christianisme* (II, *Les Apôtres*), Paris, 1866.

———— *Histoire du peuple d'Israel*, Paris, 1887ff.

RIEHM, *Alttestamentliche Theologie*, Halle, 1889.

SCHMIDT, *Der Prophet Amos*, Tübingen, 1917.

SCHÜRER, *Geschichte des jüdischen Volkes im Zeitalter Jesu Christi*, II, Leipzig, 1907.

SEINICKE, *Geschichte des Volkes Israel*, I, Göttingen, 1876.

SELLIN, *Die alttestamentliche Religion im Rahmen der andern altorientalischen*, Leipzig, 1908.

———— *Der alttestamentliche Prophetismus*, Leipzig, 1912.

SMEND, *Lehrbuch der alttestamentlichen Religionsgeschichte*, Freiburg i.B., 1899.

SOLOWJOFF, *Jewrejsko-christjansky wapros*, tr. into German by Keuchel under the title of *Judentum und Christentum*, Dresden, 1911.

STADE, *Geschichte des Volkes Israel*, Berlin, 1887ff.

STAERK, *Neutestamentliche Zeitgeschichte*, I, Leipzig, 1907.

———— *Das Werk Moses und seine Geschichte (Neue Jüdische Monatshefte*, Heft 9-12), Berlin, 1919.

STERNBERG, *Die Ethik des Deuteronomiums*, Berlin, 1908.

STOSCH, *Die Prophetie Israels in religionsgeschichtlicher Würdigung*, Gütersloh, 1907.

—— *Die Universalität des absoluten Gottes bei Jesaja* (*Evang. Kirchenztg.*, Nr. 21-25), Berlin, 1915.

TORGE, *Aus Israels Propheten*, Tübingen, 1914.

VALETON, *Amos und Hosea*, Gieszen, 1898.

VOLZ, *Mose*, Tübingen, 1907.

WALTER, *Die Propheten in ihrem sozialen Beruf und das Wirtschaftsleben ihrer Zeit*, Freiburg i.B., 1900.

WEBER, *Jüdische Theologie auf Grund des Talmud und verwandter Schriften*, Leipzig, 1897.

WEIGL, *Das Judentum*, Berlin, 1911.

WELLHAUSEN, *Israelitische und jüdische Geschichte*, Berlin, 1907.

WILKE, *Das Frauenideal und die Schätzung des Weibes im Alten Testament*, Leipzig, 1907.

[BAILEY AND KENT, *History of the Hebrew Commonwealth*, New York, Scribner's, 1922.—Tr.]

GENERAL INDEX*

Abba Areka, 74 (V, 9).

Abraham, 20 (I, 1), 139-140 (VI, 2).

Abstinence, 198-199 (VII, 1), 206-207 (VII, 21), 219 (V, 1), 220 (V, 3).

Action, the moral, 33 (VII, 2), 33-34 (VII, 5), 51-52, 62 (VII, 11), 66-67 (VIII, 3), 69-71, 83 (VII, 17), 85-86 (VIII, 2), 114 (VII, 2).

Akiba, R., 28 (V, 3), 35 (VII, 7), 55 (V, 7), 85 (VIII, 1), 108 (V, 1), 115 (VII, 4), 167 (VII, 15).

All men God's children, 164 (VII, 5), 170-171 (VII, 24), 174 (VIII, 8), 174-175 (VIII, 9), 175 (VIII, 10).

Amos, 41 (VIII, 5), 172 (VIII, 2), 181-182 (VIII, 26).

Antigonos of Socho, 137 (V, 1), 140-141 (VI, 3), 143 (VII, 7).

Antoninus, 156 (V, 5).

Arrogance, 30-31 (VI, 4).

Asceticism, not in accord with Judaism, 60-61, (VII, 7), 61-62 VII, 9), 188-189, 192-193 (III, 2), 193-194 (V, 4, 5, 6, 7, 8), 195-196 (VI, 3, 4, 5), 196-197 (VI, 7), 198 (VI, 12), 198-199 (VII, 1), 200-201 (VII, 4, 5, 6), 201-202 (VII, 7), 203 (VII, 9, 10), 205 (VII, 16, 18), 206 (VII, 20), 206-207 (VII, 21), 208 (VII, 27), 210 (VIII, 1, 2), 210-211 (VIII, 3), 211-212 (VIII, 5), 212-213 (VIII, 6, 7), 216 (VIII, 16, 17), 221 (VI, 3).

Atonement, 19, 165-166 (VII, 11).

Belief, 51-52, 57 (VI, 4), 58-59 (VII, 1), 63 (VII, 12), 170-171 (VII, 24).

Ben Azzai, 28 (V, 3), 54 (V, 3), 142 (VII, 4).

Beneficence, 34 (VII, 5). See also Mercifulness and Love of fellowmen.

Benevolence, 65 (VII, 17).

Ben-Sira, 173 (VIII, 4), 178 (VIII, 18).

Ben Soma, 34-35 (VII, 7).

Bestowing benefits, 25-26 (III, 3).

Bliss, 26 (III, 4), 80 (VII, 5), 165 (VII, 9), 177 (VIII, 15), 180 (VIII, 23), 231-232 (VI, 10). See also Happiness.

Blood, shedding of, 21 (I, 6), 52-53 (I, 3), 193 (V, 3).

Body, care of, 192 (III, 1), 194 (V, 6), 195 (VI, 1, 2), 197 (VI, 8), 197-198 (VI, 10), 198 (VI, 11), 205 (VII, 16), 205-206 (VII, 19), 213 (VIII, 8), 215-216 (VIII, 14), 219 (III, 1), 221 (VI, 4), 222 (VII, 2).

The figures in parentheses after page numerals indicate section and number of passages cited.

Bribes, 21 (I, 6), 22 (I, 10), 28 (V, 4).
Brotherhood of man, 180-181 (VIII, 25), 181-182 (VIII, 26), 183 (VIII, 27, 28).

Character, moral, 225-226.
Chastity, 31 (VI, 6), 78 (VI, 11), 219 (V, 1).
Chillul ha-Shem, see Profanation of the Divine Name.
Chiyya, R., 55 (V, 8).
Commandments, 21 (I, 4), 24 (IIa, 4), 25 (III, 1), 31 (VI, 6).
Compassion and mercy, to love, 22 (I, 9), 24 (IIa, 4).
Covenant, new and old, 87-88 (VIII, 7).
Culpable thought, 81-82 (VII, 9), 86-87 (VIII, 5), 89 (VIII, 14), 138 (V, 8).

Decalogue, 87 (VIII, 6), 117-118 (VII, 10).
Democracy, First development of ideals of, 180-181 (VIII, 25), 181-182 (VIII, 26), 183 (VIII, 27, 28).
Determinism, see Freedom of will.
Deutero-Isaiah, 175 (VIII, 10).
Devotion, 83 (VII, 17).
Disposition, moral, 56-57 (VI, 2), 60 (VII, 6), see also Moral-mindedness.
Dissemblers, 69-71, 76-77 (VI, 6), 82-83 (VII, 13).
Divine Presence as manifested on earth, see Shechinah.
Divine service, see God, awe and worship of.
Dogmas in Judaism, 31 (VI, 7), 51.
Doing and believing, 52 (I, 1, 2), 54 (V, 1), 57 (VI, 3), 57-58 (VI, 5), 59 (VII, 2-4), 63 (VII, 12, 13), 63-64 (VII, 14), 66 (VIII, 1, 2), 66-67 (VIII, 3).
Doing and learning (studying), 54 (V, 1-3), 55 (V, 4-9), 56 (V, 11, 12), 61 (VII, 8), 62 (VII, 10), 67-68 (VIII, 6).
Dualism between the temporal and the eternal, see Nature and morality.
Dualism of mind and matter, see Nature and morality.
Duties, of the heart and of the hands, 69, 75-76 (VI, 1).
Duties to fellowmen, 180-181 (VIII, 25), 181-182 (VIII, 26), 183 (VIII, 27, 28).
Duty, fulfillment of, 58-59 (VII, 1), 59 (VII, 3), 64 (VII, 15), 75-76 (VI, 1), 78-79 (VII, 1), 83 (VII, 17), 225-226.

Ecclesiasticus, see Ben-Sira.
Education, 234 (VIII, 1, 2).
Eleasar ben Asarja, R., 85 (VIII, 1).
Election, of Israel, 151, 154 (III, 4), 164 (VII, 5), 177 (VIII, 16), 178 (VIII, 18).
Elieser, R., 84 (VIII, 1).
Eliphaz, 144 (VIII, 1).
Emunah, see Belief.
Epicureanism, 192-193 (III, 2), 198 (VI, 12), 208-209 (VII, 28), 214-215 (VIII, 11).
Equality of all human beings, 150-151, 152 (I, 1-3), 152-153 (I, 4), 153 (I, 5, 6; IIa, 1), 153-154 (III, 1), 154 (III, 2-4), 154-155 (III, 5), 155 (III, 6; V, 1, 2), 156 (V, 3,

4, 6, 7), 156-157 (V, 8), 157 (V, 9), 157-158 (V, 10), 158 (V, 11, 12), 159 (V, 14-17), 160 (V, 18, 19), 161 (VI, 2), 162 (VI, 4), 162-163 (VII, 1), 163 (VII, 2, 3), 164 (VII, 4), 164-165 (VII, 7), 165 (VII, 8-10), 165-166 (VIII, 11), 166-167 (VIII, 13), 167 (VIII, 14), 170 (VII, 23), 170-171 (VII, 24), 173 (VIII, 5), 173-174 (VIII, 6), 174 (VIII, 8), 176 (VIII, 12), 177 (VIII, 13, 14), 180 (VIII, 24).

Erudition and practice, see Doing and learning.

Eschatology, see Reward and punishment.

Ethical character of Judaism, 17, 33 (VII, 2), 33-34 (VII, 4), 34 (VII, 6), 35-36 (VII, 9), 44 (VIII, 13, 14), 45 (VIII, 15), 48-49 (VIII, 25), 61-62 (VII, 9), 67 (VIII, 4), 146 (VIII, 5), 172 (VIII, 2).

Ethical-mindedness, see Moral-mindedness.

Ethics of Judaism universal, 169 (VII, 19).

Evil, not from God, 105 (IIa, 3), 109 (V, 11, 12), 110 (VI, 2), 110-111 (VI, 5).

———, to hate, 22 (I, 12), 22-23 (I, 13), 24 (IIa, 1, 2), 53 (I, 4, 5, 6), 55-56 (V, 10), 73 (V, 3), 78 (VI, 11), 87 (VIII, 6), 89 (VIII, 14).

Ezekiel, 48-49 (VIII, 25), 102-103, 118 (VII, 12), 120 (VIII, 3), 126-127, 145 (VIII, 3), 145-146 (VIII, 4).

Fanaticism, 200 (VII, 5).

Fasting, see Asceticism.

Fate, 118 (VII, 11), see also Determinism, and Predestination, doctrine of.

Fellowmen, 22 (I, 10), 28-29 (V, 4), 163 (VII, 3).

Fellowmen, duties to, see Duties to Fellowmen.

Fellowmen, love of, 24 (IIa, 4), 25 (III, 2), 30 (VI, 2), 31-32 (VI, 8), 33 (VII, 3), 34 (VII, 5), 34-35 (VII, 7), 35 (VII, 8), 36 (VII, 10), 38 (VII, 18), 40-41 (VIII, 3), 43 (VIII, 11), 47 (VIII, 20), 65 (VII, 17), 87 (VIII, 6), 180 (VIII, 23), see also Mercifulness and Beneficence.

Fidelity, 183 (VIII, 27).

Fortitude, 53-54 (III, 1).

Freedom of will, see Will, freedom of.

Freedom, moral, 18-19, 228 (V, 4).

Fundamental rights of man, 180-181 (VIII, 25), 181-182 (VIII, 26), 183 (VIII, 28).

Gamaliel, 39-40 (VIII, 1).

Goal (purpose), 19-20, 33-34 (VII, 4), 37 (VII, 14), 47 (VIII, 21).

God, awe and worship of, 25 (III, 2), 26 (III, 5; V, 1), 31 (VI, 5), 34 (VII, 6), 36 (VII, 10), 40 (VIII, 2), 66-67 (VIII, 3), 75-76 (VI, 1), 76 (VI, 2), 82 (VII, 12), 130 (I, 6), 190 (I, 4), 231 (VI, 9), 232 (VII, 2), 233 (VII, 4), 234-235 (VIII, 3).

God, love of, 20 (I, 3), 30 (VI, 3), 31 (VI, 5), 33 (VII, 3), 33-34 (VII, 4), 40-41 (VIII, 3), 69, 74 (V, 10, 11, 13),

77 (VI, 7, 9), 79 (VII, 2), 80 (VII, 5), 89 (VIII, 12), 89-90 (VIII, 15), 90 (VIII, 17), 130 (I, 6), 139-140 (VI, 2), 140-141 (VI, 3), 142-143 (VII, 5), 143 (VII, 6), 170 (VII, 22), 230 (VI, 5), 231 (VI, 9).

God, the fear of, 20 (I, 3), 22 (I, 10, 12), 22-23 (I, 13), 24 (IIa, 1), 28 (V, 4), 31 (VI, 6), 43 (VIII, 11), 47 (VIII, 20), 53 (I, 5), 55 (V, 9), 73 (V, 6), 85-86 (VIII, 2), 86-87 (VIII, 5), 89-90 (VIII, 15), 90 (VIII, 17), 109 (V, 10), 137 (V, 1), 143 (VII, 7), 153 (IIa, 1), 228 (V, 2), 231 (VI, 8, 9).

God, to know, 32-33 (VII, 1), 33-34 (VII, 4), 36-37 (VII, 13), 46 (VIII, 18), 51, 58-59 (VII, 1), 74 (V, 12), 129-130 (I, 4), 231 (VI, 7), see also Knowledge of God.

God's children, see All men God's children.

God's covenant, 21-22 (I, 8).

God's grace, 142 (VII, 3).

God's holiness, 20 (I, 2), 31 (VI, 7), 36 (VII, 11), 38 (VII, 20), 43 (VIII, 11), 44 (VIII, 13), 46-47 (VIII, 19), 177 (VIII, 16).

God's law, 41 (VIII, 4), 47-48 (VIII, 23), 69-71, 77-78 (VI, 10).

God's mercy, 30 (VI, 3).

God's mountain, 22 (I, 10), 28 (V, 4), 71 (I, 5), 152 (I, 1, 3), 152-153 (I, 4).

God's nature, 32-33 (VII, 1), 58-59 (VII, 1).

God's omniscience, 103-104.

God's spirit immanent in the world (Shechinah), 30 (VI, 1), 193 (V, 1).

God's unity, 42-43 (VIII, 9), 76 (VI, 2), 80 (VII, 4), 170-171 (VII, 24), 176 (VIII, 12).

God's ways, 20 (I, 3), 30 (VI, 3), 32-33 (VII, 1), 36 (VII, 12), 37 (VII, 16), 59 (VII, 2), 170 (VII, 22).

God's will, 60 (VII, 6), 234 (VIII, 1).

Good, do, 32-33 (VII, 1), 53 (I, 5, 6), 55-56 (V, 10), 56 (VI, 1), 56-57 (VI, 2), 58 (VII, 1), 62 (VII, 11), 63-64 (VII, 14).

————, love the, 53 (I, 4).

Guile, 53 (I, 5), 55-56 (V, 10).

Guilt, 120 (VIII, 3), 123 (VIII, 12), see also Reward and punishment.

Habakkuk, 28-29 (V, 4).

Hammurabi, code of, 47 (VIII, 22), 87 (VIII, 6).

Happiness, 170 (VII, 21), see also Bliss.

Harmony, 26 (III, 4), 53 (III, 1).

Hatred, see Remove hatred.

Heart, a pure, 69, 82 (VII, 12), 113-114 (VII, 1), see also Whole-heartedness and Moral-mindedness and Purity of heart.

Heart, ethics of the, see Moral-mindedness.

Heathens, see Non-Jews and Proselytes.

Hereditary sin, denial of, see Original sin.

GENERAL INDEX 251

Hillel, 27 (V, 2), 34-35 (VII, 7), 35 (VII, 8), 39-40 (VIII, 1), 84-85 (VIII, 1), 194 (V, 6), 205-206 (VII, 19).
Holiness, 20 (I, 2), 31 (VI, 6), 32-33 (VII, 1), 36 (VII, 11), 37-38 (VII, 17), 38 (VII, 20), 41-42 (VIII, 6), 42 (VIII, 8), 46-47 (VIII, 19), 81-82 (VII, 9), 83 (VII, 15), 97-98 (VII, 2), 168 (VII, 16), 198-199 (VII, 1), 201 (VII, 6), 219 (V, 1), 220 (V, 3), 234 (VIII, 1).
Hosea, 183 (VIII, 27).
Human destiny, 36 (VII, 12).
────── life, preservation of (pikkuach nefesh), 193 (V, 3).
Humanity, 174 (VIII, 7, 8).
Humility, 82-83 (VII, 13).
──────, before God, 22 (I, 9), 28-29 (V, 4).
Hypocrites, see Dissemblers.

Idolatry, 52-53 (I, 3), 130 (I, 6, 7), 131-132 (I, 11), 160-161 (V, 20), 170 (VII, 23), 193 (V, 3).
Imitating God, 25-26 (III, 3), 30 (VI, 3), 37 (VII, 16).
Immortality, 153-154 (III, 1), 227 (IIb, 1).
Impulse, the evil, see Inclination, the evil.
Incest, 193 (V, 3).
Inclination, the evil (yetzer ha-ra), 93-94, 95 (V, 5), 95-96 (V, 6), 98 (VII, 4), 100-101 (VIII, 1), 107 (III, 1-3), 108 (V, 2-5), 109 (V, 6-8), 116-117 (VII, 8).
──────, the good (yetzer ha-tob), 116-117 (VII, 8).
Inclination to sin, see Inclination, the evil.
Individualism, 145 (VIII, 3), 145-146 (VIII, 4), 147 (VIII, 8).
Indulgence, undue, see Epicureanism.
Instruction of all classes, 233 (VII, 5), 235 (VIII, 4).
Intention, good, 138 (V, 8, 9).
Interest, lending at, 22 (I, 10), 28-29 (V, 4), 131-132 (I, 11).
Isaac Luria, 189.
Isaiah, 28-29 (V, 4), 46-47 (VIII, 19), 120-121 (VIII, 4), 231 (VI, 9), see also Deutero-Isaiah.
Ishmael, R., 84-85 (VIII, 1).
Israel's moral code the basis of everyday life of all great democracies of the present, 183 (VIII, 28).

Jacob, 158-159 (V, 13).
Jeremiah, 90-91 (VIII, 18), 120 (VIII, 3), 126-127, 145 (VIII, 3), 174-175 (VIII, 9), 175 (VIII, 10).
Jeremiah, R., 157-158 (V, 10).
Job, 142-143 (VII, 5).
Jose, R., 158 (V, 11).
Joseph, 213-214 (VIII, 9).
Judah, 213-214 (VIII, 9).
Justice, 20 (I, 1), 21 (I, 5, 7), 22 (I, 9), 23-24 (I, 14), 28-29 (V, 4), 52-53 (I, 3), 181-182 (VIII, 26), 183 (VIII, 27).

Kant, 41 (VIII, 4).
Kiddush ha-Shem, see Sanctification of the Divine Name.
Kindness, acts of, 26 (V, 1).

————, religion of, 181-182 (VIII, 26), 183 (VIII, 27).
Kingdom of God, 147-148 (VIII, 9), 172 (VIII, 1), 172-173 (VIII, 3), 177-178 (VIII, 17), 188, 213-214 (VIII, 9).
Knowledge, 225-226.
Knowledge, of God, 18, 234 (VIII, 1).
———— and morality, 225-226, 226 (I, 1, 2), 227 (IIa, 1; IIb, 1, 2), 227-228 (IV, 1), 228 (IV, 2; V, 1, 3, 4, 5); 229 (VI, 1, 2), 230 (VI, 4, 5), 231 (VI, 9), 232 (VII, 1), 232-233 (VII, 3).

Labor, 203 (VII, 11), 215-216 (VIII, 14).
"Legalistic religion," 69-71, 80 (VII, 4).
Liberty, human, 180-181 (VIII, 25), 183 (VIII, 28).
License, see Epicureanism.
Life, 59 (VII, 2-4), 60 (VII, 5), 60-61 (VII, 7), 64 (VII, 15).
————, affirmation of, 187-188, 199 (VII, 2), 200-201 (VII, 5), 204-205 (VI, 15), 205 (VII, 17), 206 (VII, 20), 208 (VII, 26), 211 (VIII, 4), 213-214 (VIII, 9), 216 (VIII, 16).
————, joy of, 189-190 (I, 1), 190 (I, 2-7), 190-191 (I, 8), 191 (I, 9-12), 192 (IIa, 1-4), 193 (V, 1-3), 195 (VI, 1, 2), 195-196 (VI, 4), 196 (VI, 5), 198-199 (VII, 1), 202 (VII, 8), 203 (VII, 9, 11), 204 (VII, 12-14), 206-207 (VII, 21), 208 (VII, 25), 208-209 (VII, 28), 213 (VIII, 8), 213-214 (VIII, 9), 214 (VIII, 10), 214-215 (VIII, 11), 215 (VIII, 12, 13), 216 (VIII, 15, 16).
————, negation of, rejected by Judaism, 199 (VII, 3), 200 (VII, 4).
Love, as a principle of action, 183 (VIII, 27).
Loyalty, 28 (V, 4), 34 (VII, 5).
Luria, see Isaac Luria.
Luther, 51.
Luxury, see Epicureanism.

Maid-servant, see Domestic servants.
Maimonides, 31 (VI, 7).
Malignity, 23-24 (I, 14).
Man, created in God's image, 28 (V, 3), 94 (I, 1, 2), 95 (V, 1), 97-98 (VII, 2), 99-100 (VII, 6), 117 (VII, 9), 119-120 (VIII, 2), 154-155 (III, 5), 162-163 (VII, 1), 164 (VII, 6), 165-166 (VII, 11), 167-168 (VII, 15), 174 (VIII, 7).
Man-servant, see Domestic servants.
Man's resembling God, 25-26 (III, 3), 30 (VI, 3).
Marriage, 200-201 (VII, 5), 210 (VIII, 2), 211-212 (VIII, 5), 216 (VIII, 17), 221 (VI, 3).
Meir, R., 156 (V, 4).
Mercifulness, 30 (VI, 3), 37 (VII, 16), 43 (VIII, 10), see also Beneficence and love of fellowmen.
Mercy of God, see God's mercy.
Messianic teaching, 19-20, 150-151, 165 (VII, 8).
Micah, 29 (V, 4), 41 (VIII, 5), 172 (VIII, 2).
Miracle, 19.

Moderation, 192-193 (III, 2), 195-196 (VI, 4), 198 (VI, 12), 202 (VII, 8), 215-216 (VIII, 14), 217 (I, 1-5), 217-218 (I, 6), 218 (IIa, 1-4), 219 (IIa, 5, 6; III, 1-3), 219-220 V, 2), 220 (V, 5, 7, 8), 220-221 (VI, 2), 221 (VI, 3, 4), 222 (VII, 1, 2), 222-223 (VII, 3), 223 (VIII, 1), 224 (VIII, 2), 227 (IIb, 2).

Modesty, 31 (VI, 6).

Monotheism, ethical, 17-18, 42-43 (VIII, 9).

Moral intent, see Moral-mindedness, and Disposition, moral.

Morality as a basic requirement of Judaism, 17-18, 34 (VII, 6), 36 (VII, 10), 37 (VII, 14-16), 38 (VII, 20), 40 (VIII, 2), 41 (VIII, 5), 43 (VIII, 11), 44 (VIII, 13, 14), 45-46 (VIII, 17), 47 (VIII, 20-22), 47-48 (VIII, 23), 48 (VIII, 24), 48-49 (VIII, 25), 51-52, 60 (VII, 5), 64 (VII, 15), 80 (VII, 6), 86 (VIII, 4), 199 (VII, 2).

———, not dependent upon practice of ceremonial precepts, 151.

Moral law, the, 33 (VII, 2, 3).

Moral-mindedness, 69-71, 71 (I, 1-7), 71-72 (IIa, 1-3), 72 (III, 1, 2; IV, 1, 2), 72-73 (V, 1, 2, 4, 5), 73-74 (V, 6), 74 (V, 7-13), 75 (V, 14-17), 75-76 (VI, 1), 76 (VI, 2-5), 76-77 (VI, 6), 77 (VI, 7), 77-78 (VI, 10), 78 (VI, 11), 78-79 (VII, 1), 79 (VII, 2, 3), 80 (VII, 4), 81 (VII, 7, 8), 82 (VII, 10), 83 (VII, 14-16), 84-85 (VIII, 1), 86 (VIII, 3), 86-87 (VIII, 5), 87-88 (VIII, 7), 88 (VIII, 8, 10), 88-89 (VIII, 11), 89 (VIII, 13), 89-90 (VIII, 15), 90 (VIII, 17), 102, see also Disposition, moral.

Moral requirements, 85-86 (VIII, 2), 86 (VIII, 3), 89-90 (VIII, 15), 90 (VIII, 16).

Moral responsibility, see Will, freedom of.

Moses, 26 (III, 4), 63 (VII, 12), 137 (V, 5), 176 (VIII, 12).

Nationalism, 121 (VIII, 7).

Nature and morality, not opposites in Judaism, 201 (VII, 6), 205-206 (VII, 19), 207 (VII, 22, 23), 207-208 (VII, 24), 212-213 (VIII, 6), 215 (VIII, 13).

Neighbor, see Fellowmen.

Noah, 168 (VII, 17).

Nobility, 155 (III, 6).

Non-Jews, 27-28 (V, 2), 156 (V, 4, 5, 7), 157 (V, 9), 157-158 (V, 10), 158 (V, 11), 159 (V, 14-17), 160 (V, 19), 160-161 (V, 20), 173 (VIII, 5), 173-174 (VIII, 6), 175 (VIII, 10), 175-176 (VIII, 11), 177 (VIII, 15), 180 (VIII, 23).

———, equal treatment of, 150-151.

Oath, 22 (I, 10, 11).

Oath, sacredness of, 22 (I, 10, 11), 28-29 (V, 4), 30-31 (VI, 4).

Obedience to God, 26 (III, 5).

Oneness of God, see Monotheism and God's unity.

Original sin, rejection of, 92-93, 98-99 (VII, 5), 102, 113 (VII, 1), 114-115 (VII, 3), 117-118 (VII, 10), 120 (VIII, 3).

Orphan, see Widow and fatherless.

Paul, 51-52, 98 (VII, 4), 210 (VIII, 2).
Peace, 30 (VI, 2), 30-31 (VI, 4), 53 (I, 5), 177 (VIII, 13).
Pharisees, religious views of the, 34 (VII, 5).
Philo, 98 (VII, 4).
Piety, 25 (III, 2), 31 (VI, 6), 34 (VII, 6), 38 (VII, 18), 52, 53-54 (III, 1), 76 (VI, 4), 88 (VIII, 9), 108 (III, 5), *see also* Religion.
Pious acts, 73 (V, 3), 233 (VII, 6).
Plato, 98 (VII, 4).
Poor, the, 23-24 (I, 14), 24 (IIa, 4), 46 (VIII, 18).
————, Protection of, 181-182 (VIII, 26).
Predestination, doctrine of, not held by Judaism, 115-116 (VII, 5), 121 (VIII, 6), *see also* Freedom of will.
Profanation of the Divine Name (*Chillul ha-Shem*), 64-65 (VII, 16).
Propitiation, 24 (IIa, 2).
Proselytes, 27-28 (V, 2), 31-32 (VI, 8), 152, 158-159 (V, 13), 160 (V, 18), 164-165 (VII, 7), 179 (VIII, 21).
Providence, *see* Determinism *and* Predestination, doctrine of.
Punishment, *see* Reward and punishment.
Purification, 29 (V, 5, 6)
Purity, 31 (VI, 6), 48-49 (VIII, 25), 90 (VIII, 17), 92-94, 94 (IV, 1), 95 (V, 2, 3, 4), 96 (VI, 1), 97-98 (VII, 2), 98 (VII, 3), 98-99 (VII, 5), 168 (VII, 16), 198-199 (VII, 1), 201 (VII, 6), 220 (V, 3), 234 (VIII, 1).
Purity of heart, 22 (I, 11), 30 (VI, 1), *see also* Heart, a pure.
————, of the senses, 81-82 (VII, 9), 82 (VII, 11).

Rab, *see* Abba Areka.
Rabbi, *see* Yedudah, R.
Racial hatred, opposed to, 166 (VII, 12).
Ray of divine holiness, *see* Shechinah.
Rebekah, 213-214 (VIII, 9).
Religion, 45, (VIII, 15), 51-52, 53-54 (III, 1), 234 (VIII, 2), *see also* Piety.
Religion, of humanity, 168 (VI, 17).
————, of kindness, *see* Kindness, religion of.
————, national, 86 (VIII, 4), 90 (VIII, 16).
Remove hatred, 31-32 (VI, 8).
Requirement, moral, *see* Moral requirements.
Requital, *see* Reward and punishment.
Responsibility, *see* Will, freedom of.
Revelation, 32-33 (VII, 1), 80 (VII, 4), 158 (V, 11, 12), 177 (VIII, 16), 178-179 (VIII, 20), 234-235 (VIII, 3).
Reward and punishment, 120 (VIII, 3), 125-128, 128 (I, 1), 128-129 (I, 2), 129 (I, 3), 129-130 (I, 4), 130 (I, 5-7), 131 (I, 8-10), 134 (I, 12-15), 134-135 (I, 16), 135 (I, 17-22), 136 (IIa, 2), 136 (III, 1), 137 (V, 5, 6), 137-138 (V, 7), 138 (V, 10, 11), 138-139 (VI, 1), 143 (VI, 6, 7), 144-145 (VIII, 2), 145 (VIII, 3), 145-146 (VIII, 4), 146 (VIII, 6), 146-147 (VIII, 7), 147 (VIII, 8), 147-148 (VIII, 9), 159 (V, 15, 17).

Righteousness, 20 (I, 1), 21 (I, 5, 6, 7), 22 (I, 9, 10), 25 (III,
1, 2), 28-29 (V, 4), 32-33 (VII, 1), 35 (VII, 8), 36 (VII,
10), 39-40 (VIII, 1, 2), 43 (VIII, 10), 46 (VIII, 18), 52-
53 (I, 3), 53 (I, 4), 53-54 (III, 1), 71 (IIa, 1), 90 (VIII,
17), 131-132 (I, 11), 136 (III, 1), 159 (V, 14), 160
(V, 18), 181-182 (VIII, 26), 183 (VIII, 27), 202 (VII,
8), 227 (IIb, 2).

Sacrament, 19.
Sage, see wise.
Samuel, Mar, 193 (V, 2).
Sanctification of the Divine Name (Kiddush ha-Shem), 64-65 (VII,
16), 70.
Self-control, 53-54 (III, 1).
Self-determination, see Will, freedom of.
Self-seeking, the Torah combats, 87 (VIII, 6).
Servants, domestic, 23-24 (I, 14).
Shammai, 27-28 (V, 2).
Share, in the world to come, 156 (V, 3, and V, 5), 161 (VI, 1),
161-162 (VI, 3).
Shechinah, see God's spirit immanent in the world.
Simeon ben Lakish, R., 159 (V, 17).
Simeon ben Menasja, R., 84-85 (VIII, 1).
Simeon, the Just, 26 (V, 1).
Simlayi, R., 28 (V, 4).
Sin, 92-94, 96-97 (VII, 1), 109 (V, 9), 200-201 (VII, 5), 202
(VII, 8), 228 (V, 1).
———, flee from, 73 (V, 3), 75 (V, 14, 15), 81-82 (VII, 9),
101 (VIII, 2, 3).
Sinfulness, see Inclination, the evil.
Sirach, see Ben-Sira.
Slander, 22 (I, 10), 28 (V, 4).
Soma, Ben, see Ben Soma.
Soul, 195 (VI, 2), 195-196 (VI, 4), 197 (VI, 7-9), 197-198
(VI, 10), 198 (VI, 11), 199 (VII, 2).
Strangers, forbidden to oppress, 31-32 (VI, 8), 52-53 (I, 3).
——— love for, 31-32 (VI, 8).
——— behavior toward, 23 (I, 14).
Study and practice, see Doing and learning.
Study of God's teaching, 228 (V, 5), 229 (V, 7-10), 230 (VI, 3),
230-231 (VI, 6), 231-232 (VI, 10), 232 (VII, 2), 233
(VII, 4, 6), 233-234 (VII, 7), 234-235 (VIII, 3).

Tanchuma, R., 156 (V, 7).
Tarfon, R., 55 (V, 7).
Teaching, see Torah.
Temperance, 217 (I, 1-5), 217-218 (I, 6), 218 (IIa, 1, 3, 4),
219 (IIa, 5, 6; III, 3), 220 (V, 3-8; VI, 1), 221 (VI, 5,
6), 224 (VIII, 2),
Tolerance, 180 (VIII, 24).
Torah (= teaching), 22 (I, 8), 26 (III, 4; V, 1), 27-28 (V, 2),
28 (V, 3), 28-29 (V, 4), 29 (V, 5), 30 (VI, 2), 31-32

(VI, 8), 33 (VII, 3), 55 (V, 5, 8), 58-59 (VII, 1), 69-71, 73 (V, 2), 125-126.
Truth, 22 (I, 10), 28-29 (V, 4).
Tzedakah, 39-40 (VIII, 1).

Unity of God, *see* God's unity.
Universalism, 86 (VIII, 4), 150-152, 164-165 (VII, 7), 165 (VII, 8), 168 (VII, 16, 17), 169 (VII, 18, 19), 170 (VII, 20, 22), 172 (VIII, 1, 2), 173 (VIII, 4), 174 (VIII, 8), 174-175 (VIII, 9), 175-176 (VIII, 11), 177 (VIII, 15, 16), 177-178 (VIII, 17), 178 (VIII, 18), 178-179 (VIII, 20), 179 (VIII, 22).
Uprightness, 28-29 (V, 4).

Virtue, 26 (III, 5), 34 (VII, 6).
Virtue is its own reward, 135 (I, 18), 136 (III, 1, 2), 137 (V, 1-4), 138-139 (VI, 1), 139-140 (VI, 2), 140 (VI, 3), 141-142 (VII, 1), 142 (VII, 2, 4).
Vows, 196-197 (VI, 6).

Whole-heartedness, *see* Moral-mindedness.
Widow and fatherless, 21 (I, 5), 23-24 (I, 14), 52-53 (I, 3).
Will, freedom of, self-determination and responsibility for oneself, 92-94, 102-104, 104 (I, 1, 2), 104-105 (I, 3), 105 (I, 4; IIa, 1-3), 105-106 (IIa, 4), 106 (IIa, 5-7), 106-107 (IIa, 8), 107 (IIa, 9), 108 (V, 1), 110 (VI, 1-4), 110-111 (VI, 5), 111-112 (VI, 6), 112 (VI, 7-9), 113 (VI, 10, 11), 113-114 (VII, 1), 114 (VII, 2), 115 (VII, 4), 115-116 (VII, 5), 116 (VII, 6, 7), 116-117 (VII, 8), 117 (VII, 9), 117-118 (VII, 10), 118 (VII, 11, 12), 119 (VIII, 1), 119-120 (VIII, 2), 121 (VIII, 6, 7), 121-122 (VIII, 8), 122 (VIII, 9), 122-123 (VIII, 10), 123 (VIII, 11, 12), 125-127, 131 (I, 10), 131-134 (I, 11), 135-136 (IIa, 1), 136 (IIa, 3).
Will to the good, 187-188.
—— to live, 187-189.
Wine, *see* Temperance.
Wisdom, *see* wise.
Wise, 59 (VII, 2), 228 (V, 2), 228-229 (V, 6), 231 (VI, 8).

Yehudah, R., 74 (V, 9), 156 (V, 5), 193 (V, 2), 228 (V, 3).
Yochanan ben Zakkai, R., 39-40 (VIII, 1), 84-85 (VIII, 1).
Yoshua ben Levi, R., 228 (V, 5).
Yoshua ben Sira, *see* Ben-Sira.

Zadok, R., 73 (V, 4).

INDEX OF PASSAGES CITED

BIBLE   PAGE

Genesis i. 27.. 94
    viii. 21.. 94
    xvii. 1... 71
    xviii. 19... 20
Exodus xx. 5-6..128
    xxxiv. 6-7....................................128-129
Leviticus xviii. 5...................................... 52
    xix. 2... 20
    xxvi. 3ff..126
    xxvi. 3-9, 14-16...................................129
Deuteronomy v. 1....................................... 52
    v. 9-10...128
    vi. 6-7...226
    vii. 9..129-130
    vii. 12...130
    x. 12... 20
    xi. 13ff...126
    xi. 13-17...130
    xi. 26-28...130
    xvi. 11.......................................189-190
    xvi. 14.......................................189-190
    xviii. 13.. 71
    xxvi. 11..190
    xxviii. 1ff..126
    xxx. 11-14.. 21
    xxx. 19...104
Isaiah i. 16-17.. 21
    ii. 2-3...152
    iii. 10-11..131
    v. 11-12..217
    xxvi. 21..131
    xxxiii. 15-16..................................... 21
    xlv. 18...190
    lvi. 1.. 21
    lvi. 3..152
    lvi. 6-7..152
    lxvi. 20-21...................................152-153
Jeremiah iii. 17.......................................153
    vii. 3-7.......................................52-53
    xii. 1..127
    xviii. 7-11.......................................104

PAGE

xxxi. 29-30 131
xxxi. 31-33 21-22
xxxi. 33 71
Ezekiel xviii. 1-32 131-134
xviii. 2 126
xviii. 31 71
xviii. 30-32 104-105
xxxvi. 26 71
Hosea iv. 11 217
Amos v. 14-15 53
Micah iv. 1-2 152
vi. 8 22
Zephaniah iii. 9 153
Psalms viii. 5-6 94
xv. 22
xxiv. 3-4 71
xxiv. 3-5 22
xxxi. 24 134
xxxiv. 12-15 53
xxxvii. 27 53
li. 12 71
lxii. 13 134
lxxiii. 1 71
c. 2 190
cxxvii. 3 190
cxxviii. 1-4 190
cxxx. 7-8 93
cxlv. 20 134
Proverbs ii. 1-5 226
v. 22 . . . . .105, 134
viii. 13 22
x. 29 134-135
xi. 31 135
xiii. 21 135
xvi. 11 135
xx. 1 217
xxi. 7 135
xxi. 17 217
xxii. 8 135
xxiii. 20-21 217
xxiii. 29-35 217-218
Job xxviii. 28 22-23
xxxi. 13-25, 29, 30, 32, 33, 38-40 23-24
Kohelet (Ecclesiastes) iii. 12-13 190
v. 17-18 190-191
vii. 15 127
vii. 29 94
viii. 15 191
ix. 7-9 191
xi. 9 191
xii. 13-14 135

PAGE

Daniel xii. 2-3 127
Nehemiah viii. 10 191

PALESTINIAN APOCRYPHA

Ben-Sira x. 19 153
    xiv. 14 192
    xv. 11-17 105
    xv. 20 105
    xix. 1-2 218
    xix. 20-21 24
    xxiii. 4-6 218
    xxx. 21-22 192
    xxxii. (=xxxv.) 5 24
    xxxiv. (=xxxi.) 25 218
    xxxiv. (=xxxi.) 27 192
    xxxv. (=xxxii.) 3-6 192
The Book of Enoch 98, 4 105
    99, 2 105-106
The Testaments of the Twelve Patriarchs ii. 5, 2 24
    iv. 14, 1-2 218
    iv. 14, 7-8 219
    iv. 16, 2 219
    iv. 20 135-136
    v. 5, 1-2 24
    viiib. 1, 6 27
    ix. 5, 3 71
    x. 1, 3-7 106
    xii. 3, 2 72
    xii. 6, 6-7 72
The Psalms of Solomon ix. 4 106
Tobit iv. 14-15 25
The Syriac Apocalypse of Baruch 54, 15 and 19 106
The Fourth Book of Ezra vii. 35 136
    vii. 105 136
    viii. 56, 60 106-107
    xiv. 34 107
Baruch iii. 14 227

GREEK APOCRYPHA

The Wisdom of Solomon vi. 15-19 227

JEWISH-HELLENISTIC LITERATURE

The Sybilline Books, Book III, 767-776 153-154
Pseudo-Phokylides, Nuthetikon 55 219
    63-64 219
    215 192
The Letter of Aristeas 144, 168 25
    221, 222 107
    237 219

PAGE

Philo: De opificio mundi...................154-155
    De specialibus legibus ii (De septenario)..............25
    De specialibus legibus ii (De colendis parentibus)........136
    De specialibus legibus iv (De judice)................25-26
    De specialibus legibus iv (De justitia)................72
    De specialibus legibus iv (De concupiscentia)........192-193
    De virtutibus (De caritate)......................26
    De virtutibus (De poenitentia)....................72
    De virtutibus (De nobilitate).....................155
    De praemiis et poenis (De execrationibus)............154
    Fragments...............................27-28
Josephus, Against Apion ii. 17...................53-54
    ii. 23...................................26
    ii. 31..................................136
The Fourth Book of Maccabees i. 18-19...............227
    ii. 6..................................107
    ii. 18.................................107
    iii. 2-5.............................107-108
    vii. 18-19.............................108

PRAYERS

Daily prayer.......................72, 94, 227-228
Service for Sabbaths and Festivals..................72
Service for the Day of Atonement.................94-95
Eighteen Benedictions 228

TALMUDICAL LITERATURE

TANNAITIC WORKS

Mishnah Sotah, i, 7.........................138
    Ethics of the Fathers i, 2....................26
            i, 3..........................137
            i, 17..........................54
            ii, 6.........................228
            ii, 17.........................73
            iii, 12.........................54
            iii, 18.......................95-96
            iii, 19........................108
            iii, 21........................228
            iii, 22.........................54
            is, 1.........................108
            iv, 2......................73, 137
            iv, 3.........................155
            iv, 7..........................73
            vi, 2.........................228
            vi, 5..........................55
Tosefta
    Peah c. 1..............................138
    Shabbat c. 15..........................193
    Yebamot c. 4...........................109
    Sanhedrin 13, 2.........................156

PAGE

Mechilta to Exodus xii. 49 155
    xix. 2 158
    xx. 2 158
Sifra to Leviticus xviii. 5 157-158
    xix. 2 219
    xix. 18 28
    Section Achare Mot .156-157
    Section Bechukkotaj 109
Sifre to Deuteronomy vi. 5 74
    vi. 6 74
    xi. 13 74
    xviii. 13 72-73
    Section Ekeb 55
Abot de R. Nathan, ii, 1 .109
    c. 17 95-96
TALMUD
PALESTINIAN TALMUD
Yerushalmi Berachot IV, 3 .228
    VIII, 6 156
    Peah I, 1 159
    Pesachim III, 7 55
    Sukkah V, 1 193
    Taanit II, 1 75
    Kiddushin IV, 12 194
    Nedarim IX, 1 108
BABYLONIAN TALMUD
Berachot 5a 109
    5b 74
    6a 138
    7b 55
    17a 29-30, 74
    29b 220
    33b 109
Shabbat 30b 193
    31a 27
    105b 95
    152b 95
Erubin 63a 229
Pesachim 109a 194
Rosh ha-Shanah 16b 137-138
Yoma 29a 75
    85b 193
Sukkah 52a 108
Nedarim 10a 194
    62a 74, 137
Taanit 11a 29
    22b 193-194
Megillah 15a 229
    16b 229
    25a 109
Ketubot 68a 220

PAGE

Sotah 3b 137
   9a 137
   31a 74
Kiddushin 30a 229
   39a 127
   40b 55
Nazir 19a 194
   23b 74
Baba Metzia 107a 95
Baba Batra 12a 228-229
Sanhedrin 44b 229
   100a 138
Makkot 23b-24a 28-29
   24a 137
Abodah Zarah 3a 156
   5b 109
   10b 109
   17b 55
   19a 108, 138
   20b 220
Chullin 13b 160-161
   44b 109
   84a 219-220
Niddah 16b 109
   30a 95

MINOR TRACTATES
Derech Eretz Zuta c. 10 75
Gerim IV, 2 160

MIDRASHIM
Midrash Tanna Debe Elijahu c. 7 220
   c. 13 159
   22, 23 75
Bereshit Rabbah c. 44 29
   c. 53 137-138
   c. 58 194
Shemot Rabbah c. 17 156-157
   c. 40 56
Vayyikra Rabbah c. 13 29
   c. 34 ....73, 194
   c. 35 55
Bamidbar Rabbah c. 8 159
   c. 10 220
   c. 19 229
Debarim Rabbah c. 7 56
Echah Rabbati, Introd., 2 74
Midrash Tehillim ti Psalm cxlvi 159
Midrash Samuel V, 9 228
Tanchuma to Genesis viii. 21 95-96
   Section Noah 220
   Section Lech Lecha 159
Pesikta Chadata to Purim 156

PAGE

Yalkut to Psalms xxxiv. 13-15...............................55-56
            lxxxiv. 11...228
            xc. 12...228-229
            cxi. 10..55
    to Isaiah, § 429 159
            § 42 157

MINOR HAGGADIC WORKS
Midrash Le-olam VI 109
Otiyyot de Rabbi Akiba....................73-74, 159, 160
        JEWISH LITERATURE OF THE MIDDLE AGES
Asher ben Yechiel, Testament................................221
Bachya ibn Pakuda 75-76, 76, 110, 195, 220, 229
Book of Morality 77
Book of the Pious 30, 77, 230
Eleazar ben Yehudah, Rokeach 30-31
Eliezer ben Isaac, Orchot Chayyim.........................231
Eliezer Halevi, Testament..............................230-231
Immanuel ben Salomo Romi, Commentary to Proverbs i. 7......231
Isaac ben Shishat, Legal Opinions.........................112
Joseph Albo, Ikkarim I, 3..................................31
        I, 8 ....77-78, 198
        I, 9 113
        I, 21 57
        III, 25 31-32
        IV, 42 161-162
Lipman Mühlhausen, Nitztzachon.............................231
Maimonides, Commentary to the Mishnah...............140-141
    Letters, II 23d ff..................................161-162
    MISHNEH TORAH:
        Hilchot Deot 30, 56-57, 196-197
        Shemittah 161
        Teshubah 77, 110-111, 138-139,
                                139-140, 161, 230
            Tumat Ochlin 197-198
        Shemonah Perakim 111-112, 112, 197, 221
Moses Cohen ben Eleazar, The smaller Book of the Pious.31, 57-58, 78
Moses from Evreux, Kol Bo.................................57
Moses ben Jacob from Coucy, The Great Law Book...........31
Moses ben Nachman, Commentary to Genesis xxii. 1..........112
Pentateuchal Tosafot to Leviticus x. 9...................221
    Numbers xxxii. 1.......................................113
Saadyah, Emunot ve-Deot 56, 96, 110, 229
Salomo Alami, Iggeret Musar 198, 231-232
Yehudah ha-Levi, Kuzari II, 50......................195-196
    II, 56 76-77
    III, 1 196
    III, 5 220-221
    III, 19 230
    V, 20 110
    V, 23 30

MODERN JEWISH AUTHORS

PAGE

Baeck...........................32-33, 33, 58-59, 59, 96-97,
141-142, 162-163, 163
Bloch 33, 198-199
Cohen, Innere Beziehg. d. Kant. Philosophie zum Judentum...33-34,
97-98
————, The Significance of Judaism for the Progress of
Religion 113-114, 232
————, Religiöse Postulate 163, 164
Dienemann, Israels Erwählung.........................164
————, Judentum u. Christentum 114, 199
Dubnow 59
Elbogen 34, 78-79
Freudenthal 34
Geiger 34-35, 114-115, 115, 164
164-165, 199-200, 200
Güdemann 60, 142, 165, 200-201, 222
Guttmann 115-116, 165-166, 201
Hirsch, E. G. 166
Hirsch, S. R., Choreb...............35, 79, 116, 201-202, 222
————, Gesammelte Schriften.........61, 98, 166-167, 167, 203,
204, 232, 232-233, 233
————, Neunzehn Briefe 60, 60-61, 202-203
Jerusalem, Der Kulturwert des Judentums.............204, 204-205
————, Du sollst zum Segen werden....................61-62
R. Jona Land-Sofer 205
Joseph 35-36, 36, 168, 205, 222-223
Kohler......................36, 80, 98, 98-99, 116-117, 117,
117-118, 142, 142-143, 143, 168-
169, 205-206, 206, 206-207, 233
Lazarus, L. 81, 81-82, 233
Lazarus, M. 36-37, 37, 62, 80-81, 81, 143,
169, 169-170, 170, 207, 207-
208, 208, 233-234
Luzzatto, M. Ch..................37, 37-38, 82, 82-83, 208
Mendelssohn 63, 170
Perles 63-64, 64, 64-65, 83
Rabbinerversammlung zu Berlin.......................170-171
Steinthal, Zu Bibel u. Religionsphilosophie.........65, 83, 99-100
————, über Juden und Judentum.....................83, 170
Venetianer 170
Wiener, Die Religion d. Propheten.............38, 118, 208-209
————, Die Anschauung d. Propheten v. d. Sittlichkeit......38, 118
Yom-Tob Lipman Heller 167-168

CHRISTIAN AUTHORS

Bailey and Kent...........180-181, 181-182, 182, 182-183, 183
Baudissin, Die alttestamentl. Religion u. d. Armen............210
————, Zur geschichte der alttestamentl. Religion............172
Baur 234
Bertholet 172, 172-173

PAGE

Bousset 39-40, 66, 84-85, 85-86, 86,
                              100-101, 119, 173, 210, 234
Budde 40, 86
Chrysanth 173, 173-174, 210-211
Cornill, Das A. T. und die Humanität................40-41, 174
———, Der israelitische Prophetismus 174-175, 175
Couard 119-120
Dingler 41, 86-87, 144
Duhm 41
Ewald, Die Geschichte d. Volkes Israel.........41-42, 42, 175-176
———, Die Lehre der Bibel von Gott.....................176
Gunkel, Was bleibt v. A. T.?............42, 66-67, 144-145, 145
———, Kriegsfrömmigkeit im A. T.......................177
Herford 234-235
Herrmann 67
Hölscher 42-43
Jeremias 87
Kautzsch, E., Die bibl. Theologie d. A. T...........43, 120, 177
———, Die bleibende Bedeutung d. A. T................87-88
Kautzsch, K. 211
Kittel 43-44
Kleinert 67
Köberle...............44, 67-68, 88, 101, 120-121, 121,
                      145-146, 146, 211-212, 212-213
König, Die Geschichte d. Reiches Gottes................213-214
———, Die Geschichte der alttestamentl. Religion..88-89, 121, 213
———, Prophetenideal, Judentum u. Christentum.............44
Löhr 89
Marti, Die Geschichte der israelit. Religion............89, 121-122
———, Die Religion des A. T........................45, 146
Meinhold 146-147
Meyer 45
Nikel 177
Nötscher 45-46, 46, 46-47, 147
Pflüger 47
Riehm 47, 89, 89-90, 90, 122, 147-148, 177
Schürer 123, 235
Sellin, Die alttestamentl. Religion....................214
———, Der alttestamentl. Prophetismus.......47, 90-91, 177-178
Solowjoff 122-123
Stade 47-48, 101, 178
Staerk 48, 48-49
Walter 123, 178, 214-215, 215, 223-224
Weber 178-179, 179
Weigl 180, 215-216, 216
Wellhausen 216
Wilke 216